T0283407

An Introduction to Bioinformatics

An Introduction to Bioinformatics

Edited by
Regan Knight

Larsen & Keller
www.larsen-keller.com

An Introduction to Bioinformatics
Edited by Regan Knight
ISBN: 978-1-63549-045-9 (Hardback)

Larsen & Keller

Published by Larsen and Keller Education,
5 Penn Plaza,
19th Floor,
New York, NY 10001, USA

Cataloging-in-Publication Data

An introduction to bioinformatics / edited by Regan Knight.
    p. cm.
Includes bibliographical references and index.
ISBN 978-1-63549-045-9
    1. Bioinformatics. 2. Biology--Data processing. 3. Computational biology.
I. Knight, Regan.
QH324.2 .I58 2017
570.28--dc23

The publisher's policy is to use permanent paper from mills that operate a sustainable forestry policy. Furthermore, the publisher ensures that the text paper and cover boards used have met acceptable environmental accreditation standards.

Printed and bound in the United States of America.

For more information regarding Larsen and Keller Education and its products, please visit the publisher's website www.larsen-keller.com

Table of Contents

Preface   **VII**

Chapter 1   **Introduction to Bioinformatics**   1

Chapter 2   **Sequence Analysis: A Comprehensive Study**   16
    a. Sequence Analysis   16
    b. Sequence Alignment   17
    c. Multiple Sequence Alignment   26
    d. Sequence Assembly   41
    e. DNA Sequencing   48

Chapter 3   **Genome Analysis: An Overview**   88
    a. Genomics   88
    b. Personal Genomics   100
    c. Oncogenomics   105
    d. Comparative Genomics   114
    e. Genome Project   119
    f. Genome-wide Association Study   123

Chapter 4   **Computational Biology: An Integrated Study**   131
    a. Computational Biology   131
    b. Gene Prediction   136
    c. Modelling Biological Systems   142
    d. Computational Genomics   146
    e. Computational and Statistical Genetics   148

Chapter 5   **Types of Bioinformatics Software**   165
    a. Biopython   165
    b. Bioconductor   170
    c. BioPerl   174
    d. BioJava   177
    e. BioJS   192
    f. BioRuby   194
    g. Bioclipse   202
    h. EMBOSS   203
    i. GenoCAD   205

Chapter 6   **Diverse Aspects of Bioinformatics**   209
    a. Structural Bioinformatics   209
    b. Modelling Biological Systems   209

    c. Protein–protein Interaction Prediction   213
    d. Interactome   217
    e. Flow Cytometry Bioinformatics   227
    f. Biodiversity Informatics   240

Permissions

Index

Preface

Bioinformatics is an amalgamation of mathematics, engineering, computer sciences and statistics. It refers to the practice of using software tools to understand biological data. This book explores all the important aspects of bioinformatics in the present day scenario. It elaborates the different branches related to the subject and their applications. While understanding the long-term perspectives of the topics, the book makes an effort in highlighting their impact as a modern tool for the growth of bioinformatics. This text, with its detailed analyses and data, will prove immensely beneficial to students involved in this area at various levels. It will be of great help to those in the fields of genetics, forensic science and evolutionary biology.

To facilitate a deeper understanding of the contents of this book a short introduction of every chapter is written below:

Chapter 1- Bioinformatics is a field of study that helps in the development of methods and software tools for developing a better understanding of biological data. It combines subjects such as computer science, statistics, mathematics and engineering. The chapter on bioinformatics offers an insightful focus, keeping in mind the complex subject matter.

Chapter 2- Sequence analysis is the process that clarifies the sequence of DNA, RNA or peptide sequence. The methods used in this are sequence alignment, searches against biological databases etc. This section also focuses on the techniques used in DNA sequencing such as Sanger sequencing, Illumina dye sequencing and ion semiconductor sequencing. The section elucidates the crucial theories and principles of sequence analysis.

Chapter 3- The study of the genome is known as genomics. It is a discipline of genetics and applies methods such as recombinant DNA and DNA sequencing. Personal genomics, oncogenomics, comparative genomics and the genome project have been explained in this section. This chapter is an overview of the subject matter incorporating all the major aspects of genome analysis.

Chapter 4- Computational biology involves the application of the theoretical methods and data analytical methods to the study of biology and social systems. This involves subjects such as computer science, statistics, chemistry, molecular biology, ecology and visualization. This chapter will provide an integrated understanding of computational biology.

Chapter 5- The software used in bioinformatics range from simple tools to complex graphical programs. The types of bioinformatics softwares elucidated in the following section are Biopython, bioconductor, BioPerl, BioJava, BioRuby and EMBOSS. Bioinformatics software is best understood in confluence with the major topics listed in the following chapter.

Chapter 6- Bioinformatics has diverse aspects; some of these are structural bioinformatics, modelling biological systems, protein-protein interaction prediction, interactome, flow cytometry bioinformatics etc. The topics discussed in the section are of great importance to broaden the existing knowledge on bioinformatics.

I owe the completion of this book to the never-ending support of my family, who supported me throughout the project.

Editor

Introduction to Bioinformatics

Bioinformatics is a field of study that helps in the development of methods and software tools for developing a better understanding of biological data. It combines subjects such as computer science, statistics, mathematics and engineering. The chapter on bioinformatics offers an insightful focus, keeping in mind the complex subject matter.

Bioinformatics is an interdisciplinary field that develops methods and software tools for understanding biological data. As an interdisciplinary field of science, bioinformatics combines computer science, statistics, mathematics, and engineering to analyze and interpret biological data. Bioinformatics has been used for *in silico* analyses of biological queries using mathematical and statistical techniques.

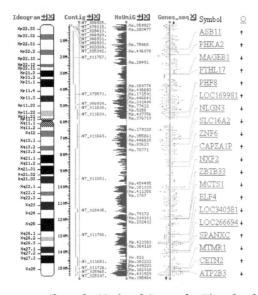

Map of the human X chromosome (from the National Center for Biotechnology Information website).

Bioinformatics is both an umbrella term for the body of biological studies that use computer programming as part of their methodology, as well as a reference to specific analysis "pipelines" that are repeatedly used, particularly in the field of genomics. Common uses of bioinformatics include the identification of candidate genes and nucleotides (SNPs). Often, such identification is made with the aim of better understanding the genetic basis of disease, unique adaptations, desirable properties (esp. in agricultural species), or differences between populations. In a less formal way, bioinformatics also tries to understand the organisational principles within nucleic acid and protein sequences, called proteomics.

Introduction

Bioinformatics has become an important part of many areas of biology. In experimental molecular biology, bioinformatics techniques such as image and signal processing allow extraction of useful results from large amounts of raw data. In the field of genetics and genomics, it aids in sequencing and annotating genomes and their observed mutations. It plays a role in the text mining of biological literature and the development of biological and gene ontologies to organize and query biological data. It also plays a role in the analysis of gene and protein expression and regulation. Bioinformatics tools aid in the comparison of genetic and genomic data and more generally in the understanding of evolutionary aspects of molecular biology. At a more integrative level, it helps analyze and catalogue the biological pathways and networks that are an important part of systems biology. In structural biology, it aids in the simulation and modeling of DNA, RNA, proteins as well as biomolecular interactions.

History

Historically, the term *bioinformatics* did not mean what it means today. Paulien Hogeweg and Ben Hesper coined it in 1970 to refer to the study of information processes in biotic systems. This definition placed bioinformatics as a field parallel to biophysics (the study of physical processes in biological systems) or biochemistry (the study of chemical processes in biological systems).

Sequences

5'ATGACGTGGGGA3'
3'TACTGCACCCCT5'

Sequences of genetic material are frequently used in bioinformatics and are easier to manage using computers than manually.

Computers became essential in molecular biology when protein sequences became available after Frederick Sanger determined the sequence of insulin in the early 1950s. Comparing multiple sequences manually turned out to be impractical. A pioneer in the field was Margaret Oakley Dayhoff, who has been hailed by David Lipman, director of the National Center for Biotechnology Information, as the "mother and father of bioinformatics." Dayhoff compiled one of the first protein sequence databases, initially published as books and pioneered methods of sequence alignment and molecular evolution. Another early contributor to bioinformatics was Elvin A. Kabat, who pioneered biological sequence analysis in 1970 with his comprehensive volumes of antibody sequences released with Tai Te Wu between 1980 and 1991.

Goals

To study how normal cellular activities are altered in different disease states, the biological data must be combined to form a comprehensive picture of these activities. Therefore, the field of bioinformatics has evolved such that the most pressing task now involves the analysis and interpretation of various types of data. This includes nucleotide and amino acid sequences, protein domains, and protein structures. The actual process of analyzing and interpreting data is referred to as computational biology. Important sub-disciplines within bioinformatics and computational biology include:

- Development and implementation of computer programs that enable efficient access to, use and management of, various types of information

- Development of new algorithms (mathematical formulas) and statistical measures that assess relationships among members of large data sets. For example, there are methods to locate a gene within a sequence, to predict protein structure and/or function, and to cluster protein sequences into families of related sequences.

The primary goal of bioinformatics is to increase the understanding of biological processes. What sets it apart from other approaches, however, is its focus on developing and applying computationally intensive techniques to achieve this goal. Examples include: pattern recognition, data mining, machine learning algorithms, and visualization. Major research efforts in the field include sequence alignment, gene finding, genome assembly, drug design, drug discovery, protein structure alignment, protein structure prediction, prediction of gene expression and protein–protein interactions, genome-wide association studies, the modeling of evolution and cell division/mitosis.

Bioinformatics now entails the creation and advancement of databases, algorithms, computational and statistical techniques, and theory to solve formal and practical problems arising from the management and analysis of biological data.

Over the past few decades, rapid developments in genomic and other molecular research technologies and developments in information technologies have combined to produce a tremendous amount of information related to molecular biology. Bioinformatics is the name given to these mathematical and computing approaches used to glean understanding of biological processes.

Common activities in bioinformatics include mapping and analyzing DNA and protein sequences, aligning DNA and protein sequences to compare them, and creating and viewing 3-D models of protein structures.

Relation to Other Fields

Bioinformatics is a science field that is similar to but distinct from biological computation, while it is often considered synonymous to computational biology. Biological computation uses bioengineering and biology to build biological computers, whereas bioinformatics uses computation to better understand biology. Bioinformatics and computational biology involve the analysis of biological data, particularly DNA, RNA, and protein sequences. The field of bioinformatics experienced explosive growth starting in the mid-1990s, driven largely by the Human Genome Project and by rapid advances in DNA sequencing technology.

Analyzing biological data to produce meaningful information involves writing and running software programs that use algorithms from graph theory, artificial intelligence, soft computing, data mining, image processing, and computer simulation. The algorithms in turn depend on theoretical foundations such as discrete mathematics, control theory, system theory, information theory, and statistics.

Sequence Analysis

```
A5ASC3.1   14 SIKLWPPSQTTRLLLVERMANNLST..PSIFTRK..YGSLSKEEARENAKQIEEVACSTANQ.....HYEKEPDGDGGSAVQLYAKECSKLILEVLK 101
84F917.1   13 SIKLWPPSESTRIMLVDRMTNNLST..ESIFSRK..YRLLGKQEAHENAKTIEELCFALADE.....HFREEPDGDGSSAVQLYAKETSKMMLEVLK 100
A9S1V2.1   23 VFKLWPPSQGTREAVRQKMALKLSS..ACFESQS..FARIELADAQEHARAIEEVAFGAAQE.....ADSGGDKTGSAVVMVYAKHASKLMLETLR 109
89G5N7.1   13 SVKLWPPGQSTRLMLVERMTKNFIT..PSFISRK..YGLLSKEEAEEDAKKIEEVAFARANQ.....HYEKQPDGDGSSAVQIYAKESSRLMLEVLK 100
Q8H0S6.1   30 SFSIWPPTQRTRDAVVRRLVDTLGG..DTILCKR..YGAVPAADAEPAARGIEAEAFDAAAA..SGEAARTASVEEGIKALQLYSKEVSRRLLDFVK 120
Q00423.2   44 SLSIWPPSQRTRDAVVRRLVQTLVR..PSILSQR..YGAVPEAEAGRAAAAVEAEAYAAVTES.SSAAAAPASVEDGIEVLQAYSKEVSRRLLELAK 135
89MVW8.1   56 SFSIWPPTQRTRDAIISRLIETLST..TSVLSKR..YGTIPKEEASEASRRIEEEAFSGAST.....VASSEKDGLEVLQLYSREISKRMLETVK 141
Q0IYC5.1   29 SFAVWPPTKRTRDAVVRRLVAVLSGDTTTALRKRYRYGAVPAADAERAARAVEAQAFDAASA....SSSSSSSVEDGIETLQLYSREVSNRLLAFVR 121
A9NW46.1   13 SIKLWPPSESTRLMLVERMTDNLSS..VSFFSRK..YGLLSKEEAAENAKRIEETAFLAAND.....HEAKEPMLDDSSVVQFYRREASKLMLEAVK 100
Q9C500.1   57 SLRIWPPTQKTRDAVLNRLIETLST..ESILSKR..YGTLKSDDATTVAKLIEEEAYGVASN.....AVSSDDDGIKILELYSKEISKRMLESVK 142
Q2HR17.1   25 MYSIWPPVQRTRDAVKNRLIETLST..FSVLTKR..YGTMSADEASAARIQIEDEAFSVANA.......SSSTSMDMVTILEVYSKEISKRMIETVK 110
Q9M7H3.1   28 SFKIWPPTQRTREAVVRRLVETLTS..QSVLSKR..YGVIPEEDATSAARIIEEEAFSVASV.ASAASTGGRPEDEWIEVLHIYSQEIXQRVVESAK 119
Q9M7N6.1   25 SFSIWPPTQRTRDAVINRLIESLST..PSILSKR..YGTLPQDEASETARLIEEEAFAAAGS.......TASDAODGIEILQVYSKEISKRMIDTVK 110
Q9LE82.1   14 SVKMWPPSKSTRLMLVERMTKNIIT..PSIFSRK..YGLLSVEEAEQDAKRIEDLAFRTANK.....HFQMEPDGDGTSAV-VYAKESSKLMLDVIK 101
Q9M6S1.2   13 SIKLWPPSLPTRKALIERITNHFSS..KTIFTEK..YGSLTKDQATENAKRIEDIAFSTANQ.....QFEREPDGDGGSAVQLYAKECSKLILEVLK 100
89R746.1   40 SLSIWPPTQRTRDAVITRLIETLSS..FSVLSKR..YGTISHDEAESAARRIEDEAFGVANT........ATSAEDDGLEILQLYSKEISRRMLDTVK 133
```

The sequences of different genes or proteins may be aligned side-by-side to measure their similarity. This alignment compares protein sequences containing WPP domains.

Since the Phage Φ-X174 was sequenced in 1977, the DNA sequences of thousands of organisms have been decoded and stored in databases. This sequence information is analyzed to determine genes that encode proteins, RNA genes, regulatory sequences, structural motifs, and repetitive sequences. A comparison of genes within a species or between different species can show similarities between protein functions, or relations between species (the use of molecular systematics to construct phylogenetic trees). With the growing amount of data, it long ago became impractical to analyze DNA sequences manually. Today, computer programs such as BLAST are used daily to search sequences from more than 260 000 organisms, containing over 190 billion nucleotides. These programs can compensate for mutations (exchanged, deleted or inserted bases) in the DNA sequence, to identify sequences that are related, but not identical. A variant of this sequence alignment is used in the sequencing process itself.

DNA Sequencing

Before sequences can be analyzed they have to be obtained. DNA sequencing is still a non-trivial problem as the raw data may be noisy or afflicted by weak signals. Algorithms have been developed for base calling for the various experimental approaches to DNA sequencing.

Sequence Assembly

Most DNA sequencing techniques produce short fragments of sequence that need to be assembled to obtain complete gene or genome sequences. The so-called shotgun sequencing technique (which was used, for example, by The Institute for Genomic Research (TIGR) to sequence the first bacterial genome, *Haemophilus influenzae*) generates the sequences of many thousands of small DNA fragments (ranging from 35 to 900 nucleotides long, depending on the sequencing technology). The ends of these fragments overlap and, when aligned properly by a genome assembly program, can be used to reconstruct the complete genome. Shotgun sequencing yields sequence data quickly, but the task of assembling the fragments can be quite complicated for larger genomes. For a genome as large as the human genome, it may take many days of CPU time on large-memory, multiprocessor computers to assemble the fragments, and the resulting assembly usually contains numerous gaps that must be filled in later. Shotgun sequencing is the method of choice for virtually all genomes sequenced today, and genome assembly algorithms are a critical area of bioinformatics research.

Genome Annotation

In the context of genomics, annotation is the process of marking the genes and other biological features in a DNA sequence. This process needs to be automated because most genomes are too large to annotate by hand, not to mention the desire to annotate as many genomes as possible, as the rate of sequencing has ceased to pose a bottleneck. Annotation is made possible by the fact that genes have recognisable start and stop regions, although the exact sequence found in these regions can vary between genes.

The first genome annotation software system was designed in 1995 by Owen White, who was part of the team at The Institute for Genomic Research that sequenced and analyzed the first genome of a free-living organism to be decoded, the bacterium *Haemophilus influenzae*. White built a software system to find the genes (fragments of genomic sequence that encode proteins), the transfer RNAs, and to make initial assignments of function to those genes. Most current genome annotation systems work similarly, but the programs available for analysis of genomic DNA, such as the GeneMark program trained and used to find protein-coding genes in *Haemophilus influenzae*, are constantly changing and improving.

Following the goals that the Human Genome Project left to achieve after its closure in 2003, a new project developed by the National Human Genome Research Institute in the U.S appeared. The so-called ENCODE project is a collaborative data collection of the functional elements of the human genome that uses next-generation DNA-sequencing technologies and genomic tiling arrays, technologies able to generate automatically large amounts of data with lower research costs but with the same quality and viability.

Computational Evolutionary Biology

Evolutionary biology is the study of the origin and descent of species, as well as their change over time. Informatics has assisted evolutionary biologists by enabling researchers to:

- trace the evolution of a large number of organisms by measuring changes in their DNA, rather than through physical taxonomy or physiological observations alone,

- more recently, compare entire genomes, which permits the study of more complex evolutionary events, such as gene duplication, horizontal gene transfer, and the prediction of factors important in bacterial speciation,

- build complex computational population genetics models to predict the outcome of the system over time

- track and share information on an increasingly large number of species and organisms

Future work endeavours to reconstruct the now more complex tree of life.

The area of research within computer science that uses genetic algorithms is sometimes confused with computational evolutionary biology, but the two areas are not necessarily related.

Comparative Genomics

The core of comparative genome analysis is the establishment of the correspondence between genes (orthology analysis) or other genomic features in different organisms. It is these intergenomic maps that make it possible to trace the evolutionary processes responsible for the divergence of two genomes. A multitude of evolutionary events acting at various organizational levels shape genome evolution. At the lowest level, point mutations affect individual nucleotides. At a higher level, large chromosomal segments undergo duplication, lateral transfer, inversion, transposition, deletion and insertion. Ultimately, whole genomes are involved in processes of hybridization, polyploidization and endosymbiosis, often leading to rapid speciation. The complexity of genome evolution poses many exciting challenges to developers of mathematical models and algorithms, who have recourse to a spectra of algorithmic, statistical and mathematical techniques, ranging from exact, heuristics, fixed parameter and approximation algorithms for problems based on parsimony models to Markov Chain Monte Carlo algorithms for Bayesian analysis of problems based on probabilistic models.

Many of these studies are based on the homology detection and protein families computation.

Pan Genomics

Pan genomics is a concept introduced in 2005 by Tettelin and Medini which eventually took root in bioinformatics. Pan genome is the complete gene repertoire of a particular taxonomic group: although initially applied to closely related strains of a species, it can be applied to a larger context like genus, phylum etc. It is divided in two parts- The Core genome: Set of genes common to all the genomes under study (These are often house-keeping genes vital for survival) and The Dispensable/Flexible Genome: Set of genes not present in all but one or some genomes under study. a bioinformatics tool BPGA can be used to characterize the Pan Genome of bacterial species.

Genetics of Disease

With the advent of next-generation sequencing we are obtaining enough sequence data to map the genes of complex diseases such as diabetes, infertility, breast cancer or Alzheimer's Disease. Genome-wide association studies are a useful approach to pinpoint the mutations responsible for such complex diseases. Through these studies, thousands of DNA variants have been identified that are associated with similar diseases and traits. Furthermore, the possibility for genes to be used at prognosis, diagnosis or treatment is one of the most essential applications. Many studies are discussing both the promising ways to choose the genes to be used and the problems and pitfalls of using genes to predict disease presence or prognosis.

Analysis of Mutations in Cancer

In cancer, the genomes of affected cells are rearranged in complex or even unpredictable ways. Massive sequencing efforts are used to identify previously unknown point mutations in a variety of genes in cancer. Bioinformaticians continue to produce specialized automated systems to manage the sheer volume of sequence data produced, and they create new algorithms and software to compare the sequencing results to the growing collection of human genome sequences and germline polymorphisms. New physical detection technologies are employed, such as oligonucleotide microarrays to identify chromosomal gains and losses (called comparative genomic hybridization), and single-nucleotide polymorphism arrays to detect known *point mutations*. These detection methods simultaneously measure several hundred thousand sites throughout the genome, and when used in high-throughput to measure thousands of samples, generate terabytes of data per experiment. Again the massive amounts and new types of data generate new opportunities for bioinformaticians. The data is often found to contain considerable variability, or noise, and thus Hidden Markov model and change-point analysis methods are being developed to infer real copy number changes.

With the breakthroughs that this next-generation sequencing technology is providing to the field of Bioinformatics, cancer genomics could drastically change. These new methods and software allow bioinformaticians to sequence many cancer genomes quickly and affordably. This could create a more flexible process for classifying types of cancer by analysis of cancer driven mutations in the genome. Furthermore, tracking of patients while the disease progresses may be possible in the future with the sequence of cancer samples.

Another type of data that requires novel informatics development is the analysis of lesions found to be recurrent among many tumors.

Gene and Protein Expression

Analysis of Gene Expression

The expression of many genes can be determined by measuring mRNA levels with multiple techniques including microarrays, expressed cDNA sequence tag (EST) sequencing, serial analysis of gene expression (SAGE) tag sequencing, massively parallel signature sequencing (MPSS), RNA-Seq, also known as "Whole Transcriptome Shotgun Sequencing" (WTSS), or various applications of multiplexed in-situ hybridization. All of these techniques are extremely noise-prone and/or subject to bias in the biological measurement, and a major research area in computational biology involves developing statistical tools to separate signal from noise in high-throughput gene expression studies. Such studies are often used to determine the genes implicated in a disorder: one might compare microarray data from cancerous epithelial cells to data from non-cancerous cells to determine the transcripts that are up-regulated and down-regulated in a particular population of cancer cells.

Analysis of Protein Expression

Protein microarrays and high throughput (HT) mass spectrometry (MS) can provide a snapshot of the proteins present in a biological sample. Bioinformatics is very much involved in making sense of protein microarray and HT MS data; the former approach faces similar problems as with microarrays targeted at mRNA, the latter involves the problem of matching large amounts of mass data against predicted masses from protein sequence databases, and the complicated statistical analysis of samples where multiple, but incomplete peptides from each protein are detected.

Analysis of Regulation

Regulation is the complex orchestration of events by which a signal, potentially an extracellular signal such as a hormone, eventually leads to an increase or decrease in the activity of one or more proteins. Bioinformatics techniques have been applied to explore various steps in this process.

For example, gene expression can be regulated by nearby elements in the genome. Promoter analysis involves the identification and study of sequence motifs in the DNA surrounding the coding region of a gene. These motifs influence the extent to which that region is transcribed into mRNA. Enhancer elements far away from the promoter can also regulate gene expression, through three-dimensional looping interactions. These interactions can be determined by bioinformatic analysis of chromosome conformation capture experiments.

Expression data can be used to infer gene regulation: one might compare microarray data from a wide variety of states of an organism to form hypotheses about the genes involved in each state. In a single-cell organism, one might compare stages of the cell cycle, along with various stress conditions (heat shock, starvation, etc.). One can then apply clustering algorithms to that expression data to determine which genes are co-expressed. For example, the upstream regions (promoters) of co-expressed genes can be searched for over-represented regulatory elements. Examples of clustering algorithms applied in gene clustering are k-means clustering, self-organizing maps (SOMs), hierarchical clustering, and consensus clustering methods.

Analysis of Cellular Organization

Several approaches have been developed to analyze the location of organelles, genes, proteins, and other components within cells. This is relevant as the location of these components affects the events within a cell and thus helps us to predict the behavior of biological systems. A gene ontology category, *cellular compartment*, has been devised to capture subcellular localization in many biological databases.

Microscopy and Image Analysis

Microscopic pictures allow us to locate both organelles as well as molecules. It may also help us to distinguish between normal and abnormal cells, e.g. in cancer.

Protein Localization

The localization of proteins helps us to evaluate the role of a protein. For instance, if a protein is found in the nucleus it may be involved in gene regulation or splicing. By contrast, if a protein is found in mitochondria, it may be involved in respiration or other metabolic processes. Protein localization is thus an important component of protein function prediction.

Chromosome Topology

Data from high-throughput chromosome conformation capture experiments, such as Hi-C (experiment) and ChIA-PET, can provide information on the spatial proximity of DNA loci. Analysis of these experiments can determine the three-dimensional structure and nuclear organization of chromatin. Bioinformatic challenges in this field include partitioning the genome into domains, such as Topologically Associating Domains (TADs), that are organised together in three-dimensional space.

Structural Bioinformatics

Protein structure prediction is another important application of bioinformatics. The amino acid sequence of a protein, the so-called primary structure, can be easily determined from the sequence on the gene that codes for it. In the vast majority of cases, this primary structure uniquely determines a structure in its native environment. (Of course, there are exceptions, such as the bovine spongiform encephalopathy – a.k.a.

Mad Cow Disease – prion.) Knowledge of this structure is vital in understanding the function of the protein. Structural information is usually classified as one of *secondary*, *tertiary* and *quaternary* structure. A viable general solution to such predictions remains an open problem. Most efforts have so far been directed towards heuristics that work most of the time.

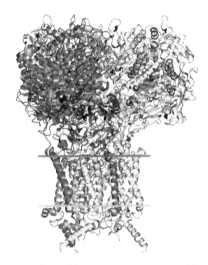

3-dimensional protein structures such as this one are common subjects in bioinformatic analyses.

One of the key ideas in bioinformatics is the notion of homology. In the genomic branch of bioinformatics, homology is used to predict the function of a gene: if the sequence of gene *A*, whose function is known, is homologous to the sequence of gene *B*, whose function is unknown, one could infer that B may share A's function. In the structural branch of bioinformatics, homology is used to determine which parts of a protein are important in structure formation and interaction with other proteins. In a technique called homology modeling, this information is used to predict the structure of a protein once the structure of a homologous protein is known. This currently remains the only way to predict protein structures reliably.

One example of this is the similar protein homology between hemoglobin in humans and the hemoglobin in legumes (leghemoglobin). Both serve the same purpose of transporting oxygen in the organism. Though both of these proteins have completely different amino acid sequences, their protein structures are virtually identical, which reflects their near identical purposes.

Other techniques for predicting protein structure include protein threading and *de novo* (from scratch) physics-based modeling.

Network and Systems Biology

Network analysis seeks to understand the relationships within biological networks such as metabolic or protein–protein interaction networks. Although biological networks can be constructed from a single type of molecule or entity (such as genes), network biology often attempts to integrate many different data types, such as proteins, small molecules, gene expression data, and others, which are all connected physically, functionally, or both.

Systems biology involves the use of computer simulations of cellular subsystems (such as the networks of metabolites and enzymes that comprise metabolism, signal transduction pathways and gene regulatory networks) to both analyze and visualize the complex connections of these cellular processes. Artificial life or virtual evolution attempts to understand evolutionary processes via the computer simulation of simple (artificial) life forms.

Molecular Interaction Networks

Interactions between proteins are frequently visualized and analyzed using networks. This network is made up of protein–protein interactions from *Treponema pallidum*, the causative agent of syphilis and other diseases.

Tens of thousands of three-dimensional protein structures have been determined by X-ray crystallography and protein nuclear magnetic resonance spectroscopy (protein NMR) and a central question in structural bioinformatics is whether it is practical to predict possible protein–protein interactions only based on these 3D shapes, without performing protein–protein interaction experiments. A variety of methods have been developed to tackle the protein–protein docking problem, though it seems that there is still much work to be done in this field.

Other interactions encountered in the field include Protein–ligand (including drug) and protein–peptide. Molecular dynamic simulation of movement of atoms about rotatable bonds is the fundamental principle behind computational algorithms, termed docking algorithms, for studying molecular interactions.

Others

Literature Analysis

The growth in the number of published literature makes it virtually impossible to read every paper, resulting in disjointed sub-fields of research. Literature analysis aims to employ computational and statistical linguistics to mine this growing library of text resources. For example:

- Abbreviation recognition – identify the long-form and abbreviation of biological terms

- Named entity recognition – recognizing biological terms such as gene names

- Protein–protein interaction – identify which proteins interact with which proteins from text

The area of research draws from statistics and computational linguistics.

High-throughput Image Analysis

Computational technologies are used to accelerate or fully automate the processing, quantification and analysis of large amounts of high-information-content biomedical imagery. Modern image analysis systems augment an observer's ability to make measurements from a large or complex set of images, by improving accuracy, objectivity, or speed. A fully developed analysis system may completely replace the observer. Although these systems are not unique to biomedical imagery, biomedical imaging is becoming more important for both diagnostics and research. Some examples are:

- high-throughput and high-fidelity quantification and sub-cellular localization (high-content screening, cytohistopathology, Bioimage informatics)

- morphometrics

- clinical image analysis and visualization

- determining the real-time air-flow patterns in breathing lungs of living animals

- quantifying occlusion size in real-time imagery from the development of and recovery during arterial injury

- making behavioral observations from extended video recordings of laboratory animals

- infrared measurements for metabolic activity determination

- inferring clone overlaps in DNA mapping, e.g. the Sulston score

High-throughput Single Cell Data Analysis

Computational techniques are used to analyse high-throughput, low-measurement single cell data, such as that obtained from flow cytometry. These methods typically involve finding populations of cells that are relevant to a particular disease state or experimental condition.

Biodiversity Informatics

Biodiversity informatics deals with the collection and analysis of biodiversity data, such as taxonomic databases, or microbiome data. Examples of such analyses include phylogenetics, niche modelling, species richness mapping, or species identification tools.

Databases

Databases are essential for bioinformatics research and applications. Many databases exist, covering various information types: for example, DNA and protein sequences, molecular structures, phenotypes and biodiversity. Databases may contain empirical data (obtained directly from experiments), predicted data (obtained from analysis), or, most commonly, both. They may be specific to a particular organism, pathway or molecule of interest. Alternatively, they can incorporate data compiled from multiple other databases. These databases vary in their format, way of accession and whether they are public or not.

Some of the most commonly used databases are listed below. For a more comprehensive list, please check the link at the beginning of the subsection.

- Used in Motif Finding: GenomeNet MOTIF Search

- Used in Gene Ontology: ToppGene FuncAssociate, Enrichr, GATHER

- Used in finding Protein Structures/Family: Pfam

- Used for Next Generation Sequencing: Sequence Read Archive

- Used in Gene Expression Analysis: GEO, ArrayExpress

- Used in Network Analysis: Interaction Analysis Databases(BioGRID, MINT, HPRD, Curated Human Signaling Network), Functional Networks (STRING, KEGG)

- Used in design of synthetic genetic circuits: GenoCAD

Software and Tools

Software tools for bioinformatics range from simple command-line tools, to more complex graphical programs and standalone web-services available from various bioinformatics companies or public institutions.

Open-source Bioinformatics Software

Many free and open-source software tools have existed and continued to grow since the 1980s. The combination of a continued need for new algorithms for the analysis of emerging types of biological readouts, the potential for innovative *in silico* experiments, and freely available open code bases have helped to create opportunities for all research groups to contribute to both bioinformatics and the range of open-source software available, regardless of their funding arrangements. The open source tools often act as incubators of ideas, or community-supported plug-ins in commercial applications. They may also provide *de facto* standards and shared object models for assisting with the challenge of bioinformation integration.

The range of open-source software packages includes titles such as Bioconductor, BioPerl, Biopython, BioJava, BioJS, BioRuby, Bioclipse, EMBOSS, .NET Bio, Orange with its bioinformatics add-on, Apache Taverna, UGENE and GenoCAD. To maintain this tradition and create further opportunities, the non-profit Open Bioinformatics Foundation have supported the annual Bioinformatics Open Source Conference (BOSC) since 2000.

An alternative method to build public bioinformatics databases is to use the MediaWiki engine with the *WikiOpener* extension. This system allows the database to be accessed and updated by all experts in the field.

Web Services in Bioinformatics

SOAP- and REST-based interfaces have been developed for a wide variety of bioinformatics applications allowing an application running on one computer in one part of the world to use algorithms, data and computing resources on servers in other parts of the world. The main advantages derive from the fact that end users do not have to deal with software and database maintenance overheads.

Basic bioinformatics services are classified by the EBI into three categories: SSS (Sequence Search Services), MSA (Multiple Sequence Alignment), and BSA (Biological Sequence Analysis). The availability of these service-oriented bioinformatics resources demonstrate the applicability of web-based bioinformatics solutions, and range from a collection of standalone tools with a common data format under a single, standalone or web-based interface, to integrative, distributed and extensible bioinformatics workflow management systems.

Bioinformatics Workflow Management Systems

A Bioinformatics workflow management system is a specialized form of a workflow management system designed specifically to compose and execute a series of computational or data manipulation steps, or a workflow, in a Bioinformatics application. Such systems are designed to

- provide an easy-to-use environment for individual application scientists themselves to create their own workflows

- provide interactive tools for the scientists enabling them to execute their workflows and view their results in real-time

- simplify the process of sharing and reusing workflows between the scientists.

- enable scientists to track the provenance of the workflow execution results and the workflow creation steps.

Some of the platforms giving this service: Galaxy, Kepler, Taverna, UGENE, Anduril.

Education Platforms

Software platforms designed to teach bioinformatics concepts and methods include Rosalind and online courses offered through the Swiss Institute of Bioinformatics Training Portal. The Canadian Bioinformatics Workshops provides videos and slides from training workshops on their website under a Creative Commons license. The 4273π project or 4273pi project also offers open source educational materials for free. The course runs on low cost raspberry pi computers and has been used to teach adults and school pupils. 4273π is actively developed by a consortium of academics and research staff who have run research level bioinformatics using raspberry pi computers and the 4273π operating system.

MOOC platforms also provide online certifications in bioinformatics and related disciplines, including Coursera's Bioinformatics Specialization (UC San Diego) and Genomic Data Science Specialization (Johns Hopkins) as well as EdX's Data Analysis for Life Sciences XSeries (Harvard).

Conferences

There are several large conferences that are concerned with bioinformatics. Some of the most notable examples are Intelligent Systems for Molecular Biology (ISMB), European Conference on Computational Biology (ECCB), and Research in Computational Molecular Biology (RECOMB).

References

- Wong, KC (2016). Computational Biology and Bioinformatics: Gene Regulation. CRC Press (Taylor & Francis Group). ISBN 9781498724975.

- Moody, Glyn (2004). Digital Code of Life: How Bioinformatics is Revolutionizing Science, Medicine, and Business. ISBN 978-0-471-32788-2.

- Chaudhari, Narendrakumar M., Vinod Kumar Gupta, and Chitra Dutta. "BPGA-an ultra-fast pan-genome analysis pipeline." Scientific Reports 6 (2016).

- McDonagh, J.L; Barker, D; Alderson, R.G. (2016). "Bringing computational science to the public". SpringerPlus. 5 (259). doi:10.1186/s40064-016-1856-7.

- Nisbet, Robert (14 May 2009). "BIOINFORMATICS". Handbook of Statistical Analysis and Data Mining Applications. John Elder IV, Gary Miner. Academic Press. p. 328. Retrieved 9 May 2014.

- "Open Bioinformatics Foundation: About us". Official website. Open Bioinformatics Foundation. Retrieved 10 May 2011.

Sequence Analysis: A Comprehensive Study

Sequence analysis is the process that clarifies the sequence of DNA, RNA or peptide sequence. The methods used in this are sequence alignment, searches against biological databases etc. This section also focuses on the techniques used in DNA sequencing such as Sanger sequencing, Illumina dye sequencing and ion semiconductor sequencing. The section elucidates the crucial theories and principles of sequence analysis.

Sequence Analysis

In bioinformatics, sequence analysis is the process of subjecting a DNA, RNA or peptide sequence to any of a wide range of analytical methods to understand its features, function, structure, or evolution. Methodologies used include sequence alignment, searches against biological databases, and others. Since the development of methods of high-throughput production of gene and protein sequences, the rate of addition of new sequences to the databases increased exponentially. Such a collection of sequences does not, by itself, increase the scientist's understanding of the biology of organisms. However, comparing these new sequences to those with known functions is a key way of understanding the biology of an organism from which the new sequence comes. Thus, sequence analysis can be used to assign function to genes and proteins by the study of the similarities between the compared sequences. Nowadays, there are many tools and techniques that provide the sequence comparisons (sequence alignment) and analyze the alignment product to understand its biology.

Sequence analysis in molecular biology includes a very wide range of relevant topics:

1. The comparison of sequences in order to find similarity, often to infer if they are related (homologous)

2. Identification of intrinsic features of the sequence such as active sites, post translational modification sites, gene-structures, reading frames, distributions of introns and exons and regulatory elements

3. Identification of sequence differences and variations such as point mutations and single nucleotide polymorphism (SNP) in order to get the genetic marker.

4. Revealing the evolution and genetic diversity of sequences and organisms

5. Identification of molecular structure from sequence alone

In chemistry, sequence analysis comprises techniques used to determine the sequence of a polymer formed of several monomers. In molecular biology and genetics, the same process is called simply "sequencing".

In marketing, sequence analysis is often used in analytical customer relationship management applications, such as NPTB models (Next Product to Buy).

In sociology, sequence methods are increasingly used to study life-course and career trajectories, patterns of organizational and national development, conversation and interaction structure, and the problem of work/family synchrony. This body of research has given rise to the emerging subfield of social sequence analysis.

History

Since the very first sequences of the insulin protein was characterised by Fred Sanger in 1951 biologists have been trying to use this knowledge to understand the function of molecules.He also contributed to DNA sequence. Not only he and his colleague's successes sequence the first DNA-based genome] . The method used in this study, which is called "Sanger method" or Sanger sequencing, was a milestone in sequencing long strand molecule such as DNA and this method was eventually used in human genome project . According to Michael Levitt, sequence analysis was born in the period from 1969-1977. In 1969 the analysis of sequences of transfer RNAs were used to infer residue interactions from correlated changes in the nucleotide sequences giving rise to a model of the tRNA secondary structure. In 1970, Saul B. Needleman and Christian D. Wunsch published the first computer algorithm for aligning two sequences. Over this time developments in obtaining nucleotide sequence greatly improved leading to the publication of the first complete genome of a bacteriophage in 1977.Robert Holley and his team in Cornell University was believed to be the first to sequence RNA molecule.

Sequence Alignment

There are millions of protein and nucleotide sequences known. These sequences fall into many groups of related sequences known as protein families or gene families. Relationships between these sequences are usually discovered by aligning them together and assigning this alignment a score. There are two main types of sequence alignment. Pair-wise sequence alignment only compares two sequences at a time and multiple sequence alignment compares many sequences in one go. Two important algorithms for aligning pairs of sequences are the Needleman-Wunsch algorithm and the Smith-Waterman algorithm. Popular tools for sequence alignment include:

- Pair-wise alignment - BLAST

- Multiple alignment - ClustalW, PROBCONS, MUSCLE, MAFFT, and T-Coffee.

A common use for pairwise sequence alignment is to take a sequence of interest and compare it to all known sequences in a database to identify homologous sequences. In general the matches in the database are ordered to show the most closely related sequences first followed by sequences with diminishing similarity. These matches are usually reported with a measure of statistical significance such as an Expectation value.

Profile Comparison

In 1987, Michael Gribskov, Andrew McLachlan, and David Eisenberg introduced the method of profile comparison for identifying distant similarities between proteins. Rather than using a single sequence, profile methods use a multiple sequence alignment to encode a profile which contains information about the conservation level of each residue. These profiles can then be used to search collections of sequences to find sequences that are related. Profiles are also known as Position Specific Scoring Matrices (PSSMs). In 1993, a probabilistic interpretation of profiles was introduced by David Haussler and colleagues using hidden Markov models. These models have become known as profile-HMMs.

In recent years, methods have been developed that allow the comparison of profiles directly to each other. These are known as profile-profile comparison methods.

Sequence Assembly

Sequence assembly refers to the reconstruction of a DNA sequence by aligning and merging small DNA fragments. It is an integral part of modern DNA sequencing. Since presently-available DNA sequencing technologies are ill-suited for reading long sequences, large pieces of DNA (such as genomes) are often sequenced by (1) cutting the DNA into small pieces, (2) reading the small fragments, and (3) reconstituting the original DNA by merging the information on various fragment.

Recently sequencing multiple species at one time is one of the top research target. Metagenomics is studying microbial communities directly obtained from environment. Different from cultured microorganism from lab, the wild sample usually contains dozens, sometimes even thousands types of microorganisms from their original habitats. Recovering the original genomes is a real challenging work. Most recently Projects:

Global Ocean survey (GOS)

Data Download

Human Microbiome Project (HMP)

Data Download

Earth Microbiome Project (EMP)

Gene Prediction

Gene prediction or gene finding refers to the process of identifying the regions of genomic DNA that encode genes. This includes protein-coding genes as well as RNA genes, but may also include prediction of other functional elements such as regulatory regions. Gene finding is one of the first and most important steps in understanding the genome of a species once it has been sequenced. In general the prediction of bacterial genes is significantly simpler and more accurate than the prediction of genes in eukaryotic species that usually have complex intron/exon patterns.Identifying genes in long sequences remains a problem, especially when the number of genes is unknown. Hidden markov model can be part of the solutions. Machine learning has been play a significant role in predicting the sequence of transcription factors. Traditional sequencing analyzing used focused on the statistical parameters of nucleotide sequence itself (The most common programs used are listed in Table 4.1). Another way is identifying homologous sequence based on other known gene sequence. Those two methods are both focusing on sequence. However, nowadays the shape feature of these molecules such as DNA and protein have also been studied and proposed to have an equivalent influence on the behaviors of these molecular as the sequence, if not higher.

Protein Structure Prediction

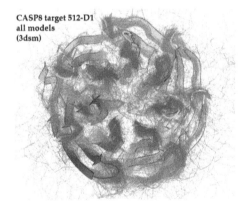

CASP8 target 512-D1
all models
(3dsm)

Target protein structure (3dsm, shown in ribbons), with Calpha backbones (in gray) of 354 predicted models for it submitted in the CASP8 structure-prediction experiment.

The 3D structures of molecules are of great importance to their functions in nature. Since structural prediction of large molecules at an atomic level is largely intractable problem, some biologists introduced ways to predict 3D structure at a primary sequence level. This includes biochemical or statistical analysis of amino acid residues in local regions and structural inference from homologs (or other potentially related proteins) with known 3D structures.

There have been a large number of diverse approaches to solve the structure prediction problem. In order to determine which methods were most effective a structure prediction competition was founded called CASP (Critical Assessment of Structure Prediction).

Methodology

The tasks that lie in the space of sequence analysis are often non-trivial to resolve and require the use of relatively complex approaches. Of the many types of methods used in practice, the most popular include:

- tools

- DNA patterns

- Dynamic programming

- Artificial Neural Network

- Hidden Markov Model

- Support Vector Machine

- Clustering

- Bayesian Network

- Regression Analysis

- Sequence mining

- Alignment-free sequence analysis

Sequence Alignment

In bioinformatics, a sequence alignment is a way of arranging the sequences of DNA, RNA, or protein to identify regions of similarity that may be a consequence of functional, structural, or evolutionary relationships between the sequences. Aligned sequences of nucleotide or amino acid residues are typically represented as rows within a matrix. Gaps are inserted between the residues so that identical or similar characters are aligned in successive columns. Sequence alignments are also used for non-biological sequences, such as calculating the edit distance cost between strings in a natural language or in financial data.

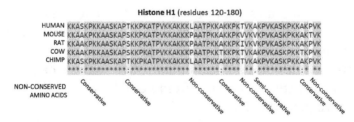

A sequence alignment, produced by ClustalO, of mammalian histone proteins.
Sequences are the amino acids for residues 120-180 of the proteins. Residues that are conserved across all sequences are highlighted in grey. Below the protein sequences is a key denoting conserved sequence (*), conservative mutations (:), semi-conservative mutations (.), and non-conservative mutations ( ).

Interpretation

If two sequences in an alignment share a common ancestor, mismatches can be interpreted as point mutations and gaps as indels (that is, insertion or deletion mutations) introduced in one or both lineages in the time since they diverged from one another. In sequence alignments of proteins, the degree of similarity between amino acids occupying a particular position in the sequence can be interpreted as a rough measure of how conserved a particular region or sequence motif is among lineages. The absence of substitutions, or the presence of only very conservative substitutions (that is, the substitution of amino acids whose side chains have similar biochemical properties) in a particular region of the sequence, suggest that this region has structural or functional importance. Although DNA and RNA nucleotide bases are more similar to each other than are amino acids, the conservation of base pairs can indicate a similar functional or structural role.

Alignment Methods

Very short or very similar sequences can be aligned by hand. However, most interesting problems require the alignment of lengthy, highly variable or extremely numerous sequences that cannot be aligned solely by human effort. Instead, human knowledge is applied in constructing algorithms to produce high-quality sequence alignments, and occasionally in adjusting the final results to reflect patterns that are difficult to represent algorithmically (especially in the case of nucleotide sequences). Computational approaches to sequence alignment generally fall into two categories: *global alignments* and *local alignments*. Calculating a global alignment is a form of global optimization that "forces" the alignment to span the entire length of all query sequences. By contrast, local alignments identify regions of similarity within long sequences that are often widely divergent overall. Local alignments are often preferable, but can be more difficult to calculate because of the additional challenge of identifying the regions of similarity. A variety of computational algorithms have been applied to the sequence alignment problem. These include slow but formally correct methods like dynamic programming. These also include efficient, heuristic algorithms or probabilistic methods designed for large-scale database search, that do not guarantee to find best matches.

Representations

Alignments are commonly represented both graphically and in text format. In almost all sequence alignment representations, sequences are written in rows arranged so that aligned residues appear in successive columns. In text formats, aligned columns containing identical or similar characters are indicated with a system of conservation symbols. As in the image above, an asterisk or pipe symbol is used to show identity between two columns; other less common symbols include a colon for conservative substitutions and a period for semiconservative substitutions. Many sequence visualization programs also use color to display information about the properties of the individual sequence elements; in DNA and RNA sequences, this equates to assigning each nucleotide its own color. In protein alignments, such as the one in the image above, color is often used to indicate amino acid properties to aid in judging the conservation of a given amino acid substitution. For multiple sequences the last row in each column is often the consensus sequence determined by the alignment; the consensus sequence is also often represented in graphical format with a sequence logo in which the size of each nucleotide or amino acid letter corresponds to its degree of conservation.

Sequence alignments can be stored in a wide variety of text-based file formats, many of which were originally developed in conjunction with a specific alignment program or implementation. Most web-based tools allow a limited number of input and output formats, such as FASTA format and GenBank format and the output is not easily editable. Several conversion programs that provide graphical and/or command line interfaces are available, such as READSEQ and EMBOSS. There are also several programming packages which provide this conversion functionality, such as BioPython, BioRuby and BioPerl.

Global and Local Alignments

Global alignments, which attempt to align every residue in every sequence, are most useful when the sequences in the query set are similar and of roughly equal size. (This does not mean global alignments cannot start and/or end in gaps.) A general global alignment technique is the Needleman–Wunsch algorithm, which is based on dynamic programming. Local alignments are more useful for dissimilar sequences that are suspected to contain regions of similarity or similar sequence motifs within their larger sequence context. The Smith–Waterman algorithm is a general local alignment method also based on dynamic programming.

Hybrid methods, known as semiglobal or "glocal" (short for global-local) methods, attempt to find the best possible alignment that includes the start and end of one or the other sequence. This can be especially useful when the downstream part of one sequence overlaps with the upstream part of the other sequence. In this case, neither global nor local alignment is entirely appropriate: a global alignment would attempt to force the alignment to extend beyond the region of overlap, while a local alignment might not fully cover the region of overlap. Another case where semiglobal alignment is useful is when one sequence is short (for example a gene sequence) and the other is very long (for example a chromosome sequence). In that case, the short sequence should be globally aligned but only a local alignment is desired for the long sequence.

Pairwise Alignment

Pairwise sequence alignment methods are used to find the best-matching piecewise (local) or global alignments of two query sequences. Pairwise alignments can only be used between two sequences at a time, but they are efficient to calculate and are often used for methods that do not require extreme precision (such as searching a database for sequences with high similarity to a query). The three primary methods of producing pairwise alignments are dot-matrix methods, dynamic programming, and word methods; however, multiple sequence alignment techniques can also align pairs of sequences. Although each method has its individual strengths and weaknesses, all three pairwise methods have difficulty with highly repetitive sequences of low information content - especially where the number of repetitions differ in the two sequences to be aligned. One way of quantifying the utility of a given pairwise alignment is the 'maximum unique match' (MUM), or the longest subsequence that occurs in both query sequences. Longer MUM sequences typically reflect closer relatedness.

Dot-matrix Methods

Self comparison of a part of a mouse strain genome. The dot-plot shows a patchwork of lines, demonstrating duplicated segments of DNA.

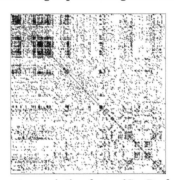

A DNA dot plot of a human zinc finger transcription factor (GenBank ID NM_002383), showing regional self-similarity. The main diagonal represents the sequence's alignment with itself; lines off the main diagonal represent similar or repetitive patterns within the sequence. This is a typical example of a recurrence plot.

The dot-matrix approach, which implicitly produces a family of alignments for individual sequence regions, is qualitative and conceptually simple, though time-consuming to analyze on a large scale. In the absence of noise, it can be easy to visually identify certain sequence features—such as insertions, deletions, repeats, or inverted repeats—from a dot-matrix plot. To construct a dot-matrix plot, the two sequences are written along the top row and leftmost column of a two-dimensional matrix and a dot is placed at any point where the characters in the appropriate columns match—this is a typical recurrence plot. Some implementations vary the size or intensity of the dot depending on the degree of similarity of the two characters, to accommodate conservative substitutions. The dot plots of very closely related sequences will appear as a single line along the matrix's main diagonal.

Problems with dot plots as an information display technique include: noise, lack of clarity, non-intuitiveness, difficulty extracting match summary statistics and match positions on the two sequences. There is also much wasted space where the match data is inherently duplicated across the diagonal and most of the actual area of the plot is taken up by either empty space or noise, and, finally, dot-plots are limited to two sequences. None of these limitations apply to Miropeats alignment diagrams but they have their own particular flaws.

Dot plots can also be used to assess repetitiveness in a single sequence. A sequence can be plotted against itself and regions that share significant similarities will appear as lines off the main diagonal. This effect can occur when a protein consists of multiple similar structural domains.

Dynamic Programming

The technique of dynamic programming can be applied to produce global alignments via the Needleman-Wunsch algorithm, and local alignments via the Smith-Waterman algorithm. In typical usage, protein alignments use a substitution matrix to assign scores to amino-acid matches or mismatches, and a gap penalty for matching an amino acid in one sequence to a gap in the other. DNA and RNA alignments may use a scoring matrix, but in practice often simply assign a positive match score, a negative mismatch score, and a negative gap penalty. (In standard dynamic programming, the score of each amino acid position is independent of the identity of its neighbors, and therefore base stacking effects are not taken into account. However, it is possible to account for such effects by modifying the algorithm.) A common extension to standard linear gap costs, is the usage of two different gap penalties for opening a gap and for extending a gap. Typically the former is much larger than the latter, e.g. -10 for gap open and -2 for gap extension. Thus, the number of gaps in an alignment is usually reduced and residues and gaps are kept together, which typically makes more biological sense. The Gotoh algorithm implements affine gap costs by using three matrices.

Dynamic programming can be useful in aligning nucleotide to protein sequences, a task complicated by the need to take into account frameshift mutations (usually insertions or deletions). The framesearch method produces a series of global or local pairwise alignments between a query nucleotide sequence and a search set of protein sequences, or vice versa. Its ability to evaluate frameshifts offset by an arbitrary number of nucleotides makes the method useful for sequences containing large numbers of indels, which can be very difficult to align with more efficient heuristic methods. In practice, the method requires large amounts of computing power or a system whose architecture is specialized for dynamic programming. The BLAST and EMBOSS suites provide basic tools for creating translated alignments (though some of these approaches take advantage of side-effects of sequence searching capabilities of the tools). More general methods are available from both commercial sources, such as *FrameSearch*, distributed as part of the Accelrys GCG package, and Open Source software such as Genewise.

The dynamic programming method is guaranteed to find an optimal alignment given a particular scoring function; however, identifying a good scoring function is often an empirical rather than a theoretical matter. Although dynamic programming is extensible to more than two sequences, it is prohibitively slow for large numbers of sequences or extremely long sequences.

Word Methods

Word methods, also known as k-tuple methods, are heuristic methods that are not guaranteed to find an optimal alignment solution, but are significantly more efficient than dynamic programming. These methods are especially useful in large-scale database searches where it is understood that a large proportion of the candidate sequences will have essentially no significant match with the query sequence. Word methods are best known for their implementation in the database search tools FASTA and the BLAST family. Word methods identify a series of short, nonoverlapping subsequences ("words") in the query sequence that are then matched to candidate database sequences. The relative positions of the word in the two sequences being compared are subtracted to obtain an offset; this will indicate a region of alignment if multiple distinct words produce the same offset. Only if this region is detected do these methods apply more sensitive alignment criteria; thus, many unnecessary comparisons with sequences of no appreciable similarity are eliminated.

In the FASTA method, the user defines a value k to use as the word length with which to search the database. The method is slower but more sensitive at lower values of k, which are also preferred for searches involving a very short query sequence. The BLAST family of search methods provides a number of algorithms optimized for particular types of queries, such as searching for distantly related sequence matches. BLAST was developed to provide a faster alternative to FASTA without sacrificing much accuracy; like FASTA, BLAST uses a word search of length k, but evaluates only the most significant word matches, rather than every word match as does FASTA. Most BLAST implementations use a fixed default word length that is optimized for the query and database type, and that is changed only under special circumstances, such as when searching with repetitive or very short query sequences. Implementations can be found via a number of web portals, such as EMBL FASTA and NCBI BLAST.

Multiple Sequence Alignment

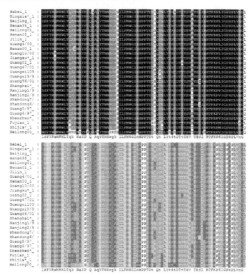

Alignment of 27 avian influenza hemagglutinin protein sequences colored by residue conservation (top) and residue properties (bottom)

Multiple sequence alignment is an extension of pairwise alignment to incorporate more than two sequences at a time. Multiple alignment methods try to align all of the sequences in a given query set. Multiple alignments are often used in identifying conserved sequence regions across a group of sequences hypothesized to be evolutionarily related. Such conserved sequence motifs can be used in conjunction with structural and mechanistic information to locate the catalytic active sites of enzymes. Alignments are also used to aid in establishing evolutionary relationships by constructing phylogenetic trees. Multiple sequence alignments are computationally difficult to produce and most formulations of the problem lead to NP-complete combinatorial optimization problems. Nevertheless, the utility of these alignments in bioinformatics has led to the development of a variety of methods suitable for aligning three or more sequences.

Dynamic Programming

The technique of dynamic programming is theoretically applicable to any number of sequences; however, because it is computationally expensive in both time and memory, it is rarely used for more than three or four sequences in its most basic form. This method requires constructing the n-dimensional equivalent of the sequence matrix formed from two sequences, where n is the number of sequences in the query. Standard dynamic programming is first used on all pairs of query sequences and then the "alignment space" is filled in by considering possible matches or gaps at intermediate positions, eventually constructing an alignment essentially between each two-sequence alignment. Although this technique is computationally expensive, its guarantee of a global optimum solution is useful in cases where only a few sequences need to be aligned accurately. One method for reducing the computational demands of dynamic programming, which relies on the "sum of pairs" objective function, has been implemented in the MSA software package.

Progressive Methods

Progressive, hierarchical, or tree methods generate a multiple sequence alignment by first aligning the most similar sequences and then adding successively less related sequences or groups to the alignment until the entire query set has been incorporated into the solution. The initial tree describing the sequence relatedness is based on pairwise comparisons that may include heuristic pairwise alignment methods similar to FASTA. Progressive alignment results are dependent on the choice of "most related" sequences and thus can be sensitive to inaccuracies in the initial pairwise alignments. Most progressive multiple sequence alignment methods additionally weight the sequences in the query set according to their relatedness, which reduces the likelihood of making a poor choice of initial sequences and thus improves alignment accuracy.

Many variations of the Clustal progressive implementation are used for multiple sequence alignment, phylogenetic tree construction, and as input for protein structure prediction. A slower but more accurate variant of the progressive method is known as T-Coffee.

Iterative Methods

Iterative methods attempt to improve on the heavy dependence on the accuracy of the initial pairwise alignments, which is the weak point of the progressive methods. Iterative methods optimize an objective function based on a selected alignment scoring method by assigning an initial global alignment and then realigning sequence subsets. The realigned subsets are then themselves aligned to produce the next iteration's multiple sequence alignment. Various ways of selecting the sequence subgroups and objective function are reviewed in.

Motif Finding

Motif finding, also known as profile analysis, constructs global multiple sequence alignments that attempt to align short conserved sequence motifs among the sequences in the query set. This is usually done by first constructing a general global multiple sequence alignment, after which the highly conserved regions are isolated and used to construct a set of profile matrices. The profile matrix for each conserved region is arranged like a scoring matrix but its frequency counts for each amino acid or nucleotide at each position are derived from the conserved region's character distribution rather than from a more general empirical distribution. The profile matrices are then used to search other sequences for occurrences of the motif they characterize. In cases where the original data set contained a small number of sequences, or only highly related sequences, pseudocounts are added to normalize the character distributions represented in the motif.

Techniques Inspired by Computer Science

A variety of general optimization algorithms commonly used in computer science have also been applied to the multiple sequence alignment problem. Hidden Markov models have been used to produce probability scores for a family of possible multiple sequence alignments for a given query set; although early HMM-based methods produced underwhelming performance, later applications have found them especially effective in detecting remotely related sequences because they are less susceptible to noise created by conservative or semiconservative substitutions. Genetic algorithms and simulated annealing have also been used in optimizing multiple sequence alignment scores as judged by a scoring function like the sum-of-pairs method. More complete details and software packages can be found in the main article multiple sequence alignment.

The Burrows–Wheeler transform has been successfully applied to fast short read alignment in popular tools such as Bowtie and BWA.

Structural Alignment

Structural alignments, which are usually specific to protein and sometimes RNA sequences, use information about the secondary and tertiary structure of the protein or RNA molecule to aid in aligning the sequences. These methods can be used for two or more sequences and typically produce local alignments; however, because they depend on the availability of structural information, they can only be used for sequences whose corresponding structures are known (usually through X-ray crystallography or NMR spectroscopy). Because both protein and RNA structure is more evolutionarily conserved than sequence, structural alignments can be more reliable between sequences that are very distantly related and that have diverged so extensively that sequence comparison cannot reliably detect their similarity.

Structural alignments are used as the "gold standard" in evaluating alignments for homology-based protein structure prediction because they explicitly align regions of the protein sequence that are structurally similar rather than relying exclusively on sequence information. However, clearly structural alignments cannot be used in structure prediction because at least one sequence in the query set is the target to be modeled, for which the structure is not known. It has been shown that, given the structural alignment between a target and a template sequence, highly accurate models of the target protein sequence can be produced; a major stumbling block in homology-based structure prediction is the production of structurally accurate alignments given only sequence information.

DALI

The DALI method, or distance matrix alignment, is a fragment-based method for constructing structural alignments based on contact similarity patterns between successive hexapeptides in the query sequences. It can generate pairwise or multiple alignments and identify a query sequence's structural neighbors in the Protein Data Bank (PDB). It has been used to construct the FSSP structural alignment database (Fold classification based on Structure-Structure alignment of Proteins, or Families of Structurally Similar Proteins). A DALI webserver can be accessed at DALI and the FSSP is located at The Dali Database.

SSAP

SSAP (sequential structure alignment program) is a dynamic programming-based method of structural alignment that uses atom-to-atom vectors in structure space as comparison points. It has been extended since its original description to include multiple as well as pairwise alignments, and has been used in the construction of the CATH (Class, Architecture, Topology, Homology) hierarchical database classification of protein folds. The CATH database can be accessed at CATH Protein Structure Classification.

Combinatorial Extension

The combinatorial extension method of structural alignment generates a pairwise structural alignment by using local geometry to align short fragments of the two proteins being analyzed and then assembles these fragments into a larger alignment. Based on measures such as rigid-body root mean square distance, residue distances, local secondary structure, and surrounding environmental features such as residue neighbor hydrophobicity, local alignments called "aligned fragment pairs" are generated and used to build a similarity matrix representing all possible structural alignments within predefined cutoff criteria. A path from one protein structure state to the other is then traced through the matrix by extending the growing alignment one fragment at a time. The optimal such path defines the combinatorial-extension alignment. A web-based server implementing the method and providing a database of pairwise alignments of structures in the Protein Data Bank is located at the Combinatorial Extension website.

Phylogenetic Analysis

Phylogenetics and sequence alignment are closely related fields due to the shared necessity of evaluating sequence relatedness. The field of phylogenetics makes extensive use of sequence alignments in the construction and interpretation of phylogenetic trees, which are used to classify the evolutionary relationships between homologous genes represented in the genomes of divergent species. The degree to which sequences in a query set differ is qualitatively related to the sequences' evolutionary distance from one another. Roughly speaking, high sequence identity suggests that the sequences in question have a comparatively young most recent common ancestor, while low identity suggests that the divergence is more ancient. This approximation, which reflects the "molecular clock" hypothesis that a roughly constant rate of evolutionary change can be used to extrapolate the elapsed time since two genes first diverged (that is, the coalescence time), assumes that the effects of mutation and selection are constant across sequence lineages. Therefore, it does not account for possible difference among organisms or species in the rates of DNA repair or the possible functional conservation of specific regions in a sequence. (In the case of nucleotide sequences, the molecular clock hypothesis in its most basic form also discounts the difference in acceptance rates between silent mutations that do not alter the meaning of a given codon and other mutations that result in a different amino acid being incorporated into the protein.) More statistically accurate methods allow the evolutionary rate on each branch of the phylogenetic tree to vary, thus producing better estimates of coalescence times for genes.

Progressive multiple alignment techniques produce a phylogenetic tree by necessity because they incorporate sequences into the growing alignment in order of relatedness. Other techniques that assemble multiple sequence alignments and phylogenetic trees score and sort trees first and calculate a multiple sequence alignment from the highest-scoring tree. Commonly used methods of phylogenetic tree construction are mainly heuristic because the problem of selecting the optimal tree, like the problem of selecting the optimal multiple sequence alignment, is NP-hard.

Assessment of Significance

Sequence alignments are useful in bioinformatics for identifying sequence similarity, producing phylogenetic trees, and developing homology models of protein structures. However, the biological relevance of sequence alignments is not always clear. Alignments are often assumed to reflect a degree of evolutionary change between sequences descended from a common ancestor; however, it is formally possible that convergent evolution can occur to produce apparent similarity between proteins that are evolutionarily unrelated but perform similar functions and have similar structures.

In database searches such as BLAST, statistical methods can determine the likelihood of a particular alignment between sequences or sequence regions arising by chance given the size and composition of the database being searched. These values can vary significantly depending on the search space. In particular, the likelihood of finding a given alignment by chance increases if the database consists only of sequences from the same organism as the query sequence. Repetitive sequences in the database or query can also distort both the search results and the assessment of statistical significance; BLAST automatically filters such repetitive sequences in the query to avoid apparent hits that are statistical artifacts.

Methods of statistical significance estimation for gapped sequence alignments are available in the literature.

Assessment of Credibility

Statistical significance indicates the probability that an alignment of a given quality could arise by chance, but does not indicate how much superior a given alignment is to alternative alignments of the same sequences. Measures of alignment credibility indicate the extent to which the best scoring alignments for a given pair of sequences are substantially similar. Methods of alignment credibility estimation for gapped sequence alignments are available in the literature.

Scoring Functions

The choice of a scoring function that reflects biological or statistical observations about known sequences is important to producing good alignments. Protein sequences are frequently aligned using substitution matrices that reflect the probabilities of given character-to-character substitutions. A series of matrices called PAM matrices (Point Accepted Mutation matrices, originally defined by Margaret Dayhoff and sometimes referred to as "Dayhoff matrices") explicitly encode evolutionary approximations regarding the rates and probabilities of particular amino acid mutations. Another common series of scoring matrices, known as BLOSUM (Blocks Substitution Matrix), encodes empirically derived substitution probabilities. Variants of both types of matrices are used to detect sequences with differing levels of divergence, thus allowing users of BLAST or FASTA to restrict searches to more closely related matches or expand to detect more divergent sequences. Gap penalties account for the introduction of a gap - on the evolutionary model, an insertion or deletion mutation - in both nucleotide and protein sequences, and therefore the penalty values should be proportional to the expected rate of such mutations. The quality of the alignments produced therefore depends on the quality of the scoring function.

It can be very useful and instructive to try the same alignment several times with different choices for scoring matrix and/or gap penalty values and compare the results. Regions where the solution is weak or non-unique can often be identified by observing which regions of the alignment are robust to variations in alignment parameters.

Other Biological Uses

Sequenced RNA, such as expressed sequence tags and full-length mRNAs, can be aligned to a sequenced genome to find where there are genes and get information about alternative splicing and RNA editing. Sequence alignment is also a part of genome assembly, where sequences are aligned to find overlap so that *contigs* (long stretches of sequence) can be formed. Another use is SNP analysis, where sequences from different individuals are aligned to find single basepairs that are often different in a population.

Non-biological Uses

The methods used for biological sequence alignment have also found applications in other fields, most notably in natural language processing and in social sciences, where the Needleman-Wunsch algorithm is usually referred to as Optimal matching. Techniques that generate the set of elements from which words will be selected in natural-language generation algorithms have borrowed multiple sequence alignment techniques from bioinformatics to produce linguistic versions of computer-generated mathematical proofs. In the field of historical and comparative linguistics, sequence alignment has been used to partially automate the comparative method by which linguists traditionally reconstruct languages. Business and marketing research has also applied multiple sequence alignment techniques in analyzing series of purchases over time.

Software

A more complete list of available software categorized by algorithm and alignment type is available at sequence alignment software, but common software tools used for general sequence alignment tasks include ClustalW2 and T-coffee for alignment, and BLAST and FASTA3x for database searching. Commercial tools such as Geneious and Pattern-Hunter are also available.

Alignment algorithms and software can be directly compared to one another using a standardized set of benchmark reference multiple sequence alignments known as BAliBASE. The data set consists of structural alignments, which can be considered a standard against which purely sequence-based methods are compared. The relative performance of many common alignment methods on frequently encountered alignment problems has been tabulated and selected results published online at BAliBASE. A comprehensive list of BAliBASE scores for many (currently 12) different alignment tools can be computed within the protein workbench STRAP.

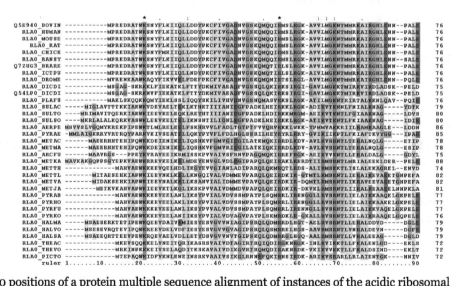

First 90 positions of a protein multiple sequence alignment of instances of the acidic ribosomal protein P0 (L10E) from several organisms. Generated with ClustalX.

A multiple sequence alignment (MSA) is a sequence alignment of three or more biological sequences, generally protein, DNA, or RNA. In many cases, the input set of query sequences are assumed to have an evolutionary relationship by which they share a lineage and are descended from a common ancestor. From the resulting MSA, sequence homology can be inferred and phylogenetic analysis can be conducted to assess the sequences' shared evolutionary origins. Visual depictions of the alignment as in the image at right illustrate mutation events such as point mutations (single amino acid or nucleotide changes) that appear as differing characters in a single alignment column, and insertion or deletion mutations (indels or gaps) that appear as hyphens in one or more of the sequences in the alignment. Multiple sequence alignment is often used to assess sequence conservation of protein domains, tertiary and secondary structures, and even individual amino acids or nucleotides.

Multiple sequence alignment also refers to the process of aligning such a sequence set. Because three or more sequences of biologically relevant length can be difficult and are almost always time-consuming to align by hand, computational algorithms are used to produce and analyze the alignments. MSAs require more sophisticated methodologies than pairwise alignment because they are more computationally complex. Most multiple sequence alignment programs use heuristic methods rather than global optimization because identifying the optimal alignment between more than a few sequences of moderate length is prohibitively computationally expensive.

Dynamic Programming and Computational Complexity

A direct method for producing an MSA uses the dynamic programming technique to identify the globally optimal alignment solution. For proteins, this method usually involves two sets of parameters: a gap penalty and a substitution matrix assigning scores or probabilities to the alignment of each possible pair of amino acids based on the similarity of the amino acids' chemical properties and the evolutionary probability of the mutation. For nucleotide sequences a similar gap penalty is used, but a much simpler substitution matrix, wherein only identical matches and mismatches are considered, is typical. The scores in the substitution matrix may be either all positive or a mix of positive and negative in the case of a global alignment, but must be both positive and negative, in the case of a local alignment.

For n individual sequences, the naive method requires constructing the n-dimensional equivalent of the matrix formed in standard pairwise sequence alignment. The search space thus increases exponentially with increasing n and is also strongly dependent on sequence length. Expressed with the big O notation commonly used to measure computational complexity, a naïve MSA takes $O(Length^{Nseqs})$ time to produce. To find the global optimum for n sequences this way has been shown to be an NP-complete problem. In 1989, based on Carrillo-Lipman Algorithm, Altschul introduced a practical method that uses pairwise alignments to constrain the n-dimensional search space. In this approach pairwise dynamic programming alignments are performed on each pair of sequences in the query set, and only the space near the n-dimensional intersection of these alignments is searched for the n-way alignment. The MSA program optimizes the sum of all of the pairs of characters at each position in the alignment (the so-called *sum of pair* score) and has been implemented in a software program for constructing multiple sequence alignments.

Progressive Alignment Construction

The most widely used approach to multiple sequence alignments uses a heuristic search known as progressive technique (also known as the hierarchical or tree method) developed by Paulien Hogeweg and Ben Hesper in 1984. Progressive alignment builds up a final MSA by combining pairwise alignments beginning with the most similar pair and progressing to the most distantly related. All progressive alignment methods require two stages: a first stage in which the relationships between the sequences are represented as a tree, called a *guide tree*, and a second step in which the MSA is built by adding the sequences sequentially to the growing MSA according to the guide tree. The initial *guide tree* is determined by an efficient clustering method such as neighbor-joining or UPGMA, and may use distances based on the number of identical two letter sub-sequences (as in FASTA rather than a dynamic programming alignment).

Progressive alignments are not guaranteed to be globally optimal. The primary problem is that when errors are made at any stage in growing the MSA, these errors are then propagated through to the final result. Performance is also particularly bad when all of the sequences in the set are rather distantly related. Most modern progressive methods modify their scoring function with a secondary weighting function that assigns scaling factors to individual members of the query set in a nonlinear fashion based on their phylogenetic distance from their nearest neighbors. This corrects for non-random selection of the sequences given to the alignment program.

Progressive alignment methods are efficient enough to implement on a large scale for many (100s to 1000s) sequences. Progressive alignment services are commonly available on publicly accessible web servers so users need not locally install the applications of interest. The most popular progressive alignment method has been the Clustal family, especially the weighted variant ClustalW to which access is provided by a large number of web portals including GenomeNet, EBI, and EMBNet. Different portals or implementations can vary in user interface and make different parameters accessible to the user. ClustalW is used extensively for phylogenetic tree construction, in spite of the author's explicit warnings that unedited alignments should not be used in such studies and as input for protein structure prediction by homology modeling. Current version of Clustal family is ClustalW2. EMBL-EBI announced that CLustalW2 will be expired in August 2015. They recommend Clustal Omega which performs based on seeded guide trees and HMM profile-profile techniques for protein alignments. They offer different MSA tools for progressive DNA alignments. One of them is MAFFT (Multiple Alignment using Fast Fourier Transform).

Another common progressive alignment method called T-Coffee is slower than Clustal and its derivatives but generally produces more accurate alignments for distantly related sequence sets. T-Coffee calculates pairwise alignments by combining the direct alignment of the pair with indirect alignments that aligns each sequence of the pair to a third sequence. It uses the output from Clustal as well as another local alignment program LALIGN, which finds multiple regions of local alignment between two sequences. The resulting alignment and phylogenetic tree are used as a guide to produce new and more accurate weighting factors.

Because progressive methods are heuristics that are not guaranteed to converge to a global optimum, alignment quality can be difficult to evaluate and their true biological significance can be obscure. A semi-progressive method that improves alignment quality and does not use a lossy heuristic while still running in polynomial time has been implemented in the program PSAlign.

Iterative Methods

A set of methods to produce MSAs while reducing the errors inherent in progressive methods are classified as "iterative" because they work similarly to progressive methods but repeatedly realign the initial sequences as well as adding new sequences to the growing MSA. One reason progressive methods are so strongly dependent on a high-quality initial alignment is the fact that these alignments are always incorporated into the final result — that is, once a sequence has been aligned into the MSA, its alignment is not considered further. This approximation improves efficiency at the cost of accuracy. By contrast, iterative methods can return to previously calculated pairwise alignments or sub-MSAs incorporating subsets of the query sequence as a means of optimizing a general objective function such as finding a high-quality alignment score.

A variety of subtly different iteration methods have been implemented and made available in software packages; reviews and comparisons have been useful but generally refrain from choosing a "best" technique. The software package PRRN/PRRP uses a hill-climbing algorithm to optimize its MSA alignment score and iteratively corrects both alignment weights and locally divergent or "gappy" regions of the growing MSA. PRRP performs best when refining an alignment previously constructed by a faster method.

Another iterative program, DIALIGN, takes an unusual approach of focusing narrowly on local alignments between sub-segments or sequence motifs without introducing a gap penalty. The alignment of individual motifs is then achieved with a matrix representation similar to a dot-matrix plot in a pairwise alignment. An alternative method that uses fast local alignments as anchor points or "seeds" for a slower global-alignment procedure is implemented in the CHAOS/DIALIGN suite.

A third popular iteration-based method called MUSCLE (multiple sequence alignment by log-expectation) improves on progressive methods with a more accurate distance measure to assess the relatedness of two sequences. The distance measure is updated between iteration stages (although, in its original form, MUSCLE contained only 2-3 iterations depending on whether refinement was enabled).

Consensus Methods

Consensus methods attempt to find the optimal multiple sequence alignment given multiple different alignments of the same set of sequences. There are two commonly used consensus methods, M-COFFEE and MergeAlign. M-COFFEE uses multiple sequence alignments generated by seven different methods to generate consensus alignments. MergeAlign is capable of generating consensus alignments from any number of input alignments generated using different models of sequence evolution or different methods of multiple sequence alignment. The default option for MergeAlign is to infer a consensus alignment using alignments generated using 91 different models of protein sequence evolution.

Hidden Markov Models

Hidden Markov models are probabilistic models that can assign likelihoods to all possible combinations of gaps, matches, and mismatches to determine the most likely MSA or set of possible MSAs. HMMs can produce a single highest-scoring output but can also generate a family of possible alignments that can then be evaluated for biological significance. HMMs can produce both global and local alignments. Although HMM-based methods have been developed relatively recently, they offer significant improvements in computational speed, especially for sequences that contain overlapping regions.

Typical HMM-based methods work by representing an MSA as a form of directed acyclic graph known as a partial-order graph, which consists of a series of nodes representing possible entries in the columns of an MSA. In this representation a column that is absolutely conserved (that is, that all the sequences in the MSA share a particular character at a particular position) is coded as a single node with as many outgoing connections as there are possible characters in the next column of the alignment. In the terms of a typical hidden Markov model, the observed states are the individual alignment columns and the "hidden" states represent the presumed ancestral sequence from which the sequences in the query set are hypothesized to have descended. An efficient search variant of the dynamic programming method, known as the Viterbi algorithm, is generally used to successively align the growing MSA to the next sequence in the query set to produce a new MSA. This is distinct from progressive alignment methods because the alignment of prior sequences is updated at each new sequence addition. However, like progressive methods, this technique can be influenced by the order in which the sequences in the query set are integrated into the alignment, especially when the sequences are distantly related.

Several software programs are available in which variants of HMM-based methods have been implemented and which are noted for their scalability and efficiency, although properly using an HMM method is more complex than using more common progressive methods. The simplest is POA (Partial-Order Alignment); a similar but more generalized method is implemented in the packages SAM (Sequence Alignment and Modeling System). and HMMER. SAM has been used as a source of alignments for protein structure prediction to participate in the CASP structure prediction experiment and to develop a database of predicted proteins in the yeast species *S. cerevisiae*. HHsearch is a software package for the detection of remotely related protein sequences based on the pairwise comparison of HMMs. A server running HHsearch (HHpred) was by far the fastest of the 10 best automatic structure prediction servers in the CASP7 and CASP8 structure prediction competitions.

Genetic Algorithms and Simulated Annealing

Standard optimization techniques in computer science — both of which were inspired by, but do not directly reproduce, physical processes — have also been used in an attempt to more efficiently produce quality MSAs. One such technique, genetic algorithms, has been used for MSA production in an attempt to broadly simulate the hypothesized evolutionary process that gave rise to the divergence in the query set. The method works by breaking a series of possible MSAs into fragments and repeatedly rearranging those fragments with the introduction of gaps at varying positions. A general objective function is optimized during the simulation, most generally the "sum of pairs" maximization function introduced in dynamic programming-based MSA methods. A technique for protein sequences has been implemented in the software program SAGA (Sequence Alignment by Genetic Algorithm) and its equivalent in RNA is called RAGA.

The technique of simulated annealing, by which an existing MSA produced by another method is refined by a series of rearrangements designed to find better regions of alignment space than the one the input alignment already occupies. Like the genetic algorithm method, simulated annealing maximizes an objective function like the sum-of-pairs function. Simulated annealing uses a metaphorical "temperature factor" that determines the rate at which rearrangements proceed and the likelihood of each rearrangement; typical usage alternates periods of high rearrangement rates with relatively low likelihood (to explore more distant regions of alignment space) with periods of lower rates and higher likelihoods to more thoroughly explore local minima near the newly "colonized" regions. This approach has been implemented in the program MSA-SA (Multiple Sequence Alignment by Simulated Annealing).

Phylogeny-aware Methods

Most multiple sequence alignment methods try to minimize the number of insertions/deletions (gaps) and, as a consequence, produce compact alignments. This causes several problems if the sequences to be aligned contain non-homologous regions, if gaps are informative in a phylogeny analysis. These problems are common in newly produced sequences that are poorly annotated and may contain frame-shifts, wrong domains or non-homologous spliced exons.

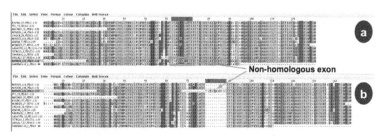

Non-homologous exon alignment by an iterative method (a), and by a phylogeny-aware method (b)

The first such method was developed in 2005 by Löytynoja and Goldman. The same authors released a software package called *PRANK* in 2008. PRANK improves alignments when insertions are present. Nevertheless, it runs slowly compared to progressive and/or iterative methods which have been developed for several years.

In 2012, two new phylogeny-aware tools appeared. One is called *PAGAN* that was developed by the same team as PRANK. The other is *ProGraphMSA* developed by Szalkowski. Both software packages were developed independently but share common features, notably the use of graph algorithms to improve the recognition of non-homologous regions, and an improvement in code making these software faster than PRANK.

Motif Finding

```
DAMMfly2R_  : MYLPERTEHQKIERLY--------------------------------------------------DSNRVN--------------AEPGQGL----
DCP1fly2R_  : ---------------MTD-----------------ECVTRNYGVGIRSPNGSENRGS-FIMADNTDAK-------------GCTPESLVVGG
DRICEfly3R  : MDATNNGESADQVGIRVGN---------------PEQPNDHTDALGSV-GSGGAGSSGLVAGSSHPY-------------GSGAIGQLANG
DECAYfly3R  : MDDTDFSLFGQKNKHK--------------------------------------------KDKADATKIA--------------HTPTSEL-;--
DRONCfly3L  : MQPPELEIGMPKRHREHIRKNLNILVEWTNYERLAMECVQQGILTVQMLRNTQDLNGK-PFNMDEKDVRVEQHRRLLLKITQRGPTAYNLLINA
STRICAfly2  : MGWWSKKSETDRSQPSQELVAQDPRTRVQTTSAATETTNTAVQNSTITDNNKQTVTFL-TTRQTVTHTQRALITETTTRRTPSQABLEALFAKI
DREDDPAfly  : MSASAIYRPFPKVKHFCIFPIAMAGSNLLIHLDTIDQNDLIYVERDMNFAQKVGLGFL-LYGDDHSDATYILQKLLAMTRSDFPQSDLLIKFAK
DREDDPBfly  : MSASAIYRPFPKVKHFCIFPIAMAGSNLLIHLDTIDQNDLIYVERDMNFAQKVGLGFL-LYGDDHSDATYILQKLLAMTRSDFPQSDLLIKFAK
DREDDPCfly  : MSASAIYRPFPKVKHFCIFPIAMAGSNLLIHLDTIDQNDLIYVERDMNFAQKVGLGFL-LYGDDHSDATYILQKLLAMTRSDFPQSDLLIKFAK
```

Alignment of the seven Drosophila caspases colored by motifs as identified by MEME. When motif positions and sequence alignments are generated independently, they often correlate well but not perfectly, as in this example.

Motif finding, also known as profile analysis, is a method of locating sequence motifs in global MSAs that is both a means of producing a better MSA and a means of producing a scoring matrix for use in searching other sequences for similar motifs. A variety of methods for isolating the motifs have been developed, but all are based on identifying short highly conserved patterns within the larger alignment and constructing a matrix similar to a substitution matrix that reflects the amino acid or nucleotide composition of each position in the putative motif. The alignment can then be refined using these matrices. In standard profile analysis, the matrix includes entries for each possible character as well as entries for gaps. Alternatively, statistical pattern-finding algorithms can identify motifs as a precursor to an MSA rather than as a derivation. In many cases when the query set contains only a small number of sequences or contains only highly related sequences, pseudocounts are added to normalize the distribution reflected in the scoring matrix. In particular, this corrects zero-probability entries in the matrix to values that are small but nonzero.

Blocks analysis is a method of motif finding that restricts motifs to ungapped regions in the alignment. Blocks can be generated from an MSA or they can be extracted from unaligned sequences using a precalculated set of common motifs previously generated from known gene families. Block scoring generally relies on the spacing of high-frequency characters rather than on the calculation of an explicit substitution matrix. The BLOCKS server provides an interactive method to locate such motifs in unaligned sequences.

Statistical pattern-matching has been implemented using both the expectation-maximization algorithm and the Gibbs sampler. One of the most common motif-finding tools, known as MEME, uses expectation maximization and hidden Markov methods to generate motifs that are then used as search tools by its companion MAST in the combined suite MEME/MAST.

Non-Coding Multiple Sequence Alignment

Non-coding DNA regions, especially TFBSs, are rather more conserved and not necessarily evolutionarily related, and may have converged from non-common ancestors. Thus, the assumptions used to align protein sequences and DNA coding regions are inherently different from those that hold for TFBS sequences. Although it is meaningful to align DNA coding regions for homologous sequences using mutation operators, alignment of binding site sequences for the same transcription factor cannot rely on evolutionary related mutation operations. Similarly, the evolutionary operator of point mutations can be used to define an edit distance for coding sequences, but this has little meaning for TFBS sequences because any sequence variation has to maintain a certain level of specificity for the binding site to function. This becomes specifically important when trying to align known TFBS sequences to build supervised models to predict unknown locations of the same TFBS. Hence, Multiple Sequence Alignment methods need to adjust the underlying evolutionary hypothesis and the operators used as in the work published incorporating neighbouring base thermodynamic information to align the binding sites searching for the lowest thermodynamic alignment conserving specificity of the binding site, EDNA .

Alignment Visualization and Quality Control

The necessary use of heuristics for multiple alignment means that for an arbitrary set of proteins, there is always a good chance that an alignment will contain errors. For example, an evaluation of several leading alignment programs using the BAliBase benchmark found that at least 24% of all pairs of aligned amino acids were incorrectly aligned. These errors can arise because of unique insertions into one or more regions of sequences, or through some more complex evolutionary process leading to proteins that do not align easily by sequence alone. As the number of sequence and their divergence increases many more errors will be made simply because of the heuristic nature of MSA algorithms. Multiple sequence alignment viewers enable alignments to be visually reviewed, often by inspecting the quality of alignment for annotated functional sites on two or more sequences. Many also enable the alignment to be edited to correct these (usually minor) errors, in order to obtain an optimal 'curated' alignment suitable for use in phylogenetic analysis or comparative modeling.

However, as the number of sequences increases and especially in genome-wide studies that involve many MSAs it is impossible to manually curate all alignments. Furthermore, manual curation is subjective. And finally, even the best expert cannot confidently align the more ambiguous cases of highly diverged sequences. In such cases it is common practice to use automatic procedures to exclude unreliably aligned regions from the MSA. For the purpose of phylogeny reconstruction the Gblocks program is widely used to remove alignment blocks suspect of low quality, according to various cutoffs on the number of gapped sequences in alignment columns. However, these criteria may excessively filter out regions with insertion/deletion events that may still be aligned reliably, and these regions might be desirable for other purposes such as detection of positive selection. A few alignment algorithms output site-specific scores that allow the selection of high-confidence regions. Such a service was first offered by the SOAP program, which tests the robustness of each column to perturbation in the parameters of the popular alignment program CLUSTALW. The T-Coffee program uses a library of alignments in the construction of the final MSA, and its output MSA is colored according to confidence scores that reflect the agreement between different alignments in the library regarding each aligned residue. Its extension, TCS : (Transitive Consistency Score), uses T-Coffee libraries of pairwise alignments to evaluate any third party MSA. Pairwise projections can be produced using fast or slow methods, thus allowing a trade-off between speed and accuracy. Another alignment program that can output an MSA with confidence scores is FSA, which uses a statistical model that allows calculation of the uncertainty in the alignment. The HoT (Heads-Or-Tails) score can be used as a measure of site-specific alignment uncertainty due to the existence of multiple co-optimal solutions. The GUIDANCE program calculates a similar site-specific confidence measure based on the robustness of the alignment to uncertainty in the guide tree that is used in progressive alignment programs. An alternative, more statistically justified approach to assess alignment uncertainty is the use of probabilistic evolutionary models for joint estimation of phylogeny and alignment. A Bayesian approach allows calculation of posterior probabilities of estimated phylogeny and alignment, which is a measure of the confidence in these estimates. In this case, a posterior probability can be calculated for each site in the alignment. Such an approach was implemented in the program BAli-Phy.

There free available programs for visualization of multiple sequence alignments: JalView, UGENE.

Use in Phylogenetics

Multiple sequence alignments can be used to create a phylogenetic tree. This is made possible by two reasons. The first is because functional domains that are known in annotated sequences can be used for alignment in non-annotated sequences. The other is that conserved regions known to be functionally important can be found. This makes it possible for multiple sequence alignments to be used to analyze and find evolutionary relationships through homology between sequences. Point mutations and insertion or deletion events (called indels) can be detected.

Multiple sequence alignments can also be used to identify functionally important sites, such as binding sites, active sites, or sites corresponding to other key functions, by locating conserved domains. When looking at multiple sequence alignments, it is useful to consider different aspects of the sequences when comparing sequences. These aspects include identity, similarity, and homology. Identity means that the sequences have identical residues at their respective positions. On the other hand, similarity has to do with the sequences being compared having similar residues quantitatively. For example, in terms of nucleotide sequences, pyrimidines are considered similar to each other, as are purines. Similarity ultimately leads to homology, in that the more similar sequences are, the closer they are to being homologous. This similarity in sequences can then go on to help find common ancestry.

Sequence Assembly

In bioinformatics, sequence assembly refers to aligning and merging fragments from a longer DNA sequence in order to reconstruct the original sequence. This is needed as DNA sequencing technology cannot read whole genomes in one go, but rather reads small pieces of between 20 and 30000 bases, depending on the technology used. Typically the short fragments, called reads, result from shotgun sequencing genomic DNA, or gene transcript (ESTs).

The problem of sequence assembly can be compared to taking many copies of a book, passing each of them through a shredder with a different cutter, and piecing the text of the book back together just by looking at the shredded pieces. Besides the obvious difficulty of this task, there are some extra practical issues: the original may have many repeated paragraphs, and some shreds may be modified during shredding to have typos. Excerpts from another book may also be added in, and some shreds may be completely unrecognizable.

Genome Assemblers

The first sequence assemblers began to appear in the late 1980s and early 1990s as variants of simpler sequence alignment programs to piece together vast quantities of fragments generated by automated sequencing instruments called DNA sequencers. As the sequenced organisms grew in size and complexity (from small viruses over plasmids to bacteria and finally eukaryotes), the assembly programs used in these genome projects needed increasingly sophisticated strategies to handle:

- terabytes of sequencing data which need processing on computing clusters;

- identical and nearly identical sequences (known as *repeats*) which can, in the worst case, increase the time and space complexity of algorithms exponentially;

- errors in the fragments from the sequencing instruments, which can confound assembly.

Faced with the challenge of assembling the first larger eukaryotic genomes—the fruit fly Drosophila melanogaster in 2000 and the human genome just a year later,—scientists developed assemblers like Celera Assembler and Arachne able to handle genomes of 100-300 million base pairs. Subsequent to these efforts, several other groups, mostly at the major genome sequencing centers, built large-scale assemblers, and an open source effort known as AMOS was launched to bring together all the innovations in genome assembly technology under the open source framework.

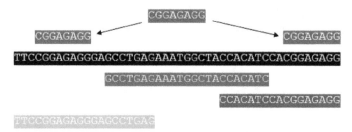

Sample sequence showing how a sequence assembler would take fragments and match by overlaps. Image also shows the potential problem of repeats in the sequence.

EST Assemblers

Expressed Sequence Tag or EST assembly differs from genome assembly in several ways. The sequences for EST assembly are the transcribed mRNA of a cell and represent only a subset of the whole genome. At a first glance, underlying algorithmical problems differ between genome and EST assembly. For instance, genomes often have large amounts of repetitive sequences, mainly in the inter-genic parts. Since ESTs represent gene transcripts, they will not contain these repeats. On the other hand, cells tend to have a certain number of genes that are constantly expressed in very high numbers (housekeeping genes), which again leads to the problem of similar sequences present in high numbers in the data set to be assembled.

Furthermore, genes sometimes overlap in the genome (sense-antisense transcription), and should ideally still be assembled separately. EST assembly is also complicated by features like (cis-) alternative splicing, trans-splicing, single-nucleotide polymorphism, and post-transcriptional modification.

De-novo vs. Mapping Assembly

In sequence assembly, two different types can be distinguished:

1. de-novo: assembling short reads to create full-length (sometimes novel) sequences

2. mapping: assembling reads against an existing backbone sequence, building a sequence that is similar but not necessarily identical to the backbone sequence

In terms of complexity and time requirements, de-novo assemblies are orders of magnitude slower and more memory intensive than mapping assemblies. This is mostly due to the fact that the assembly algorithm needs to compare every read with every other read (an operation that has a naive time complexity of $O(n^2)$; using a hash this can be reduced significantly). Referring to the comparison drawn to shredded books in the introduction: while for mapping assemblies one would have a very similar book as template (perhaps with the names of the main characters and a few locations changed), the de-novo assemblies are more hardcore in a sense as one would not know beforehand whether this would become a science book, a novel, a catalogue, or even several books. Also, every shred would be compared with every other shred.

Influence of Technological Changes

The complexity of sequence assembly is driven by two major factors: the number of fragments and their lengths. While more and longer fragments allow better identification of sequence overlaps, they also pose problems as the underlying algorithms show quadratic or even exponential complexity behaviour to both number of fragments and their length. And while shorter sequences are faster to align, they also complicate the layout phase of an assembly as shorter reads are more difficult to use with repeats or near identical repeats.

In the earliest days of DNA sequencing, scientists could only gain a few sequences of short length (some dozen bases) after weeks of work in laboratories. Hence, these sequences could be aligned in a few minutes by hand.

In 1975, the *Dideoxy termination* method (AKA *Sanger sequencing*) was invented and until shortly after 2000, the technology was improved up to a point where fully automated machines could churn out sequences in a highly parallelised mode 24 hours a day. Large genome centers around the world housed complete farms of these sequencing machines, which in turn led to the necessity of assemblers to be optimised for sequences from whole-genome shotgun sequencing projects where the reads

- are about 800–900 bases long

- contain sequencing artifacts like sequencing and cloning vectors

- have error rates between 0.5 and 10%

With the Sanger technology, bacterial projects with 20,000 to 200,000 reads could easily be assembled on one computer. Larger projects, like the human genome with approximately 35 million reads, needed large computing farms and distributed computing.

By 2004 / 2005, pyrosequencing had been brought to commercial viability by 454 Life Sciences. This new sequencing method generated reads much shorter than those of Sanger sequencing: initially about 100 bases, now 400-500 bases. Its much higher throughput and lower cost (compared to Sanger sequencing) pushed the adoption of this technology by genome centers, which in turn pushed development of sequence assemblers that could efficiently handle the read sets. The sheer amount of data coupled with technology-specific error patterns in the reads delayed development of assemblers; at the beginning in 2004 only the Newbler assembler from 454 was available. Released in mid-2007, the hybrid version of the MIRA assembler by Chevreux et al. was the first freely available assembler that could assemble 454 reads as well as mixtures of 454 reads and Sanger reads. Assembling sequences from different sequencing technologies was subsequently coined *hybrid assembly*.

From 2006, the Illumina (previously Solexa) technology has been available and can generate about 100 million reads per run on a single sequencing machine. Compare this to the 35 million reads of the human genome project which needed several years to be produced on hundreds of sequencing machines. Illumina was initially limited to a length of only 36 bases, making it less suitable for de novo assembly (such as de novo transcriptome assembly), but newer iterations of the technology achieve read lengths above 100 bases from both ends of a 3-400bp clone. Announced at the end of 2007, the SHARCGS assembler by Dohm et al. was the first published assembler that was used for an assembly with Solexa reads. It was quickly followed by a number of others.

Later, new technologies like SOLiD from Applied Biosystems, Ion Torrent and SMRT were released and new technologies (e.g. Nanopore sequencing) continue to emerge.

Greedy Algorithm

Given a set of sequence fragments the object is to find the shortest common supersequence.

1. Calculate pairwise alignments of all fragments.

2. Choose two fragments with the largest overlap.

3. Merge chosen fragments.

4. Repeat step 2 and 3 until only one fragment is left.

The result need not be an optimal solution to the problem.

Available Assemblers

The following table lists assemblers that have a de-novo assembly capability on at least one of the supported technologies.

Name	Type	Technologies	Author	Presented / Last updated	Licence*
ABySS	(large) genomes	Solexa, SOLiD	Simpson, J. et al.	2008 / 2014	NC-A
ALL-PATHS-LG	(large) genomes	Solexa, SOLiD	Gnerre, S. et al.	2011	OS
AMOS	genomes	Sanger, 454	Salzberg, S. et al.	2002? / 2011	OS
Arapan-M	Medium Genomes (e.g. E.coli)	All	Sahli, M. & Shibuya, T.	2011 / 2012	OS
Arapan-S	Small Genomes (Viruses and Bacteria)	All	Sahli, M. & Shibuya, T.	2011 / 2012	OS
Celera WGA Assembler / CABOG	(large) genomes	Sanger, 454, Solexa	Myers, G. et al.; Miller G. et al.	2004 / 2015	OS
CLC Genomics Workbench & CLC Assembly Cell	genomes	Sanger, 454, Solexa, SOLiD	CLC bio	2008 / 2010 / 2014	C
Cortex	genomes	Solexa, SOLiD	Iqbal, Z. *et al.*	2011	OS
DBG2OLC	(large) genomes	Illumina, PacBio, Oxford Nanopore	Ye, C. et al	2014/2016	OS
DNA Baser Assembler	(small) genomes	Sanger, 454	Heracle BioSoft SRL	04.2016	C
DNA Dragon	genomes	Illumina, SOLiD, Complete Genomics, 454, Sanger	SequentiX	2011	C
DNAnexus	genomes	Illumina, SOLiD, Complete Genomics	DNAnexus	2011	C
DNASTAR Lasergene Genomics Suite	(large) genomes, exomes, transcriptomes, metagenomes, ESTs	Illumina, ABI SOLiD, Roche 454, Ion Torrent, Solexa, Sanger	DNASTAR	2007 / 2016	C

Name	Type	Technologies	Author	Presented / Last updated	Licence*
Edena	genomes	Illumina	D. Hernandez, P. François, L. Farinelli, M. Osteras, and J. Schrenzel.	2008/2013	OS
Euler	genomes	Sanger, 454 (,Solexa ?)	Pevzner, P. et al.	2001 / 2006?	(C / NC-A?)
Euler-sr	genomes	454, Solexa	Chaisson, MJ. et al.	2008	NC-A
Fermi	(large) genomes	Illumina	Li, H.	2012	OS
Forge	(large) genomes, EST, metagenomes	454, Solexa, SOLID, Sanger	Platt, DM, Evers, D.	2010	OS
Geneious	genomes	Sano	Biomatters Ltd	2009 / 2013	C
Graph Constructor	(large) genomes	Sanger, 454, Solexa, SOLiD	Convey Computer Corporation	2011	C
HINGE	genomes	PacBio/Oxford Nanopore	Kamath, Shomorony, Xia et. al.	2016	OS
IDBA (Iterative De Bruijn graph short read Assembler)	(large) genomes	Sanger,454,Solexa	Yu Peng, Henry C. M. Leung, Siu-Ming Yiu, Francis Y. L. Chin	2010	(C / NC-A?)
LIGR Assembler (derived from TIGR Assembler)	genomic	Sanger	-	2009/ 2012	OS
MaSuRCA (Maryland Super Read - Celera Assembler)	(large) genomes	Sanger, Illumina, 454	Aleksey Zimin, Guillaume Marçais, Daniela Puiu, Michael Roberts, Steven L. Salzberg, James A. Yorke	2012 / 2013	OS

Name	Type	Technologies	Author	Presented / Last updated	Licence*
MIRA (Mimicking Intelligent Read Assembly)	genomes, ESTs	Sanger, 454, Solexa	Chevreux, B.	1998 / 2014	OS
NextGENe	(small genomes?)	454, Solexa, SOLiD	Softgenetics	2008	C
Newbler	genomes, ESTs	454, Sanger	454/Roche	2004/2012	C
PADENA	genomes	454, Sanger	454/Roche	2010	OS
PASHA	(large) genomes	Illumina	Liu, Schmidt, Maskell	2011	OS
Phrap	genomes	Sanger, 454, Solexa	Green, P.	1994 / 2008	C / NC-A
TIGR Assembler	genomic	Sanger	-	1995 / 2003	OS
Trinity	Transcriptomes	short reads (paired, oriented, mixed) Illumina, 454, Solid,...	Grabher, MG et al.	2011/2016	OS
Ray	genomes	Illumina, mix of Illumina and 454, paired or not	Sébastien Boisvert, François Laviolette & Jacques Corbeil.	2010	OS [GNU General Public License]
Sequencher	genomes	traditional and next generation sequence data	Gene Codes Corporation	1991 / 2009 / 2011	C
SGA	(large) genomes	Illumina, Sanger (Roche 454?, Ion Torrent?)	Simpson, J.T. et al.	2011 / 2012	OS
SHARCGS	(small) genomes	Solexa	Dohm et al.	2007 / 2007	OS
SOPRA	genomes	Illumina, SOLiD, Sanger, 454	Dayarian, A. et al.	2010 / 2011	OS
Sparse-Assembler	(large) genomes	Illumina, 454, Ion torrent	Ye, C. et al.	2012 / 2012	OS
SSAKE	(small) genomes	Solexa (SOLiD? Helicos?)	Warren, R. et al.	2007 / 2014	OS

Name	Type	Technologies	Author	Presented / Last updated	Licence*
SOAPdeno-vo	genomes	Solexa	Luo, R. et al.	2009 / 2013	OS
SPAdes	(small) genomes, single-cell	Illumi-na, Solexa, Sanger, 454, Ion Torrent, PacBio, Oxford Nanopore	Bankevich, A et al.	2012 / 2015	OS
Staden gap4 package	BACs (, small ge-nomes?)	Sanger	Staden et al.	1991 / 2008	OS
Taipan	(small) genomes	Illumina	Schmidt, B. *et al.*	2009 / 2009	OS
VCAKE	(small) ge-nomes	Solexa (SOLiD?, Helicos?)	Jeck, W. et al.	2007 / 2009	OS
Phusion as-sembler	(large) ge-nomes	Sanger	Mullikin JC, *et al.*	2003 / 2006	OS
Quality Value Guid-ed SRA (QSRA)	genomes	Sanger, Solexa	Bryant DW, *et al.*	2009 / 2009	OS
Velvet	(small) ge-nomes	Sanger, 454, Solexa, SOLiD	Zerbino, D. et al.	2007 / 2011	OS
*Licences: OS = Open Source; C = Com-mercial; C / NC-A = Commer-cial but free for non-com-mercial and academics; Brackets = unclear, but most likely C / NC-A					

DNA Sequencing

DNA sequencing is the process of determining the precise order of nucleotides within a DNA molecule. It includes any method or technology that is used to determine the order of the four bases—adenine, guanine, cytosine, and thymine—in a strand of DNA. The advent of rapid DNA sequencing methods has greatly accelerated biological and medical research and discovery.

Knowledge of DNA sequences has become indispensable for basic biological research, and in numerous applied fields such as medical diagnosis, biotechnology, forensic biology, virology and biological systematics. The rapid speed of sequencing attained with modern DNA sequencing technology has been instrumental in the sequencing of complete DNA sequences, or genomes of numerous types and species of life, including the human genome and other complete DNA sequences of many animal, plant, and microbial species.

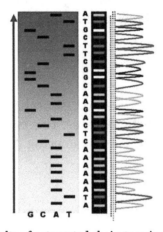

An example of the results of automated chain-termination DNA sequencing.

The first DNA sequences were obtained in the early 1970s by academic researchers using laborious methods based on two-dimensional chromatography. Following the development of fluorescence-based sequencing methods with a DNA sequencer, DNA sequencing has become easier and orders of magnitude faster.

Applications

DNA sequencing may be used to determine the sequence of individual genes, larger genetic regions (i.e. clusters of genes or operons), full chromosomes or entire genomes, of any organism. DNA sequencing is also the most efficient way to sequence RNA or proteins (via their open reading frames). In fact, DNA sequencing has become a key technology in many areas of biology and other sciences such as medicine, forensics, or anthropology. Some applications include:-

Molecular Biology

Sequencing is used in molecular biology to study genomes and the proteins they encode. Information obtained using sequencing allows researchers to identify changes in genes, associations with diseases and phenotypes, and identify potential drug targets.

Evolutionary Biology

Since DNA is an informative macromolecule in terms of transmission from one generation to another, DNA sequencing is used in evolutionary biology to study how different organisms are related and how they evolved.

Metagenomics

The field of [metagenomics] involves identification of organisms present in a body of water, [sewage], dirt, debris filtered from the air, or swab samples from organisms. Knowing which organisms are present in a particular environment is critical to research in ecology, epidemiology, microbiology, and other fields. Sequencing enables researchers to determine which types of microbes may be present in a [microbiome], for example.

Medicine

Medical technicians may sequence genes (or, theoretically, full genomes) from patients to determine if there is risk of genetic diseases. This is a form of genetic testing, though some genetic tests may not involve DNA sequencing.

Forensics

DNA sequencing may be used along with DNA profiling methods for forensic identification and paternity testing.

The Four Canonical Bases

The canonical structure of DNA has four bases: thymine (T), adenine (A), cytosine (C), and guanine (G). DNA sequencing is the determination of the physical order of these bases in a molecule of DNA. However, there are many other bases that may be present in a molecule. In some viruses (specifically, bacteriophage), cytosine may be replaced by hydroxy methyl or hydroxy methyl glucose cytosine. In mammalian DNA, variant bases with methyl groups or phosphosulfate may be found. Depending on the sequencing technique, a particular modification, e.g., the 5mC (5 methyl cytosine) common in humans, may or may not be detected.

History

Deoxyribonucleic acid (DNA) was first discovered and isolated by Friedrich Miescher in 1869, but it remained understudied for many decades because proteins, rather than DNA, were thought to hold the genetic blueprint to life. This situation changed after 1944 as a result of some experiments by Oswald Avery, Colin MacLeod, and Maclyn McCarty demonstrating that purified DNA could change one strain of bacteria into another. This was the first time that DNA was shown capable of transforming the properties of cells.

In 1953 James Watson and Francis Crick put forward their double-helix model of DNA, based on crystallized X-ray structures being studied by Rosalind Franklin. According to the model, DNA is composed of two strands of nucleotides coiled around each other, linked together by hydrogen bonds and running in opposite directions. Each strand is composed of four complementary nucleotides – adenine (A), cytosine (C), guanine (G) and thymine (T) – with an A on one strand always paired with T on the other, and C always paired with G. They proposed such a structure allowed each strand to be used to reconstruct the other, an idea central to the passing on of hereditary information between generations.

Frederick Sanger, a pioneer of sequencing. Sanger is one of the few scientists who was awarded two Nobel prizes, one for the sequencing of proteins, and the other for the sequencing of DNA.

The foundation for sequencing proteins was first laid by the work of Fred Sanger who by 1955 had completed the sequence of all the amino acids in insulin, a small protein secreted by the pancreas. This provided the first conclusive evidence that proteins were chemical entities with a specific molecular pattern rather than a random mixture of material suspended in fluid. Sanger's success in sequencing insulin greatly electrified x-ray crystallographers, including Watson and Crick who by now were trying to understand how DNA directed the formation of proteins within a cell. Soon after attending a series of lectures given by Fred Sanger in October 1954, Crick began to develop a theory which argued that the arrangement of nucleotides in DNA determined the sequence of amino acids in proteins which in turn helped determine the function of a protein. He published this theory in 1958.

RNA Sequencing

RNA sequencing was one of the earliest forms of nucleotide sequencing. The major landmark of RNA sequencing is the sequence of the first complete gene and the complete genome of Bacteriophage MS2, identified and published by Walter Fiers and his coworkers at the University of Ghent (Ghent, Belgium), in 1972 and 1976. Traditional RNA sequencing methods require the creation of a cDNA molecule which must be sequenced. In August 2016, scientists at Oxford Nanopore Technologies published a pre-print indicating that direct RNA sequencing could be performed in real time using nanopore technology.

Early DNA Sequencing Methods

The first method for determining DNA sequences involved a location-specific primer extension strategy established by Ray Wu at Cornell University in 1970. DNA polymerase catalysis and specific nucleotide labeling, both of which figure prominently in current sequencing schemes, were used to sequence the cohesive ends of lambda phage DNA. Between 1970 and 1973, Wu, R Padmanabhan and colleagues demonstrated that this method can be employed to determine any DNA sequence using synthetic location-specific primers. Frederick Sanger then adopted this primer-extension strategy to develop more rapid DNA sequencing methods at the MRC Centre, Cambridge, UK and published a method for "DNA sequencing with chain-terminating inhibitors" in 1977. Walter Gilbert and Allan Maxam at Harvard also developed sequencing methods, including one for "DNA sequencing by chemical degradation". In 1973, Gilbert and Maxam reported the sequence of 24 basepairs using a method known as wandering-spot analysis. Advancements in sequencing were aided by the concurrent development of recombinant DNA technology, allowing DNA samples to be isolated from sources other than viruses.

Sequencing of Full Genomes

The first full DNA genome to be sequenced was that of bacteriophage φX174 in 1977. Medical Research Council scientists deciphered the complete DNA sequence of the Epstein-Barr virus in 1984, finding it contained 172,282 nucleotides. Completion of the sequence marked a significant turning point in DNA sequencing because it was achieved with no prior genetic profile knowledge of the virus.

A non-radioactive method for transferring the DNA molecules of sequencing reaction mixtures onto an immobilizing matrix during electrophoresis was developed by Pohl and co-workers in the early 1980s. Followed by the commercialization of the DNA sequencer "Direct-Blotting-Electrophoresis-System GATC 1500" by GATC Biotech, which was intensively used in the framework of the EU genome-sequencing programme, the complete DNA sequence of the yeast *Saccharomyces cerevisiae* chromosome II. Leroy E. Hood's laboratory at the California Institute of Technology announced the first semi-automated DNA sequencing machine in 1986. This was followed by Applied Biosystems' marketing of the first fully automated sequencing machine, the ABI 370, in 1987 and by Dupont's Genesis 2000 which used a novel fluorescent labeling technique enabling all four dideoxynucleotides to be identified in a single lane. By 1990, the U.S. National Institutes of Health (NIH) had begun large-scale sequencing trials on *Mycoplasma capricolum, Escherichia coli, Caenorhabditis elegans*, and *Saccharomyces cerevisiae* at a cost of US$0.75 per base. Meanwhile, sequencing of human cDNA sequences called expressed sequence tags began in Craig Venter's lab, an attempt to capture the coding fraction of the human genome. In 1995, Venter, Hamilton Smith, and colleagues at The Institute for Genomic Research (TIGR) published the first complete genome of a free-living organism, the bacterium *Haemophilus influenzae*. The circular chromosome contains 1,830,137 bases and its publication in the journal Science marked the first published use of whole-genome shotgun sequencing, eliminating the need for initial mapping efforts.

By 2001, shotgun sequencing methods had been used to produce a draft sequence of the human genome.

High-throughput Sequencing (HTP) Methods

Several new methods for DNA sequencing were developed in the mid to late 1990s and were implemented in commercial DNA sequencers by the year 2000. Together these were called the "next-generation" sequencing methods.

On October 26, 1990, [Roger Tsien], Pepi Ross, Margaret Fahnestock and Allan J Johnston filed a patent describing stepwise ("base-by-base") sequencing with removable 3' blockers on DNA arrays (blots and single DNA molecules). In 1996, Pål Nyrén and his student Mostafa Ronaghi at the Royal Institute of Technology in Stockholm published their method of pyrosequencing.

On April 1, 1997, Pascal Mayer and Laurent Farinelli submitted patents to the World Intellectual Property Organization describing DNA colony sequencing. The DNA sample preparation and random surface-PCR arraying methods described in this patent, coupled to Roger Tsien et al.'s "base-by-base" sequencing method, is now implemented in Illumina's Hi-Seq genome sequencers.

Lynx Therapeutics published and marketed Massively parallel signature sequencing (MPSS), in 2000. This method incorporated a parallelized, adapter/ligation-mediated, bead-based sequencing technology and served as the first commercially available "next-generation" sequencing method, though no DNA sequencers were sold to independent laboratories.

In 2004, 454 Life Sciences marketed a parallelized version of pyrosequencing. The first version of their machine reduced sequencing costs 6-fold compared to automated Sanger sequencing, and was the second of the new generation of sequencing technologies, after MPSS.

The large quantities of data produced by DNA sequencing have also required development of new methods and programs for sequence analysis. Phil Green and Brent Ewing of the University of Washington described their phred quality score for sequencer data analysis in 1998.

Basic Methods

Maxam-Gilbert Sequencing

Allan Maxam and Walter Gilbert published a DNA sequencing method in 1977 based on chemical modification of DNA and subsequent cleavage at specific bases. Also known as chemical sequencing, this method allowed purified samples of double-stranded DNA to be used without further cloning. This method's use of radioactive labeling and its technical complexity discouraged extensive use after refinements in the Sanger methods had been made.

Maxam-Gilbert sequencing requires radioactive labeling at one 5' end of the DNA and purification of the DNA fragment to be sequenced. Chemical treatment then generates breaks at a small proportion of one or two of the four nucleotide bases in each of four reactions (G, A+G, C, C+T). The concentration of the modifying chemicals is controlled to introduce on average one modification per DNA molecule. Thus a series of labeled fragments is generated, from the radiolabeled end to the first "cut" site in each molecule. The fragments in the four reactions are electrophoresed side by side in denaturing acrylamide gels for size separation. To visualize the fragments, the gel is exposed to X-ray film for autoradiography, yielding a series of dark bands each corresponding to a radiolabeled DNA fragment, from which the sequence may be inferred.

Chain-termination Methods

The chain-termination method developed by Frederick Sanger and coworkers in 1977 soon became the method of choice, owing to its relative ease and reliability. When invented, the chain-terminator method used fewer toxic chemicals and lower amounts of radioactivity than the Maxam and Gilbert method. Because of its comparative ease, the Sanger method was soon automated and was the method used in the first generation of DNA sequencers.

Sanger sequencing is the method which prevailed from the 1980s until the mid-2000s. Over that period, great advances were made in the technique, such as fluorescent labelling, capillary electrophoresis, and general automation. These developments allowed much more efficient sequencing, leading to lower costs. The Sanger method, in mass production form, is the technology which produced the first human genome in 2001, ushering in the age of genomics. However, later in the decade, radically different approaches reached the market, bringing the cost per genome down from $100 million in 2001 to $10,000 in 2011.

Advanced Methods and De Novo Sequencing

Large-scale sequencing often aims at sequencing very long DNA pieces, such as whole chromosomes, although large-scale sequencing can also be used to generate very large numbers of short sequences, such as found in phage display. For longer targets such as chromosomes, common approaches consist of cutting (with restriction enzymes) or shearing (with mechanical forces) large DNA fragments into shorter DNA fragments. The fragmented DNA may then be cloned into a DNA vector and amplified in a bacterial host such as *Escherichia coli*. Short DNA fragments purified from individual bacterial colonies are individually sequenced and assembled electronically into one long, contiguous sequence. Studies have shown that adding a size selection step to collect DNA fragments of uniform size can improve sequencing efficiency and accuracy of the genome assembly. In these studies, automated sizing has proven to be more reproducible and precise than manual gel sizing.

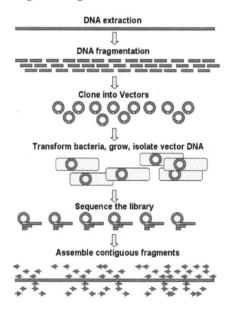

Genomic DNA is fragmented into random pieces and cloned as a bacterial library. DNA from individual bacterial clones is sequenced and the sequence is assembled by using overlapping DNA regions.

The term "*de novo* sequencing" specifically refers to methods used to determine the sequence of DNA with no previously known sequence. *De novo* translates from Latin as "from the beginning". Gaps in the assembled sequence may be filled by primer walking. The different strategies have different tradeoffs in speed and accuracy; shotgun methods are often used for sequencing large genomes, but its assembly is complex and difficult, particularly with sequence repeats often causing gaps in genome assembly.

Most sequencing approaches use an *in vitro* cloning step to amplify individual DNA molecules, because their molecular detection methods are not sensitive enough for single molecule sequencing. Emulsion PCR isolates individual DNA molecules along with primer-coated beads in aqueous droplets within an oil phase. A polymerase chain reaction (PCR) then coats each bead with clonal copies of the DNA molecule followed by immobilization for later sequencing. Emulsion PCR is used in the methods developed by Marguilis et al. (commercialized by 454 Life Sciences), Shendure and Porreca et al. (also known as "Polony sequencing") and SOLiD sequencing, (developed by Agencourt, later Applied Biosystems, now Life Technologies). Emulsion PCR is also used in the GemCode and Chromium platforms developed by 10x Genomics.

Shotgun Sequencing

Shotgun sequencing is a sequencing method designed for analysis of DNA sequences longer than 1000 base pairs, up to and including entire chromosomes. This method requires the target DNA to be broken into random fragments. After sequencing individual fragments, the sequences can be reassembled on the basis of their overlapping regions.

Bridge PCR

Another method for *in vitro* clonal amplification is bridge PCR, in which fragments are amplified upon primers attached to a solid surface and form "DNA colonies" or "DNA clusters". This method is used in the Illumina Genome Analyzer sequencers. Single-molecule methods, such as that developed by Stephen Quake's laboratory (later commercialized by Helicos) are an exception: they use bright fluorophores and laser excitation to detect base addition events from individual DNA molecules fixed to a surface, eliminating the need for molecular amplification.

High-throughput Methods

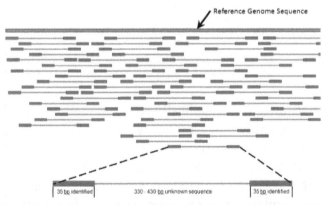

Multiple, fragmented sequence reads must be assembled together on the basis of their overlapping areas.

High-throughput (formerly "next-generation") sequencing applies to genome sequencing, genome resequencing, transcriptome profiling (RNA-Seq), DNA-protein interactions (ChIP-sequencing), and epigenome characterization. Resequencing is necessary, because the genome of a single individual of a species will not indicate all of the genome variations among other individuals of the same species.

The high demand for low-cost sequencing has driven the development of high-throughput sequencing technologies that parallelize the sequencing process, producing thousands or millions of sequences concurrently. High-throughput sequencing technologies are intended to lower the cost of DNA sequencing beyond what is possible with standard dye-terminator methods. In ultra-high-throughput sequencing as many as 500,000 sequencing-by-synthesis operations may be run in parallel.

Comparison of high-throughput sequencing methods							
Method	Read length	Accuracy (single read not consensus)	Reads per run	Time per run	Cost per 1 million bases (in US$)	Advantages	Disadvantages
Single-molecule real-time sequencing (Pacific Biosciences)	10,000 bp to 15,000 bp avg (14,000 bp N50); maximum read length >40,000 bases	87% single-read accuracy	50,000 per SMRT cell, or 500–1000 megabases	30 minutes to 4 hours	$0.13–$0.60	Longest read length. Fast. Detects 4mC, 5mC, 6mA.	Moderate throughput. Equipment can be very expensive.
Ion semiconductor (Ion Torrent sequencing)	up to 400 bp	98%	up to 80 million	2 hours	$1	Less expensive equipment. Fast.	Homopolymer errors.
Pyrosequencing (454)	700 bp	99.9%	1 million	24 hours	$10	Long read size. Fast.	Runs are expensive. Homopolymer errors.
Sequencing by synthesis (Illumina)	MiniSeq, NextSeq: 75-300 bp; MiSeq: 50-600 bp; HiSeq 2500: 50-500 bp; HiSeq 3/4000: 50-300 bp; HiSeq X: 300 bp	99.9% (Phred30)	MiniSeq/MiSeq: 1-25 Million; NextSeq: 130-00 Million, HiSeq 2500: 300 million - 2 billion, HiSeq 3/4000 2.5 billion, HiSeq X: 3 billion	1 to 11 days, depending upon sequencer and specified read length	$0.05 to $0.15	Potential for high sequence yield, depending upon sequencer model and desired application.	Equipment can be very expensive. Requires high concentrations of DNA.
Sequencing by ligation (SOLiD sequencing)	50+35 or 50+50 bp	99.9%	1.2 to 1.4 billion	1 to 2 weeks	$0.13	Low cost per base.	Slower than other methods. Has issues sequencing palindromic sequences.

Nanopore Sequenc-ing (Min-ION - Oxford Nanopore)	5.4 kb av-erage (Up to 300 kb reported)	~90% single read (up to 99% consen-sus)	4.4 Mil-lion	1 min to 48 hrs	$0.11 - 0.5	Very long reads, Af-fordable equip-ment (MinION starter kit is only $1000 USD), Portable (Palm sized)	Lower throughput than other machines, Only 90% single read accuracy
Chain ter-mination (Sanger se-quencing)	400 to 900 bp	99.9%	N/A	20 min-utes to 3 hours	$2400	Long in-dividual reads. Useful for many applica-tions.	More ex-pensive and impractical for larger sequencing projects. This meth-od also requires the time consuming step of plas-mid cloning or PCR.

Massively Parallel Signature Sequencing (MPSS)

The first of the high-throughput sequencing technologies, massively parallel signature sequencing (or MPSS), was developed in the 1990s at Lynx Therapeutics, a company founded in 1992 by Sydney Brenner and Sam Eletr. MPSS was a bead-based method that used a complex approach of adapter ligation followed by adapter decoding, read-ing the sequence in increments of four nucleotides. This method made it susceptible to sequence-specific bias or loss of specific sequences. Because the technology was so complex, MPSS was only performed 'in-house' by Lynx Therapeutics and no DNA se-quencing machines were sold to independent laboratories. Lynx Therapeutics merged with Solexa (later acquired by Illumina) in 2004, leading to the development of se-quencing-by-synthesis, a simpler approach acquired from Manteia Predictive Medi-cine, which rendered MPSS obsolete. However, the essential properties of the MPSS output were typical of later high-throughput data types, including hundreds of thou-sands of short DNA sequences. In the case of MPSS, these were typically used for se-quencing cDNA for measurements of gene expression levels.

Polony Sequencing

The Polony sequencing method, developed in the laboratory of George M. Church at

Harvard, was among the first high-throughput sequencing systems and was used to sequence a full *E. coli* genome in 2005. It combined an in vitro paired-tag library with emulsion PCR, an automated microscope, and ligation-based sequencing chemistry to sequence an *E. coli* genome at an accuracy of >99.9999% and a cost approximately 1/9 that of Sanger sequencing. The technology was licensed to Agencourt Biosciences, subsequently spun out into Agencourt Personal Genomics, and eventually incorporated into the Applied Biosystems SOLiD platform. Applied Biosystems was later acquired by Life Technologies, now part of Thermo Fisher Scientific.

454 Pyrosequencing

A parallelized version of pyrosequencing was developed by 454 Life Sciences, which has since been acquired by Roche Diagnostics. The method amplifies DNA inside water droplets in an oil solution (emulsion PCR), with each droplet containing a single DNA template attached to a single primer-coated bead that then forms a clonal colony. The sequencing machine contains many picoliter-volume wells each containing a single bead and sequencing enzymes. Pyrosequencing uses luciferase to generate light for detection of the individual nucleotides added to the nascent DNA, and the combined data are used to generate sequence read-outs. This technology provides intermediate read length and price per base compared to Sanger sequencing on one end and Solexa and SOLiD on the other.

Illumina (Solexa) Sequencing

Solexa, now part of Illumina, was founded by Shankar Balasubramanian and David Klenerman in 1998, and developed a sequencing method based on reversible dye-terminators technology, and engineered polymerases. The reversible terminated chemistry concept was invented by Bruno Canard and Simon Sarfati at the Pasteur Institute in Paris. It was developed internally at Solexa by those named on the relevant patents. In 2004, Solexa acquired the company Manteia Predictive Medicine in order to gain a massivelly parallel sequencing technology invented in 1997 by Pascal Mayer and Laurent Farinelli. It is based on "DNA Clusters" or "DNA colonies", which involves the clonal amplification of DNA on a surface. The cluster technology was co-acquired with Lynx Therapeutics of California. Solexa Ltd. later merged with Lynx to form Solexa Inc.

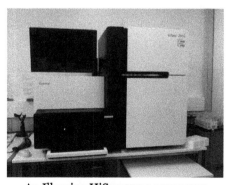

An Illumina HiSeq 2500 sequencer

In this method, DNA molecules and primers are first attached on a slide or flow cell and amplified with polymerase so that local clonal DNA colonies, later coined "DNA clusters", are formed. To determine the sequence, four types of reversible terminator bases (RT-bases) are added and non-incorporated nucleotides are washed away. A camera takes images of the fluorescently labeled nucleotides. Then the dye, along with the terminal 3' blocker, is chemically removed from the DNA, allowing for the next cycle to begin. Unlike pyrosequencing, the DNA chains are extended one nucleotide at a time and image acquisition can be performed at a delayed moment, allowing for very large arrays of DNA colonies to be captured by sequential images taken from a single camera.

An Illumina MiSeq sequencer

Decoupling the enzymatic reaction and the image capture allows for optimal throughput and theoretically unlimited sequencing capacity. With an optimal configuration, the ultimately reachable instrument throughput is thus dictated solely by the analog-to-digital conversion rate of the camera, multiplied by the number of cameras and divided by the number of pixels per DNA colony required for visualizing them optimally (approximately 10 pixels/colony). In 2012, with cameras operating at more than 10 MHz A/D conversion rates and available optics, fluidics and enzymatics, throughput can be multiples of 1 million nucleotides/second, corresponding roughly to 1 human genome equivalent at 1x coverage per hour per instrument, and 1 human genome re-sequenced (at approx. 30x) per day per instrument (equipped with a single camera).

SOLiD Sequencing

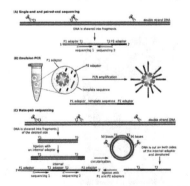

Library preparation for the SOLiD platform

Applied Biosystems' (now a Life Technologies brand) SOLiD technology employs sequencing by ligation. Here, a pool of all possible oligonucleotides of a fixed length are labeled according to the sequenced position. Oligonucleotides are annealed and ligated; the preferential ligation by DNA ligase for matching sequences results in a signal informative of the nucleotide at that position. Before sequencing, the DNA is amplified by emulsion PCR. The resulting beads, each containing single copies of the same DNA molecule, are deposited on a glass slide. The result is sequences of quantities and lengths comparable to Illumina sequencing. This sequencing by ligation method has been reported to have some issue sequencing palindromic sequences.

Ion Torrent Semiconductor Sequencing

Ion Torrent Systems Inc. (now owned by Life Technologies) developed a system based on using standard sequencing chemistry, but with a novel, semiconductor based detection system. This method of sequencing is based on the detection of hydrogen ions that are released during the polymerisation of DNA, as opposed to the optical methods used in other sequencing systems. A microwell containing a template DNA strand to be sequenced is flooded with a single type of nucleotide. If the introduced nucleotide is complementary to the leading template nucleotide it is incorporated into the growing complementary strand. This causes the release of a hydrogen ion that triggers a hypersensitive ion sensor, which indicates that a reaction has occurred. If homopolymer repeats are present in the template sequence multiple nucleotides will be incorporated in a single cycle. This leads to a corresponding number of released hydrogens and a proportionally higher electronic signal.

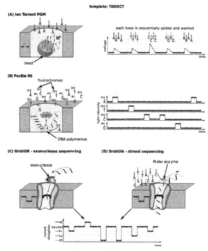

Sequencing of the TAGGCT template with IonTorrent, PacBioRS and GridION

DNA Nanoball Sequencing

DNA nanoball sequencing is a type of high throughput sequencing technology used to determine the entire genomic sequence of an organism. The company Complete Genomics uses this technology to sequence samples submitted by independent researchers. The method uses rolling circle replication to amplify small fragments of genomic DNA into DNA nanoballs. Unchained sequencing by ligation is then used to determine the nucleotide sequence. This method of DNA sequencing allows large numbers of DNA nanoballs to be sequenced per run and at low reagent costs compared to other high-throughput sequencing platforms. However, only short sequences of DNA are determined from each DNA nanoball which makes mapping the short reads to a reference genome difficult. This technology has been used for multiple genome sequencing projects and is scheduled to be used for more.

Heliscope Single Molecule Sequencing

Heliscope sequencing is a method of single-molecule sequencing developed by Helicos Biosciences. It uses DNA fragments with added poly-A tail adapters which are attached to the flow cell surface. The next steps involve extension-based sequencing with cyclic washes of the flow cell with fluorescently labeled nucleotides (one nucleotide type at a time, as with the Sanger method). The reads are performed by the Heliscope sequencer. The reads are short, averaging 35 bp. In 2009 a human genome was sequenced using the Heliscope, however in 2012 the company went bankrupt.

Single Molecule Real Time (SMRT) Sequencing

SMRT sequencing is based on the sequencing by synthesis approach. The DNA is synthesized in zero-mode wave-guides (ZMWs) – small well-like containers with the capturing tools located at the bottom of the well. The sequencing is performed with use of unmodified polymerase (attached to the ZMW bottom) and fluorescently labelled nucleotides flowing freely in the solution. The wells are constructed in a way that only the fluorescence occurring by the bottom of the well is detected. The fluorescent label is detached from the nucleotide upon its incorporation into the DNA strand, leaving an unmodified DNA strand. According to Pacific Biosciences (PacBio), the SMRT technology developer, this methodology allows detection of nucleotide modifications (such as cytosine methylation). This happens through the observation of polymerase kinetics. This approach allows reads of 20,000 nucleotides or more, with average read lengths of 5 kilobases. In 2015, Pacific Biosciences announced the launch of a new sequencing instrument called the Sequel System, with 1 million ZMWs compared to 150,000 ZMWs in the PacBio RS II instrument.

Nanopore DNA Sequencing

The DNA passing through the nanopore changes its ion current. This change is dependent on the shape, size and length of the DNA sequence. Each type of the nucleotide blocks the ion flow through the pore for a different period of time. The method does not require modified nucleotides and is performed in real time.

Early industrial research into this method was based on a technique called 'Exonuclease sequencing', where the readout of electrical signals occurring at nucleotides passing by alpha-hemolysin pores covalently bound with cyclodextrin. However the subsequently commercial method, 'strand sequencing' sequencing DNA bases in an intact strand. In 2014, Oxford Nanopore Technologies, a United Kingdom-based company, released the MinION portable DNA sequencer into an early access community and the first dataset became available in June 2014. The MinION was subsequently launched commercially in 2015 and the launch of the 'R9' nanopore in 2016 resulted in reports of performance improvements in accuracy and yield. in autumn 2016, the MinION handheld sequencer is capable of generating more than 2 Gigabases of sequencing data in one run. it is used in multiple scientific applications such as pathogen analysis/surveillance, metagenomics, cancer research and environmental analysis and a version has also been recently installed on the ISS by NASA.

Two main areas of nanopore sequencing in development are solid state nanopore sequencing, and protein based nanopore sequencing. Protein nanopore sequencing utilizes membrane protein complexes such as ∝-Hemolysin, MspA (Mycobacterium Smegmatis Porin A) or CssG, which show great promise given their ability to distinguish between individual and groups of nucleotides. In contrast, solid-state nanopore sequencing utilizes synthetic materials such as silicon nitride and aluminum oxide and it is preferred for its superior mechanical ability and thermal and chemical stability. The fabrication method is essential for this type of sequencing given that the nanopore array can contain hundreds of pores with diameters smaller than eight nanometers.

The concept originated from the idea that single stranded DNA or RNA molecules can be electrophoretically driven in a strict linear sequence through a biological pore that can be less than eight nanometers, and can be detected given that the molecules release an ionic current while moving through the pore. The pore contains a detection region capable of recognizing different bases, with each base generating various time specific signals corresponding to the sequence of bases as they cross the pore which are then evaluated. Precise control over the DNA transport through the pore is crucial for success. Various enzymes such as exonucleases and polymerases have been used to moderate this process by positioning them near the pore's entrance.

Methods in Development

DNA sequencing methods currently under development include reading the sequence as a DNA strand transits through nanopores (a method that is now commercial but subsequent generations such as solid-state nanopores are still in development), and microscopy-based techniques, such as atomic force microscopy or transmission electron microscopy that are used to identify the positions of individual nucleotides within long DNA fragments (>5,000 bp) by nucleotide labeling with heavier elements (e.g., halogens) for visual detection and recording. Third generation technologies aim to increase throughput and decrease the time to result and cost by eliminating the need for excessive reagents and harnessing the processivity of DNA polymerase.

Tunnelling Currents DNA Sequencing

Another approach uses measurements of the electrical tunnelling currents across single-strand DNA as it moves through a channel. Depending on its electronic structure, each base affects the tunnelling current differently, allowing differentiation between different bases.

The use of tunnelling currents has the potential to sequence orders of magnitude faster than ionic current methods and the sequencing of several DNA oligomers and micro-RNA has already been achieved.

Sequencing by Hybridization

Sequencing by hybridization is a non-enzymatic method that uses a DNA microarray. A single pool of DNA whose sequence is to be determined is fluorescently labeled and hybridized to an array containing known sequences. Strong hybridization signals from a given spot on the array identifies its sequence in the DNA being sequenced.

This method of sequencing utilizes binding characteristics of a library of short single stranded DNA molecules (oligonucleotides), also called DNA probes, to reconstruct a target DNA sequence. Non-specific hybrids are removed by washing and the target DNA is eluted. Hybrids are re-arranged such that the DNA sequence can be reconstructed. The benefit of this sequencing type is its ability to capture a large number of targets with a homogenous coverage. A large number of chemicals and starting DNA is usually required. However, with the advent of solution-based hybridization, much less equipment and chemicals are necessary.

Sequencing with Mass Spectrometry

Mass spectrometry may be used to determine DNA sequences. Matrix-assisted laser desorption ionization time-of-flight mass spectrometry, or MALDI-TOF MS, has specifically been investigated as an alternative method to gel electrophoresis for visualizing DNA fragments. With this method, DNA fragments generated by chain-termination sequencing reactions are compared by mass rather than by size. The mass of each nucleotide is different from the others and this difference is detectable by mass spectrometry. Single-nucleotide mutations in a fragment can be more easily detected with MS than by gel electrophoresis alone. MALDI-TOF MS can more easily detect differences between RNA fragments, so researchers may indirectly sequence DNA with MS-based methods by converting it to RNA first.

The higher resolution of DNA fragments permitted by MS-based methods is of special interest to researchers in forensic science, as they may wish to find single-nucleotide polymorphisms in human DNA samples to identify individuals. These samples may be highly degraded so forensic researchers often prefer mitochondrial DNA for its higher stability and applications for lineage studies. MS-based sequencing methods have been used to compare the sequences of human mitochondrial DNA from samples in a Federal Bureau of Investigation database and from bones found in mass graves of World War I soldiers.

Early chain-termination and TOF MS methods demonstrated read lengths of up to 100 base pairs. Researchers have been unable to exceed this average read size; like chain-termination sequencing alone, MS-based DNA sequencing may not be suitable for large *de novo* sequencing projects. Even so, a recent study did use the short sequence reads and mass spectroscopy to compare single-nucleotide polymorphisms in pathogenic *Streptococcus* strains.

Microfluidic Sanger Sequencing

In microfluidic Sanger sequencing the entire thermocycling amplification of DNA fragments as well as their separation by electrophoresis is done on a single glass wafer (approximately 10 cm in diameter) thus reducing the reagent usage as well as cost. In some instances researchers have shown that they can increase the throughput of conventional sequencing through the use of microchips. Research will still need to be done in order to make this use of technology effective.

Microscopy-based Techniques

This approach directly visualizes the sequence of DNA molecules using electron microscopy. The first identification of DNA base pairs within intact DNA molecules by enzymatically incorporating modified bases, which contain atoms of increased atomic number, direct visualization and identification of individually labeled bases within a synthetic 3,272 base-pair DNA molecule and a 7,249 base-pair viral genome has been demonstrated.

RNAP Sequencing

This method is based on use of RNA polymerase (RNAP), which is attached to a polystyrene bead. One end of DNA to be sequenced is attached to another bead, with both beads being placed in optical traps. RNAP motion during transcription brings the beads in closer and their relative distance changes, which can then be recorded at a single nucleotide resolution. The sequence is deduced based on the four readouts with lowered concentrations of each of the four nucleotide types, similarly to the Sanger method. A comparison is made between regions and sequence information is deduced by comparing the known sequence regions to the unknown sequence regions.

In Vitro Virus High-throughput Sequencing

A method has been developed to analyze full sets of protein interactions using a combination of 454 pyrosequencing and an *in vitro* virus mRNA display method. Specifically, this method covalently links proteins of interest to the mRNAs encoding them, then detects the mRNA pieces using reverse transcription PCRs. The mRNA may then be amplified and sequenced. The combined method was titled IVV-HiTSeq and can be performed under cell-free conditions, though its results may not be representative of *in vivo* conditions.

Sample Preparation

The success of a DNA sequencing protocol is dependent on the sample preparation. A successful DNA extraction will yield a sample with long, non-degraded strands of DNA which require further preparation according to the sequencing technology to be used. For Sanger sequencing, either cloning procedures or PCR are required prior to sequencing. In the case of next generation sequencing methods, library preparation is required before processing.

With the advent of next generation sequencing, Illumina and Roche 454 methods have become a common approach to transcriptomic studies (RNAseq). RNA can be extracted from tissues of interest and converted to complementary DNA (cDNA) using reverse transcriptase—a DNA polymerase that synthesizes a complimentary DNA based on existing strands of RNA in a PCR-like manner. Complementary DNA can be processed the same way as genomic DNA, allowing the expression levels of RNAs to be determined for the tissue selected.

Development Initiatives

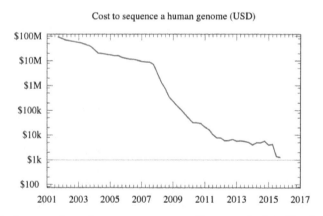

Cost to sequence a human genome (USD)

Total cost of sequencing a human genome over time as calculated by the NHGRI.

In October 2006, the X Prize Foundation established an initiative to promote the development of full genome sequencing technologies, called the Archon X Prize, intending to award $10 million to "the first Team that can build a device and use it to sequence 100 human genomes within 10 days or less, with an accuracy of no more than one error in every 100,000 bases sequenced, with sequences accurately covering at least 98% of the genome, and at a recurring cost of no more than $10,000 (US) per genome."

Each year the National Human Genome Research Institute, or NHGRI, promotes grants for new research and developments in genomics. 2010 grants and 2011 candidates include continuing work in microfluidic, polony and base-heavy sequencing methodologies.

Computational Challenges

The sequencing technologies described here produce raw data that needs to be assembled into longer sequences such as complete genomes (sequence assembly). There are many computational challenges to achieve this, such as the evaluation of the raw sequence data which is done by programs and algorithms such as Phred and Phrap. Other challenges have to deal with repetitive sequences that often prevent complete genome assemblies because they occur in many places of the genome. As a consequence, many sequences may not be assigned to particular chromosomes. The production of raw sequence data is only the beginning of its detailed bioinformatical analysis. Yet new methods for sequencing and correcting sequencing errors were developed.

Read Trimming

Sometimes, the raw reads produced by the sequencer are correct and precise only in a fraction of their length. Using the entire read may introduce artifacts in the downstream analyses like genome assembly, snp calling, or gene expression estimation. Two classes of trimming programs have been introduced, based on the window-based or the running-sum classes of algorithms. This is a partial list of the trimming algorithms currently available, specifying the algorithm class they belong to:

Read Trimming Algorithms	
Name of algorithm	**Type of algorithm**
Cutadapt	Running sum
ConDeTri	Window based
ERNE-FILTER	Running sum
FASTX quality trimmer	Window based
PRINSEQ	Window based
Trimmomatic	Window based
SolexaQA	Window based
SolexaQA-BWA	Running sum
Sickle	Window based

Ethical Issues

Human genetics have been included within the field of bioethics since the early 1970s and the growth in the use of DNA sequencing (particularly high-throughput sequencing) has introduced a number of ethical issues. One key issue is the ownership of an individual's DNA and the data produced when that DNA is sequenced. Regarding the DNA molecule itself, the leading legal case on this topic, *Moore v. Regents of the University of California* (1990) ruled that individuals have no property rights to discarded cells or any profits made using these cells (for instance, as a patented cell line). However, individuals have a right to informed consent regarding removal and use of cells. Regarding the data produced through DNA sequencing, *Moore* gives the individual no rights to the information derived from their DNA.

As DNA sequencing becomes more widespread, the storage, security and sharing of genomic data has also become more important. For instance, one concern is that insurers may use an individual's genomic data to modify their quote, depending on the perceived future health of the individual based on their DNA. In May 2008, the Genetic Information Nondiscrimination Act (GINA) was signed in the United States, prohibiting discrimination on the basis of genetic information with respect to health insurance and employment. In 2012, the US Presidential Commission for the Study of Bioethical Issues reported that existing privacy legislation for DNA sequencing data such as GINA and the Health Insurance Portability and Accountability Act were insufficient, noting that whole-genome sequencing data was particularly sensitive, as it could be used to identify not only the individual from which the data was created, but also their relatives.

Ethical issues have also been raised by the increasing use of genetic variation screening, both in newborns, and in adults by companies such as 23andMe. It has been asserted that screening for genetic variations can be harmful, increasing anxiety in individuals who have been found to have an increased risk of disease. For example, in one case noted in *Time*, doctors screening an ill baby for genetic variants chose not to inform the parents of an unrelated variant linked to dementia due to the harm it would cause to the parents. However, a 2011 study in *The New England Journal of Medicine* has shown that individuals undergoing disease risk profiling did not show increased levels of anxiety.

Methods and Techniques of DNA Sequencing

Sanger Sequencing

Sanger sequencing is a method of DNA sequencing first commercialized by Applied Biosystems, based on the selective incorporation of chain-terminating dideoxynucleotides by DNA polymerase during in vitro DNA replication. Developed by Frederick Sanger and colleagues in 1977, it was the most widely used sequencing method for approximately 39 years. More recently, higher volume Sanger sequencing has been supplanted by "Next-Gen" sequencing methods, especially for large-scale, automated genome analyses. However, the Sanger method remains in wide use, for smaller-scale projects, validation of Next-Gen results and for obtaining especially long contiguous DNA sequence reads (> 500 nucleotides).

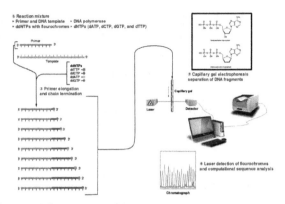

The Sanger (chain-termination) method for DNA sequencing.

Method

The classical chain-termination method requires a single-stranded DNA template, a DNA primer, a DNA polymerase, normal deoxynucleosidetriphosphates (dNTPs), and modified di-deoxynucleosidetriphosphates (ddNTPs), the latter of which terminate DNA strand elongation. These chain-terminating nucleotides lack a 3'-OH group required for the formation of a phosphodiester bond between two nucleotides, causing DNA polymerase to cease extension of DNA when a modified ddNTP is incorporated. The ddNTPs may be radioactively or fluorescently labeled for detection in automated sequencing machines.

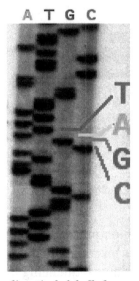

Part of a radioactively labelled sequencing gel

The DNA sample is divided into four separate sequencing reactions, containing all four of the standard deoxynucleotides (dATP, dGTP, dCTP and dTTP) and the DNA polymerase. To each reaction is added only one of the four dideoxynucleotides (ddATP, ddGTP, ddCTP, or ddTTP), while the other added nucleotides are ordinary ones. The dideoxynucleotide is added to be approximately 100-fold lower in concentration than the corresponding deoxynucleotide (e.g. 0.005mM ddATP : 0.5mM dATP) allowing for enough fragments to be produced while still transcribing the complete sequence. Putting it in a more sensible order, four separate reactions are needed in this process to test all four ddNTPs. Following rounds of template DNA extension from the bound primer, the resulting DNA fragments are heat denatured and separated by size using gel electrophoresis. In the original publication of 1977, the formation of base-paired loops of ssDNA was a cause of serious difficulty in resolving bands at some locations. This is frequently performed using a denaturing polyacrylamide-urea gel with each of the four reactions run in one of four individual lanes (lanes A, T, G, C). The DNA bands may then be visualized by autoradiography or UV light and the DNA sequence can be directly read off the X-ray film or gel image.

In the image on the right, X-ray film was exposed to the gel, and the dark bands correspond to DNA fragments of different lengths. A dark band in a lane indicates a DNA fragment that is the result of chain termination after incorporation of a dideoxynucleotide (ddATP, ddGTP, ddCTP, or ddTTP). The relative positions of the different bands among the four lanes, from bottom to top, are then used to read the DNA sequence.

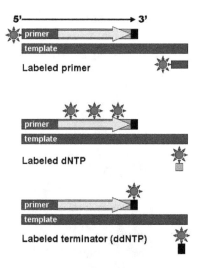

DNA fragments are labelled with a radioactive or fluorescent tag on the primer (1), in the new DNA strand with a labeled dNTP, or with a labeled ddNTP.

Technical variations of chain-termination sequencing include tagging with nucleotides containing radioactive phosphorus for radiolabelling, or using a primer labeled at the 5' end with a fluorescent dye. Dye-primer sequencing facilitates reading in an optical system for faster and more economical analysis and automation. The later development by Leroy Hood and coworkers of fluorescently labeled ddNTPs and primers set the stage for automated, high-throughput DNA sequencing.

Chain-termination methods have greatly simplified DNA sequencing. For example, chain-termination-based kits are commercially available that contain the reagents needed for sequencing, pre-aliquoted and ready to use. Limitations include non-specific binding of the primer to the DNA, affecting accurate read-out of the DNA sequence, and DNA secondary structures affecting the fidelity of the sequence.

Dye-terminator Sequencing

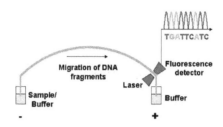

Capillary electrophoresis

Dye-terminator sequencing utilizes labelling of the chain terminator ddNTPs, which permits sequencing in a single reaction, rather than four reactions as in the labelled-primer method. In dye-terminator sequencing, each of the four dideoxynucleotide chain terminators is labelled with fluorescent dyes, each of which emit light at different wavelengths.

Owing to its greater expediency and speed, dye-terminator sequencing is now the mainstay in automated sequencing. Its limitations include dye effects due to differences in the incorporation of the dye-labelled chain terminators into the DNA fragment, resulting in unequal peak heights and shapes in the electronic DNA sequence trace chromatogram after capillary electrophoresis.

This problem has been addressed with the use of modified DNA polymerase enzyme systems and dyes that minimize incorporation variability, as well as methods for eliminating "dye blobs". The dye-terminator sequencing method, along with automated high-throughput DNA sequence analyzers, is now being used for the vast majority of sequencing projects.

Automation and Sample Preparation

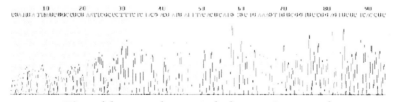

View of the start of an example dye-terminator read

Automated DNA-sequencing instruments (DNA sequencers) can sequence up to 384 DNA samples in a single batch. Batch runs may occur up to 24 times a day. DNA sequencers separate strands by size (or length) using capillary electrophoresis, they detect and record dye fluorescence, and output data as fluorescent peak trace chromato-grams. Sequencing reactions (thermocycling and labelling), cleanup and re-suspension of samples in a buffer solution are performed separately, before loading samples onto the sequencer. A number of commercial and non-commercial software packages can trim low-quality DNA traces automatically. These programs score the quality of each peak and remove low-quality base peaks (which are generally located at the ends of the sequence). The accuracy of such algorithms is inferior to visual examination by a human operator, but is adequate for automated processing of large sequence data sets.

Challenges

Common challenges of DNA sequencing with the Sanger method include poor quality in the first 15-40 bases of the sequence due to primer binding and deteriorating quality of sequencing traces after 700-900 bases. Base calling software such as Phred typically provides an estimate of quality to aid in trimming of low-quality regions of sequences.

In cases where DNA fragments are cloned before sequencing, the resulting sequence may contain parts of the cloning vector. In contrast, PCR-based cloning and next-gen-eration sequencing technologies based on pyrosequencing often avoid using cloning vectors. Recently, one-step Sanger sequencing (combined amplification and sequenc-ing) methods such as Ampliseq and SeqSharp have been developed that allow rapid sequencing of target genes without cloning or prior amplification.

Current methods can directly sequence only relatively short (300-1000 nucleotides long) DNA fragments in a single reaction. The main obstacle to sequencing DNA frag-ments above this size limit is insufficient power of separation for resolving large DNA fragments that differ in length by only one nucleotide.

Microfluidic Sanger Sequencing

Microfluidic Sanger sequencing is a lab-on-a-chip application for DNA sequencing, in which the Sanger sequencing steps (thermal cycling, sample purification, and capil-lary electrophoresis) are integrated on a wafer-scale chip using nanoliter-scale sample volumes. This technology generates long and accurate sequence reads, while obviating many of the significant shortcomings of the conventional Sanger method (e.g. high con-sumption of expensive reagents, reliance on expensive equipment, personnel-intensive manipulations, etc.) by integrating and automating the Sanger sequencing steps.

In its modern inception, high-throughput genome sequencing involves fragmenting the genome into small single-stranded pieces, followed by amplification of the frag-ments by Polymerase Chain Reaction (PCR). Adopting the Sanger method, each DNA fragment is irreversibly terminated with the incorporation of a fluorescently labeled dideoxy chain-terminating nucleotide, thereby producing a DNA "ladder" of fragments that each differ in length by one base and bear a base-specific fluorescent label at the terminal base. Amplified base ladders are then separated by Capillary Array Electrophoresis (CAE) with automated, *in situ* "finish-line" detection of the fluorescently labeled ssDNA fragments, which provides an ordered sequence of the fragments. These sequence reads are then computer assembled into overlapping or contiguous sequences (termed "contigs") which resemble the full genomic sequence once fully assembled.

Sanger methods achieve read lengths of approximately 800bp (typically 500-600bp with non-enriched DNA). The longer read lengths in Sanger methods display significant advantages over other sequencing methods especially in terms of sequencing repetitive regions of the genome. A challenge of short-read sequence data is particularly an issue in sequencing new genomes *(de novo)* and in sequencing highly rearranged genome segments, typically those seen of cancer genomes or in regions of chromosomes that exhibit structural variation.

Applications of Microfluidic Sequencing Technologies

Other useful applications of DNA sequencing include single nucleotide polymorphism (SNP) detection, single-strand conformation polymorphism (SSCP) heteroduplex analysis, and short tandem repeat (STR) analysis. Resolving DNA fragments according to differences in size and/or conformation is the most critical step in studying these features of the genome.

Device Design

The sequencing chip has a four-layer construction, consisting of three 100-mm-diameter glass wafers (on which device elements are microfabricated) and a polydimethylsiloxane (PDMS) membrane. Reaction chambers and capillary electrophoresis channels are etched between the top two glass wafers, which are thermally bonded. Three-dimensional channel interconnections and microvalves are formed by the PDMS and bottom manifold glass wafer.

The device consists of three functional units, each corresponding to the Sanger sequencing steps. The Thermal Cycling (TC) unit is a 250-nanoliter reaction chamber with integrated resistive temperature detector, microvalves, and a surface heater. Movement of reagent between the top all-glass layer and the lower glass-PDMS layer occurs through 500-μm-diameter via-holes. After thermal-cycling, the reaction mixture undergoes purification in the capture/purification chamber, and then is injected into the capillary electrophoresis (CE) chamber. The CE unit consists of a 30-cm capillary which is folded into a compact switchback pattern via 65-μm-wide turns.

Sequencing Chemistry

- Thermal cycling

In the TC reaction chamber, dye-terminator sequencing reagent, template DNA, and primers are loaded into the TC chamber and thermal-cycled for 35 cycles (at 95 °C for 12 seconds and at 60 °C for 55 seconds).

- Purification

The charged reaction mixture (containing extension fragments, template DNA, and excess sequencing reagent) is conducted through a capture/purification chamber at 30 °C via a 33-Volts/cm electric field applied between capture outlet and inlet ports. The capture gel through which the sample is driven, consists of 40 μM of oligonucleotide (complementary to the primers) covalently bound to a polyacrylamide matrix. Extension fragments are immobilized by the gel matrix, and excess primer, template, free nucleotides, and salts are eluted through the capture waste port. The capture gel is heated to 67-75 °C to release extension fragments.

- Capillary electrophoresis

Extension fragments are injected into the CE chamber where they are electrophoresed through a 125-167-V/cm field.

Platforms

The Apollo 100 platform (Microchip Biotechnologies Inc., Dublin, CA) integrates the first two Sanger sequencing steps (thermal cycling and purification) in a fully automated system. The manufacturer claims that samples are ready for capillary electrophoresis within three hours of the sample and reagents being loaded into the system. The Apollo 100 platform requires sub-microliter volumes of reagents.

Comparisons to Other Sequencing Techniques

Performance values for genome sequencing technologies including Sanger methods and next-generation methods. Data is from 2008 and has since changed drastically.							
Technology	Number of Lanes	Injection Volume (nL)	Analysis Time	Average Read Length	Throughput (including analysis; Mb/hr)	Gel Pouring	Lane Tracking
Slab Gel	96	500-1000	6–8 hours	700bp	0.0672	Yes	Yes
Capillary Array Electrophoresis	96	1-5	1–3 hours	700bp	0.166	No	No
Microchip	96	0.1-0.5	6–30 minutes	430bp	0.660	No	No
454/Roche FLX		< 0.001	4 hours	200-300bp	20-30	No	
Illumina/Solexa			2–3 days	30-100bp	20	No	
ABI/SOLiD			8 days	35bp	5-15	No	

The ultimate goal of high-throughput sequencing is to develop systems that are low-cost, and extremely efficient at obtaining extended (longer) read lengths. Longer read lengths of each single electrophoretic separation, substantially reduces the cost associated with de novo DNA sequencing and the number of templates needed to sequence DNA contigs at a given redundancy. Microfluidics may allow for faster, cheaper and easier sequence assembly.

Illumina Dye Sequencing

Illumina dye sequencing is a technique used to determine the series of base pairs in DNA, also known as DNA sequencing. The reversible terminated chemistry concept was invented by Bruno Canard and Simon Sarfati at the Pasteur Institute in Paris. It was developed by Shankar Balasubramanian and David Klenerman of Cambridge University, who subsequently founded Solexa, a company later acquired by Illumina. This sequencing method is based on reversible dye-terminators that enable the identification of single bases as they are introduced into DNA strands. It can also be used for whole-genome and region sequencing, transcriptome analysis, metagenomics, small RNA discovery, methylation profiling, and genome-wide protein-nucleic acid interaction analysis.

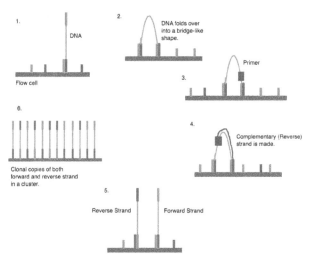

The DNA attaches to the flow cell via complementary sequences. The strand bends over and attaches to a second oligo forming a bridge. A polymerase synthesizes the reverse strand. The two strands release and straighten. Each forms a new bridge (bridge amplification). The result is a cluster of DNA forward and reverse strands clones.

Overview

Illumina sequencing technology works in three basic steps: amplify, sequence, and analyze. The process begins with purified DNA. The DNA gets chopped up into smaller pieces and given adapters, indices, and other kinds of molecular modifications that act as reference points during amplification, sequencing, and analysis. The modified DNA is loaded onto a specialized chip where amplification and sequencing will take place. Along the bottom of the chip are hundreds of thousands of oligonucleotides (short, synthetic pieces of DNA). They are anchored to the chip and able to grab DNA fragments that have complementary sequences. Once the fragments have attached, a phase called cluster generation begins. This step makes about a thousand copies of each fragment of DNA. Next, primers and modified nucleotides enter the chip. These nucleotides have reversible 3' blockers that force the primers to add on only one nucleotide at a time as well as fluorescent tags. After each round of synthesis, a camera takes a picture of the chip. A computer determines what base was added by the wavelength of the fluorescent tag and records it for every spot on the chip. After each round, non-incorporated molecules are washed away. A chemical deblocking step is then used in the removal of the 3' terminal blocking group and the dye in a single step. The process continues until the full DNA molecule is sequenced. With this technology, thousands of places throughout the genome are sequenced at once via massive parallel sequencing.

Procedure

Tagmentation

The first step after DNA purification is tagmentation. Enzymes called transposomes randomly cut the DNA into short segments ("tags"). Adapters are added on either side of the cut points (ligation). Strands that fail to have adapters ligated are washed away.

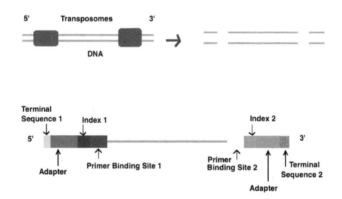

Double stranded DNA is cleaved by transposomes. The cut ends are repaired and adapters, indices, primer binding sites, and terminal sites are added to each strand of the DNA. Image based in part on illumina's sequencing video

Reduced Cycle Amplification

The next step is called reduced cycle amplification. During this step, sequences for primer binding, indices, and terminal sequences are added. Indices are usually six base pairs long and are used during DNA sequence analysis to identify samples. Indices allow for up to 96 different samples to be run together. During analysis, the computer will group all reads with the same index together. The terminal sequences are used for attaching the DNA strand to the flow cell. Illumina uses a "sequence by synthesis" approach. This process takes place inside of an acrylamide-coated glass flow cell. The flow cell has oligonucleotides (short nucleotide sequences) coating the bottom of the cell, and they serve to hold the DNA strands in place during sequencing. The oligos match the two kinds of terminal sequences added to the DNA during reduced cycle amplification. As the DNA enters the flow cell, one of the adapters attaches to a complementary oligo.

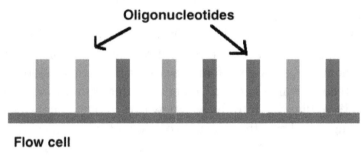

Oligonucleotides

Flow cell

Millions of oligos line the bottom of each flow cell lane.

Bridge Amplification

Once attached, cluster generation can begin. The goal is to create hundreds of identical strands of DNA. Some will be the forward strand; the rest, the reverse. Clusters are generated through bridge amplification. Polymerases move along a strand of DNA, creating its complementary strand. The original strand is washed away, leaving only the reverse strand. At the top of the reverse strand there is an adapter sequence. The DNA strand bends and attaches to the oligo that is complementary to the top adapter sequence. Polymerases attach to the reverse strand, and its complementary strand (which is identical to the original) is made. The now double stranded DNA is denatured so that each strand can separately attach to an oligonucleotide sequence anchored to the flow cell. One will be the reverse strand; the other, the forward. This process is called bridge amplification, and it happens for thousands of clusters all over the flow cell at once.

Clonal Amplification

Over and over again, DNA strands will bend and attach to oligos. Polymerases will synthesize a new strand to create a double stranded segment, and that will be denatured so that all of the DNA strands in one area are from a single source (clonal amplification). Clonal amplification is important for quality control purposes. If a strand is found to have an odd sequence, then scientists can check the reverse strand to make sure that it has the complement of the same oddity. The forward and reverse strands act as checks to guard against artifacts. Because Illumina sequencing uses polymerases, base substitution errors have been observed, especially at the 3' end. Paired end reads combined with cluster generation can confirm an error took place. The reverse and forward strands should be complementary to each other, all reverse reads should match each other, and all forward reads should match each other. If a read is not similar enough to its counterparts (with which it should be a clone), an error may have occurred. A minimum threshold of 97% similarity has been used in some labs' analyses.

Sequence by Synthesis

At the end of bridge amplification, all of the reverse strands are washed off the flow cell, leaving only forward strands. Primers attach to the forward strands and add fluorescently tagged nucleotides to the DNA strand. Only one base is added per round. A reversible terminator is on every nucleotide to prevent multiple additions in one round. Using the four-colour chemistry, each of the four bases has a unique emission, and after each round, the machine records which base was added. Starting with the launch of the NextSeq and later the MiniSeq, Illumina introduced a new two-colour sequencing chemistry. Nucleotides are distinguished by either one of two colours (red or green), no colour ("black") or binding both colours (appreading orange as a mixture between red and green).

Tagged nucleotides are added in order to the DNA strand. Each of the four nucleotides have an identifying label that can be excited to emit a characteristic wavelength. A computer records all of the emissions, and from this data, base calls are made.

Once the DNA strand has been read, the strand that was just added is washed away. Then, the index 1 primer attaches, polymerizes the index 1 sequence, and is washed away. The strand forms a bridge again, and the 3' end of the DNA strand attaches to an oligo on the flow cell. The index 2 primer attaches, polymerizes the sequence, and is washed away.

A polymerase sequences the complementary strand on top of the arched strand. They separate, and the 3' end of each strand is blocked. The forward strand is washed away, and the process of sequence by synthesis repeats for the reverse strand.

Data Analysis

The sequencing occurs for millions of clusters at once, and each cluster has ~1,000 identical copies of a DNA insert. The sequence data is analyzed by finding fragments with overlapping areas, called contigs, and lining them up. If a reference sequence is known, the contigs are then compared to it for variant identification.

This piecemeal process allows scientists to see the complete sequence even though an unfragmented sequence was never run; however, because Illumina read lengths are not very long (HiSeq sequencing can produce read lengths around 90 bp long), it can be a struggle to resolve short tandem repeat areas. Also, if the sequence is de novo and so a reference doesn't exist, repeated areas can cause a lot of difficulty in sequence assembly. Additional difficulties include base substitutions (especially at the 3' end of reads) by inaccurate polymerases, chimeric sequences, and PCR-bias, all of which can contribute to generating an incorrect sequence.

Comparison with Other Sequencing Methods

This technique offers a number of advantages over traditional sequencing methods such as Sanger sequencing. Due to the automated nature of Illumina dye sequencing it is possible to sequence multiple strands at once and gain actual sequencing data quickly. Additionally, this method only uses DNA polymerase as opposed to multiple, expensive enzymes required by other sequencing techniques (i.e. pyrosequencing).

Examples of Use

Illumina sequencing has been used to research transcriptomes of the sweet potato and the gymnosperm genus *Taxus*.

Ion Semiconductor Sequencing

Ion semiconductor sequencing is a method of DNA sequencing based on the detection of hydrogen ions that are released during the polymerization of DNA. This is a method of "sequencing by synthesis", during which a complementary strand is built based on the sequence of a template strand.

A Ion Proton semiconductor sequencer

A microwell containing a template DNA strand to be sequenced is flooded with a single species of deoxyribonucleotide triphosphate (dNTP). If the introduced dNTP is complementary to the leading template nucleotide, it is incorporated into the growing complementary strand. This causes the release of a hydrogen ion that triggers an ISFET ion sensor, which indicates that a reaction has occurred. If homopolymer repeats are present in the template sequence, multiple dNTP molecules will be incorporated in a single cycle. This leads to a corresponding number of released hydrogens and a proportionally higher electronic signal.

This technology differs from other sequencing technologies in that no modified nucleotides or optics are used. Ion semiconductor sequencing may also be referred to as Ion Torrent sequencing, pH-mediated sequencing, silicon sequencing, or semiconductor sequencing.

Technology Development History

The technology was licensed from DNA Electronics Ltd, developed by Ion Torrent Systems Inc. and was released in February 2010. Ion Torrent have marketed their machine as a rapid, compact and economical sequencer that can be utilized in a large number of laboratories as a bench top machine. Roche's 454 Life Sciences is partnering with DNA Electronics on the development of a long-read, high-density semiconductor sequencing platform using this technology.

Technology

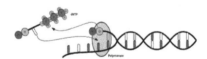

Polymerase integrates a nucleotide.

Hydrogen and pyrophosphate are released.

The incorporation of deoxyribonucleotide Triphosphate into a growing DNA strand causes the release of hydrogen and pyrophosphate.

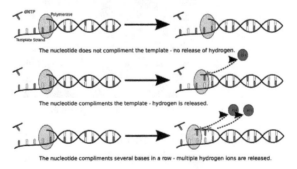

The release of hydrogen ions indicate if zero, one or more nucleotides were incorporated.

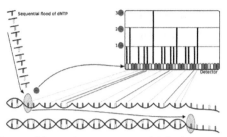

Released hydrogens ions are detected by an ion sensor. Multiple incorporations lead to a corresponding number of released hydrogens and intensity of signal.

Sequencing Chemistry

In nature, the incorporation of a deoxyribonucleoside triphosphate (dNTP) into a growing DNA strand involves the formation of a covalent bond and the release of pyrophosphate and a positively charged hydrogen ion. A dNTP will only be incorporated if it is complementary to the leading unpaired template nucleotide. Ion semiconductor sequencing exploits these facts by determining if a hydrogen ion is released upon providing a single species of dNTP to the reaction.

Microwells on a semiconductor chip that each contain many copies of one single-stranded template DNA molecule to be sequenced and DNA polymerase are sequentially flooded with unmodified A, C, G or T dNTP. If an introduced dNTP is complementary to the next unpaired nucleotide on the template strand it is incorporated into the growing complementary strand by the DNA polymerase. If the introduced dNTP is not complementary there is no incorporation and no biochemical reaction. The hydrogen ion that is released in the reaction changes the pH of the solution, which is detected by an ISFET. The unattached dNTP molecules are washed out before the next cycle when a different dNTP species is introduced.

Signal Detection

Beneath the layer of microwells is an ion sensitive layer, below which is an ISFET ion sensor. All layers are contained within a CMOS semiconductor chip, similar to that used in the electronics industry.

Each chip contains an array of microwells with corresponding ISFET detectors. Each released hydrogen ion then triggers the ISFET ion sensor. The series of electrical pulses transmitted from the chip to a computer is translated into a DNA sequence, with no intermediate signal conversion required. Because nucleotide incorporation events are measured directly by electronics, the use of labeled nucleotides and optical measurements are avoided. Signal processing and DNA assembly can then be carried out in software.

Sequencing Characteristics

The per base accuracy achieved in house by Ion Torrent on the Ion Torrent Ion semiconductor sequencer as of February 2011 was 99.6% based on 50 base reads, with 100 Mb per run. The read-length as of February 2011 was 100 base pairs. The accuracy for homopolymer repeats of 5 repeats in length was 98%. Later releases show a read length of 400 base pairs It should be noted that these figures have not yet been independently verified outside of the company.

Strengths

The major benefits of ion semiconductor sequencing are rapid sequencing speed and low upfront and operating costs. This has been enabled by the avoidance of modified nucleotides and optical measurements.

Because the system records natural polymerase-mediated nucleotide incorporation events, sequencing can occur in real-time. In reality, the sequencing rate is limited by the cycling of substrate nucleotides through the system. Ion Torrent Systems Inc., the developer of the technology, claims that each incorporation measurement takes 4 seconds and each run takes about one hour, during which 100-200 nucleotides are sequenced. If the semiconductor chips are improved (as predicted by Moore's law), the number of reads per chip (and therefore per run) should increase.

The cost of acquiring a pH-mediated sequencer from Ion Torrent Systems Inc. at time of launch was priced at around $50,000 USD, excluding sample preparation equipment and a server for data analysis. The cost per run is also significantly lower than that of alternative automated sequencing methods, at roughly $1,000.

Limitations

If homopolymer repeats of the same nucleotide (e.g. TTTTT) are present on the template strand (strand to be sequenced) then multiple introduced nucleotides are incorporated and more hydrogen ions are released in a single cycle. This results in a greater pH change and a proportionally greater electronic signal. This is a limitation of the system in that it is difficult to enumerate long repeats. This limitation is shared by other techniques that detect single nucleotide additions such as pyrosequencing. Signals generated from a high repeat number are difficult to differentiate from repeats of a similar but different number; e.g., homorepeats of length 7 are difficult to differentiate from those of length 8.

Another limitation of this system is the short read length compared to other sequencing methods such as Sanger sequencing or pyrosequencing. Longer read lengths are beneficial for de novo genome assembly. Ion Torrent semiconductor sequencers produce an average read length of approximately 400 nucleotides per read.

The throughput is currently lower than that of other high-throughput sequencing technologies, although the developers hope to change this by increasing the density of the chip.

Application

The developers of Ion Torrent semiconductor sequencing have marketed it as a rapid, compact and economical sequencer that can be utilized in a large number of laboratories as a bench top machine. The company hopes that their system will take sequencing outside of specialized centers and into the reach of hospitals and smaller laboratories. A January 2011 New York Times article, "Taking DNA Sequencing to the Masses", underlines these ambitions.

Due to the ability of alternative sequencing methods to achieve a greater read length (and therefore being more suited to whole genome analysis) this technology may be best suited to small scale applications such as microbial genome sequencing, microbial transcriptome sequencing, targeted sequencing, amplicon sequencing, or for quality testing of sequencing libraries.

Threading (Protein Sequence)

Protein threading, also known as fold recognition, is a method of protein modeling which is used to model those proteins which have the same fold as proteins of known structures, but do not have homologous proteins with known structure. It differs from the homology modeling method of structure prediction as it (protein threading) is used for proteins which do not have their homologous protein structures deposited in the Protein Data Bank (PDB), whereas homology modeling is used for those proteins which do. Threading works by using statistical knowledge of the relationship between the structures deposited in the PDB and the sequence of the protein which one wishes to model.

The prediction is made by "threading" (i.e. placing, aligning) each amino acid in the target sequence to a position in the template structure, and evaluating how well the target fits the template. After the best-fit template is selected, the structural model of the sequence is built based on the alignment with the chosen template. Protein threading is based on two basic observations: that the number of different folds in nature is fairly small (approximately 1300); and that 90% of the new structures submitted to the PDB in the past three years have similar structural folds to ones already in the PDB.

Classification of Protein Structure

The Structural Classification of Proteins (SCOP) database provides a detailed and comprehensive description of the structural and evolutionary relationships of known structure. Proteins are classified to reflect both structural and evolutionary relatedness. Many levels exist in the hierarchy, but the principal levels are family, superfamily and fold, as described below.

Family (clear evolutionary relationship): Proteins clustered together into families are clearly evolutionarily related. Generally, this means that pairwise residue identities between the proteins are 30% and greater. However, in some cases similar functions and structures provide definitive evidence of common descent in the absence of high sequence identity; for example, many globins form a family though some members have sequence identities of only 15%.

Superfamily (probable common evolutionary origin): Proteins that have low sequence identities, but whose structural and functional features suggest that a common evolutionary origin is probable, are placed together in superfamilies. For example, actin, the ATPase domain of the heat shock protein, and hexakinase together form a superfamily.

Fold (major structural similarity): Proteins are defined as having a common fold if they have the same major secondary structures in the same arrangement and with the same topological connections. Different proteins with the same fold often have peripheral elements of secondary structure and turn regions that differ in size and conformation. In some cases, these differing peripheral regions may comprise half the structure. Proteins placed together in the same fold category may not have a common evolutionary origin: the structural similarities could arise just from the physics and chemistry of proteins favoring certain packing arrangements and chain topologies.

Method

A general paradigm of protein threading consists of the following four steps:

The construction of a structure template database: Select protein structures from the protein structure databases as structural templates. This generally involves selecting protein structures from databases such as PDB, FSSP, SCOP, or CATH, after removing protein structures with high sequence similarities.

The design of the scoring function: Design a good scoring function to measure the fitness between target sequences and templates based on the knowledge of the known relationships between the structures and the sequences. A good scoring function should contain mutation potential, environment fitness potential, pairwise potential, secondary structure compatibilities, and gap penalties. The quality of the energy function is closely related to the prediction accuracy, especially the alignment accuracy.

Threading alignment: Align the target sequence with each of the structure templates by optimizing the designed scoring function. This step is one of the major tasks of all threading-based structure prediction programs that take into account the pairwise contact potential; otherwise, a dynamic programming algorithm can fulfill it.

Threading prediction: Select the threading alignment that is statistically most probable as the threading prediction. Then construct a structure model for the target by placing the backbone atoms of the target sequence at their aligned backbone positions of the selected structural template.

Comparison with Homology Modeling

Homology modeling and protein threading are both template-based methods and there is no rigorous boundary between them in terms of prediction techniques. But the protein structures of their targets are different. Homology modeling is for those targets which have homologous proteins with known structure (usually/maybe of same family), while protein threading is for those targets with only fold-level homology found. In other words, homology modeling is for "easier" targets and protein threading is for "harder" targets.

Homology modeling treats the template in an alignment as a sequence, and only sequence homology is used for prediction. Protein threading treats the template in an alignment as a structure, and both sequence and structure information extracted from the alignment are used for prediction. When there is no significant homology found, protein threading can make a prediction based on the structure information. That also explains why protein threading may be more effective than homology modeling in many cases.

In practice, when the sequence identity in a sequence sequence alignment is low (i.e. <25%), homology modeling may not produce a significant prediction. In this case, if there is distant homology found for the target, protein threading can generate a good prediction.

More About Threading

Fold recognition methods can be broadly divided into two types: 1, those that derive a 1-D profile for each structure in the fold library and align the target sequence to these profiles; and 2, those that consider the full 3-D structure of the protein template. A simple example of a profile representation would be to take each amino acid in the structure and simply label it according to whether it is buried in the core of the protein or exposed on the surface. More elaborate profiles might take into account the local secondary structure (e.g. whether the amino acid is part of an alpha helix) or even evolutionary information (how conserved the amino acid is). In the 3-D representation, the structure is modeled as a set of inter-atomic distances, i.e. the distances are calculated between some or all of the atom pairs in the structure. This is a much richer and far more flexible description of the structure, but is much harder to use in calculating an alignment. The profile-based fold recognition approach was first described by Bowie, Lüthy and Eisenberg in 1991. The term *threading* was first coined by Jones, Taylor and Thornton in 1992, and originally referred specifically to the use of a full 3-D structure atomic representation of the protein template in fold recognition. Today, the terms threading and fold recognition are frequently (though somewhat incorrectly) used interchangeably.

Fold recognition methods are widely used and effective because it is believed that there are a strictly limited number of different protein folds in nature, mostly as a result of evolution but also due to constraints imposed by the basic physics and chemistry of polypeptide chains. There is, therefore, a good chance (currently 70-80%) that a protein which has a similar fold to the target protein has already been studied by X-ray crystallography or nuclear magnetic resonance (NMR) spectroscopy and can be found in the PDB. Currently there are nearly 1300 different protein folds known, but new folds are still being discovered every year due in significant part to the ongoing structural genomics projects.

Many different algorithms have been proposed for finding the correct threading of a sequence onto a structure, though many make use of dynamic programming in some form. For full 3-D threading, the problem of identifying the best alignment is very difficult (it is an NP-hard problem for some models of threading). Researchers have made use of many combinatorial optimization methods such as Conditional random fields, simulated annealing, branch and bound and linear programming, searching to arrive at heuristic solutions. Louisiana It is interesting to compare threading methods to methods which attempt to align two protein structures (protein structural alignment), and indeed many of the same algorithms have been applied to both problems.

Protein Threading Software

- HHpred is a popular threading server which runs HHsearch, a widely used software for remote homology detection based on pairwise comparison of hidden Markov models.

- RAPTOR (software) is an integer programming based protein threading software. It has been replaced by a new protein threading program RaptorX / software for protein modeling and analysis, which employs probabilistic graphical models and statistical inference to both single template and multi-template based protein threading. RaptorX significantly outperforms RAPTOR and is especially good at aligning proteins with sparse sequence profile. The RaptorX server is free to public.

- Phyre is a popular threading server combining HHsearch with *ab initio* and multiple-template modelling.

- MUSTER is a standard threading algorithm based on dynamic programming and sequence profile-profile alignment. It also combines multiple structural resources to assist the sequence profile alignment.

- SPARKS X is a probabilistic-based sequence-to-structure matching between predicted one-dimensional structural properties of query and corresponding native properties of templates.

- BioShell is a threading algorithm using optimized profile-to-profile dynamic programming algorithm combined with predicted secondary structure.

References

- Kalb, Gilbert; Moxley, Robert (1992). Massively Parallel, Optical, and Neural Computing in the United States. IOS Press. ISBN 90-5199-097-9.

- Kim N; Lee C (2008). "Bioinformatics detection of alternative splicing". Methods Mol. Biol. Methods in Molecular Biology™. 452: 179–97. doi:10.1007/978-1-60327-159-2_9. ISBN 978-1-58829-707-5.

- Canard, Bruno; Sarfati, Simon (13 Oct 1994), Novel derivatives usable for the sequencing of nucleic acids, retrieved 2016-03-09.

- "Publications Landing | Oxford Nanopore: Community". publications.nanoporetech.com. Retrieved 2016-08-17.

- "NASA prepares for first-ever in-space DNA sequencing experiment | NASASpaceFlight.com". www.nasaspaceflight.com. Retrieved 2016-08-17.

- Canard, Bruno; Sarfati, Simon (13 Oct 1994), Novel derivatives usable for the sequencing of nucleic acids, retrieved 2016-03-09.

- Henderson, Mark. "Human genome sequencing: the real ethical dilemmas". The Guardian. Retrieved 20 May 2015.

Genome Analysis: An Overview

The study of the genome is known as genomics. It is a discipline of genetics and applies methods such as recombinant DNA and DNA sequencing. Personal genomics, oncogenomics, comparative genomics and the genome project have been explained in this section. This chapter is an overview of the subject matter incorporating all the major aspects of genome analysis.

Genomics

Genomics refers to the study of the genome in contrast to genetics which refers to the study of genes and their roles in inheritance. Genomics can be considered a discipline in genetics. It applies recombinant DNA, DNA sequencing methods, and bioinformatics to sequence, assemble, and analyze the function and structure of genomes (the *complete* set of DNA within a single cell of an organism). Advances in genomics have triggered a revolution in discovery-based research to understand even the most complex biological systems such as the brain. The field includes efforts to determine the entire DNA sequence of organisms and fine-scale genetic mapping. The field also includes studies of intragenomic phenomena such as heterosis, epistasis, pleiotropy and other interactions between loci and alleles within the genome. In contrast, the investigation of the roles and functions of single genes is a primary focus of molecular biology or genetics and is a common topic of modern medical and biological research. Research carried out into single genes does not generally fall into the definition of genomics unless the aim of this genetic, pathway, and functional information analysis is to elucidate its effect on, place in, and response to the entire genomes networks.

History

Etymology

From the *gen*, "gene" (gamma, epsilon, nu, epsilon) meaning "become, cre-ate, creation, birth", and subsequent variants: genealogy, genesis, genetics, genic, genomere, genotype, genus etc. While the word *genome* (from the German *Genom*, attributed to Hans Winkler) was in use in English as early as 1926, the term *genomics* was coined by Tom Roderick, a geneticist at the Jackson Laboratory (Bar Harbor, Maine), over beer at a meeting held in Maryland on the mapping of the human genome in 1986.

Early Sequencing Efforts

Following Rosalind Franklin's confirmation of the helical structure of DNA, James D. Watson and Francis Crick's publication of the structure of DNA in 1953 and Fred Sanger's publication of the Amino acid sequence of insulin in 1955, nucleic acid sequencing became a major target of early molecular biologists. In 1964, Robert W. Holley and colleagues published the first nucleic acid sequence ever determined, the ribonucleotide sequence of alanine transfer RNA. Extending this work, Marshall Nirenberg and Philip Leder revealed the triplet nature of the genetic code and were able to determine the sequences of 54 out of 64 codons in their experiments. In 1972, Walter Fiers and his team at the Laboratory of Molecular Biology of the University of Ghent (Ghent, Belgium) were the first to determine the sequence of a gene: the gene for Bacteriophage MS2 coat protein. Fiers' group expanded on their MS2 coat protein work, determining the complete nucleotide-sequence of bacteriophage MS2-RNA (whose genome encodes just four genes in 3569 base pairs [bp]) and Simian virus 40 in 1976 and 1978, respectively.

DNA-sequencing Technology Developed

Walter Gilbert   Frederick Sanger

Frederick Sanger and Walter Gilbert shared half of the 1980 Nobel Prize in chemistry for independently developing methods for the sequencing of DNA.

In addition to his seminal work on the amino acid sequence of insulin, Frederick Sanger and his colleagues played a key role in the development of DNA sequencing techniques that enabled the establishment of comprehensive genome sequencing projects. In 1975, he and Alan Coulson published a sequencing procedure using DNA polymerase with radiolabelled nucleotides that he called the *Plus and Minus technique*. This involved two closely related methods that generated short oligonucleotides with defined 3' termini. These could be fractionated by electrophoresis on a polyacrylamide gel and visualised using autoradiography. The procedure could sequence up to 80 nucleotides in one go and was a big improvement, but was still very laborious. Nevertheless, in 1977 his group was able to sequence most of the 5,386 nucleotides of the single-stranded bacteriophage φX174, completing the first fully sequenced DNA-based genome. The refinement of the *Plus and Minus* method resulted in the chain-termination, or Sanger method, which formed the basis of the techniques of DNA sequencing, genome mapping, data storage, and bioinformatic analysis most widely used in the following quarter-century of research. In the same year Walter Gilbert and Allan Maxam of Harvard University independently developed the Maxam-Gilbert method (also known as the *chemical method*) of DNA sequencing, involving the preferential cleavage of DNA at known bases, a less efficient method. For their groundbreaking work in the sequencing of nucleic acids, Gilbert and Sanger shared half the 1980 Nobel Prize in chemistry with Paul Berg (recombinant DNA).

Complete Genomes

The advent of these technologies resulted in a rapid intensification in the scope and speed of completion of genome sequencing projects. The first complete genome sequence of an eukaryotic organelle, the human mitochondrion (16,568 bp, about 16.6 kb [kilobase]), was reported in 1981, and the first chloroplast genomes followed in 1986. In 1992, the first eukaryotic chromosome, chromosome III of brewer's yeast *Saccharomyces cerevisiae* (315 kb) was sequenced. The first free-living organism to be sequenced was that of *Haemophilus influenzae* (1.8 Mb [megabase]) in 1995. The following year a consortium of researchers from laboratories across North America, Europe, and Japan announced the completion of the first complete genome sequence of a eukaryote, *S. cerevisiae* (12.1 Mb), and since then genomes have continued being sequenced at an exponentially growing pace. As of October 2011, the complete sequences are available for: 2,719 viruses, 1,115 archaea and bacteria, and 36 eukaryotes, of which about half are fungi.

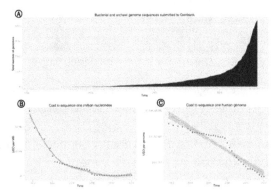

The number of genome projects has increased as technological improvements continue to lower the cost of sequencing. (A) Exponential growth of genome sequence databases since 1995. (B) The cost in US Dollars (USD) to sequence one million bases. (C) The cost in USD to sequence a 3,000 Mb (human-sized) genome on a log-transformed scale.

Most of the microorganisms whose genomes have been completely sequenced are problematic pathogens, such as *Haemophilus influenzae*, which has resulted in a pronounced bias in their phylogenetic distribution compared to the breadth of microbial diversity. Of the other sequenced species, most were chosen because they were well-studied model organisms or promised to become good models. Yeast (*Saccharomyces cerevisiae*) has long been an important model organism for the eukaryotic cell, while the fruit fly *Drosophila melanogaster* has been a very important tool (notably in early pre-molecular genetics). The worm *Caenorhabditis elegans* is an often used simple model for multicellular organisms. The zebrafish *Brachydanio rerio* is used for many developmental studies on the molecular level, and the flower *Arabidopsis thaliana* is a model organism for flowering plants. The Japanese pufferfish (*Takifugu rubripes*) and the spotted green pufferfish (*Tetraodon nigroviridis*) are interesting because of their small and compact genomes, which contain very little noncoding DNA compared to most species. The mammals dog (*Canis familiaris*), brown rat (*Rattus norvegicus*), mouse (*Mus musculus*), and chimpanzee (*Pan troglodytes*) are all important model animals in medical research.

A rough draft of the human genome was completed by the Human Genome Project in early 2001, creating much fanfare. This project, completed in 2003, sequenced the entire genome for one specific person, and by 2007 this sequence was declared "finished" (less than one error in 20,000 bases and all chromosomes assembled). In the years since then, the genomes of many other individuals have been sequenced, partly under the auspices of the 1000 Genomes Project, which announced the sequencing of 1,092 genomes in October 2012. Completion of this project was made possible by the development of dramatically more efficient sequencing technologies and required the commitment of significant bioinformatics resources from a large international collaboration. The continued analysis of human genomic data has profound political and social repercussions for human societies.

The "Omics" Revolution

The English-language neologism omics informally refers to a field of study in biology ending in -*omics*, such as genomics, proteomics or metabolomics. The related suffix -ome is used to address the objects of study of such fields, such as the genome, proteome or metabolome respectively. The suffix -*ome* as used in molecular biology refers to a *totality* of some sort; similarly omics has come to refer generally to the study of large, comprehensive biological data sets. While the growth in the use of the term has led some scientists (Jonathan Eisen, among others) to claim that it has been oversold, it reflects the change in orientation towards the quantitative analysis of complete or near-complete assortment of all the constituents of a system. In the study of symbioses, for example, researchers which were once limited to the study of a single gene product can now simultaneously compare the total complement of several types of biological molecules.

Genome Analysis

After an organism has been selected, genome projects involve three components: the sequencing of DNA, the assembly of that sequence to create a representation of the original chromosome, and the annotation and analysis of that representation.

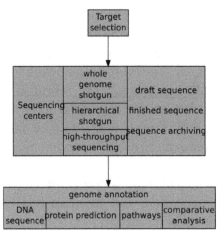

Overview of a genome project. First, the genome must be selected, which involves several factors including cost and relevance. Second, the sequence is generated and assembled at a given sequencing center (such as BGI or DOE JGI). Third, the genome sequence is annotated at several levels: DNA, protein, gene pathways, or comparatively.

Sequencing

Historically, sequencing was done in *sequencing centers*, centralized facilities (ranging from large independent institutions such as Joint Genome Institute which sequence dozens of terabases a year, to local molecular biology core facilities) which contain research laboratories with the costly instrumentation and technical support necessary. As sequencing technology continues to improve, however, a new generation of effective fast turnaround benchtop sequencers has come within reach of the average academic laboratory. On the whole, genome sequencing approaches fall into two broad categories, *shotgun* and *high-throughput* (aka *next-generation*) sequencing.

Shotgun Sequencing

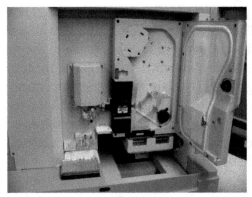

An ABI PRISM 3100 Genetic Analyzer. Such capillary sequencers automated early large-scale genome sequencing efforts.

Shotgun sequencing (Sanger sequencing is used interchangeably) is a sequencing method designed for analysis of DNA sequences longer than 1000 base pairs, up to and including entire chromosomes. It is named by analogy with the rapidly expanding, quasi-random firing pattern of a shotgun. Since the chain termination method of DNA sequencing can only be used for fairly short strands (100 to 1000 base pairs), longer DNA sequences must be broken into random small segments which are then sequenced to obtain *reads*. Multiple overlapping reads for the target DNA are obtained by performing several rounds of this fragmentation and sequencing. Computer programs then use the overlapping ends of different reads to assemble them into a continuous sequence. Shotgun sequencing is a random sampling process, requiring over-sampling to ensure a given nucleotide is represented in the reconstructed sequence; the average number of reads by which a genome is over-sampled is referred to as coverage.

For much of its history, the technology underlying shotgun sequencing was the classical chain-termination method, which is based on the selective incorporation of chain-terminating dideoxynucleotides by DNA polymerase during in vitro DNA replication. Developed by Frederick Sanger and colleagues in 1977, it was the most widely used sequencing method for approximately 25 years. More recently, Sanger sequencing has been supplanted by "Next-Gen" sequencing methods, especially for large-scale, automated genome analyses. However, the Sanger method remains in wide use in 2013, primarily for smaller-scale projects and for obtaining especially long contiguous DNA sequence reads (>500 nucleotides). Chain-termination methods require a single-stranded DNA template, a DNA primer, a DNA polymerase, normal deoxynucleosidetriphosphates (dNTPs), and modified nucleotides (dideoxyNTPs) that terminate DNA strand elongation. These chain-terminating nucleotides lack a 3'-OH group required for the formation of a phosphodiester bond between two nucleotides, causing DNA polymerase to cease extension of DNA when a ddNTP is incorporated. The ddNTPs may be radioactively or fluorescently labelled for detection in automated sequencing machines. Typically, these automated DNA-sequencing instruments (DNA sequencers) can sequence up to 96 DNA samples in a single batch (run) in up to 48 runs a day.

High-throughput Sequencing

The high demand for low-cost sequencing has driven the development of high-throughput sequencing (or next-generation sequencing [NGS]) technologies that parallelize the sequencing process, producing thousands or millions of sequences at once. High-throughput sequencing technologies are intended to lower the cost of DNA sequencing beyond what is possible with standard dye-terminator methods. In ultra-high-throughput sequencing as many as 500,000 sequencing-by-synthesis operations may be run in parallel.

Illumina (Solexa) Sequencing

Solexa, now part of Illumina, developed a sequencing method based on reversible dye-terminators technology acquired from Manteia Predictive Medicine in 2004. This technology had been invented and developed in late 1996 at Glaxo-Welcome's Geneva

Biomedical Research Institute (GBRI), by Dr. Pascal Mayer and Dr Laurent Farinelli. In this method, DNA molecules and primers are first attached on a slide and amplified with polymerase so that local clonal colonies, initially coined "DNA colonies", are formed. To determine the sequence, four types of reversible terminator bases (RT-bases) are added and non-incorporated nucleotides are washed away. Unlike pyrosequencing, the DNA chains are extended one nucleotide at a time and image acquisition can be performed at a delayed moment, allowing for very large arrays of DNA colonies to be captured by sequential images taken from a single camera.

Illumina Genome Analyzer II System. Illumina technologies have set the standard for high throughput massively parallel sequencing.

Decoupling the enzymatic reaction and the image capture allows for optimal throughput and theoretically unlimited sequencing capacity. With an optimal configuration, the ultimately reachable instrument throughput is thus dictated solely by the analogic-to-digital conversion rate of the camera, multiplied by the number of cameras and divided by the number of pixels per DNA colony required for visualizing them optimally (approximately 10 pixels/colony). In 2012, with cameras operating at more than 10 MHz A/D conversion rates and available optics, fluidics and enzymatics, throughput can be multiples of 1 million nucleotides/second, corresponding roughly to 1 human genome equivalent at 1x coverage per hour per instrument, and 1 human genome re-sequenced (at approx. 30x) per day per instrument (equipped with a single camera). The camera takes images of the fluorescently labeled nucleotides, then the dye along with the terminal 3' blocker is chemically removed from the DNA, allowing the next cycle.

Ion Torrent

Ion Torrent Systems Inc. developed a sequencing approach based on standard DNA replication chemistry. This technology measures the release of a hydrogen ion each time a base is incorporated. A microwell containing template DNA is flooded with a single nucleotide, if the nucleotide is complementary to the template strand it will be incorporated and a hydrogen ion will be released. This release triggers an ISFET ion sensor. If a homopolymer is present in the template sequence multiple nucleotides will be incorporated in a single flood cycle, and the detected electrical signal will be proportionally higher.

Assembly

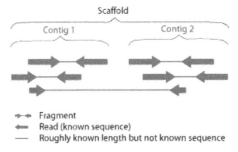

Overlapping reads form contigs; contigs and gaps of known length form scaffolds.

Multiple, fragmented sequence reads must be assembled together on the basis of their overlapping areas.

Sequence assembly refers to aligning and merging fragments of a much longer DNA sequence in order to reconstruct the original sequence. This is needed as current DNA sequencing technology cannot read whole genomes as a continuous sequence, but rather reads small pieces of between 20 and 1000 bases, depending on the technology used. Typically the short fragments, called reads, result from shotgun sequencing genomic DNA, or gene transcripts (ESTs).

Assembly Approaches

Assembly can be broadly categorized into two approaches: *de novo* assembly, for genomes which are not similar to any sequenced in the past, and comparative assembly, which uses the existing sequence of a closely related organism as a reference during assembly. Relative to comparative assembly, *de novo* assembly is computationally difficult (NP-hard), making it less favorable for short-read NGS technologies.

Finishing

Finished genomes are defined as having a single contiguous sequence with no ambiguities representing each replicon.

Annotation

The DNA sequence assembly alone is of little value without additional analysis. Genome annotation is the process of attaching biological information to sequences, and consists of three main steps:

1. identifying portions of the genome that do not code for proteins

2. identifying elements on the genome, a process called gene prediction, and

3. attaching biological information to these elements.

Automatic annotation tools try to perform these steps *in silico*, as opposed to manual annotation (a.k.a. curation) which involves human expertise and potential experimental verification. Ideally, these approaches co-exist and complement each other in the same annotation pipeline.

Traditionally, the basic level of annotation is using BLAST for finding similarities, and then annotating genomes based on homologues. More recently, additional information is added to the annotation platform. The additional information allows manual annotators to deconvolute discrepancies between genes that are given the same annotation. Some databases use genome context information, similarity scores, experimental data, and integrations of other resources to provide genome annotations through their Subsystems approach. Other databases (e.g. Ensembl) rely on both curated data sources as well as a range of software tools in their automated genome annotation pipeline. *Structural annotation* consists of the identification of genomic elements, primarily ORFs and their localisation, or gene structure. *Functional annotation* consists of attaching biological information to genomic elements.

Sequencing Pipelines and Databases

The need for reproducibility and efficient management of the large amount of data associated with genome projects mean that computational pipelines have important applications in genomics.

Research Areas

Functional Genomics

Functional genomics is a field of molecular biology that attempts to make use of the vast wealth of data produced by genomic projects (such as genome sequencing projects) to describe gene (and protein) functions and interactions. Functional genomics focuses on the dynamic aspects such as gene transcription, translation, and protein–protein interactions, as opposed to the static aspects of the genomic information such as DNA sequence or structures. Functional genomics attempts to answer questions about the function of DNA at the levels of genes, RNA transcripts, and protein products. A key characteristic of functional genomics studies is their genome-wide approach to these questions, generally involving high-throughput methods rather than a more traditional "gene-by-gene" approach.

A major branch of genomics is still concerned with sequencing the genomes of various organisms, but the knowledge of full genomes has created the possibility for the field of functional genomics, mainly concerned with patterns of gene expression during various conditions. The most important tools here are microarrays and bioinformatics.

Structural Genomics

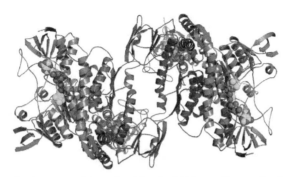

An example of a protein structure determined by the Midwest Center for Structural Genomics.

Structural genomics seeks to describe the 3-dimensional structure of every protein encoded by a given genome. This genome-based approach allows for a high-throughput method of structure determination by a combination of experimental and modeling approaches. The principal difference between structural genomics and traditional structural prediction is that structural genomics attempts to determine the structure of every protein encoded by the genome, rather than focusing on one particular protein. With full-genome sequences available, structure prediction can be done more quickly through a combination of experimental and modeling approaches, especially because the availability of large numbers of sequenced genomes and previously solved protein structures allow scientists to model protein structure on the structures of previously solved homologs. Structural genomics involves taking a large number of approaches to structure determination, including experimental methods using genomic sequences or modeling-based approaches based on sequence or structural homology to a protein of known structure or based on chemical and physical principles for a protein with no homology to any known structure. As opposed to traditional structural biology, the determination of a protein structure through a structural genomics effort often (but not always) comes before anything is known regarding the protein function. This raises new challenges in structural bioinformatics, i.e. determining protein function from its 3D structure.

Epigenomics

Epigenomics is the study of the complete set of epigenetic modifications on the genetic material of a cell, known as the epigenome. Epigenetic modifications are reversible modifications on a cell's DNA or histones that affect gene expression without altering the DNA sequence. Two of the most characterized epigenetic modifications are DNA methylation and histone modification. Epigenetic modifications play an important role in gene expression and regulation, and are involved in numerous cellular processes such as in differentiation/development and tumorigenesis. The study of epigenetics on a global level has been made possible only recently through the adaptation of genomic high-throughput assays.

Metagenomics

Environmental Shotgun Sequencing (ESS) is a key technique in metagenomics. (A) Sampling from habitat; (B) filtering particles, typically by size; (C) Lysis and DNA extraction; (D) cloning and library construction; (E) sequencing the clones; (F) sequence assembly into contigs and scaffolds.

Metagenomics is the study of *metagenomes*, genetic material recovered directly from environmental samples. The broad field may also be referred to as environmental genomics, ecogenomics or community genomics. While traditional microbiology and microbial genome sequencing rely upon cultivated clonal cultures, early environmental gene sequencing cloned specific genes (often the 16S rRNA gene) to produce a profile of diversity in a natural sample. Such work revealed that the vast majority of microbial biodiversity had been missed by cultivation-based methods. Recent studies use "shotgun" Sanger sequencing or massively parallel pyrosequencing to get largely unbiased samples of all genes from all the members of the sampled communities. Because of its power to reveal the previously hidden diversity of microscopic life, metagenomics offers a powerful lens for viewing the microbial world that has the potential to revolutionize understanding of the entire living world.

Study Systems

Viruses and Bacteriophages

Bacteriophages have played and continue to play a key role in bacterial genetics and molecular biology. Historically, they were used to define gene structure and gene regulation. Also the first genome to be sequenced was a bacteriophage. However, bacteriophage research did not lead the genomics revolution, which is clearly dominated by bacterial genomics. Only very recently has the study of bacteriophage genomes become prominent, thereby enabling researchers to understand the mechanisms underlying phage evolution. Bacteriophage genome sequences can be obtained through direct sequencing of isolated bacteriophages, but can also be derived as part of microbial genomes. Analysis of bacterial genomes has shown that a substantial amount of microbial DNA consists of prophage sequences and prophage-like elements. A detailed database mining of these sequences offers insights into the role of prophages in shaping the bacterial genome.

Cyanobacteria

At present there are 24 cyanobacteria for which a total genome sequence is available. 15 of these cyanobacteria come from the marine environment. These are six *Prochlorococcus* strains, seven marine *Synechococcus* strains, *Trichodesmium erythraeum* IMS101 and *Crocosphaera watsonii* WH8501. Several studies have demonstrated how these sequences could be used very successfully to infer important ecological and physiological characteristics of marine cyanobacteria. However, there are many more genome projects currently in progress, amongst those there are further *Prochlorococcus* and marine *Synechococcus* isolates, *Acaryochloris* and *Prochloron*, the N_2-fixing filamentous cyanobacteria *Nodularia spumigena*, *Lyngbya aestuarii* and *Lyngbya majuscula*, as well as bacteriophages infecting marine cyanobaceria. Thus, the growing body of genome information can also be tapped in a more general way to address global problems by applying a comparative approach. Some new and exciting examples of progress in this field are the identification of genes for regulatory RNAs, insights into the evolutionary origin of photosynthesis, or estimation of the contribution of horizontal gene transfer to the genomes that have been analyzed.

Human Genomics

Applications of Genomics

Genomics has provided applications in many fields, including medicine, biotechnology, anthropology and other social sciences.

Genomic Medicine

Next-generation genomic technologies allow clinicians and biomedical researchers to drastically increase the amount of genomic data collected on large study populations. When combined with new informatics approaches that integrate many kinds of data with genomic data in disease research, this allows researchers to better understand the genetic bases of drug response and disease.

Synthetic Biology and Bioengineering

The growth of genomic knowledge has enabled increasingly sophisticated applications of synthetic biology. In 2010 researchers at the J. Craig Venter Institute announced the creation of a partially synthetic species of bacterium, *Mycoplasma laboratorium*, derived from the genome of *Mycoplasma genitalium*.

Conservation Genomics

Conservationists can use the information gathered by genomic sequencing in order to better evaluate genetic factors key to species conservation, such as the genetic diversity of a population or whether an individual is heterozygous for a recessive inherited genetic disorder. By using genomic data to evaluate the effects of evolutionary processes and to detect patterns in variation throughout a given population, conservationists can formulate plans to aid a given species without as many variables left unknown as those unaddressed by standard genetic approaches.

Personal Genomics

Personal genomics is the branch of genomics concerned with the sequencing and analysis of the genome of an individual. The genotyping stage employs different techniques, including single-nucleotide polymorphism (SNP) analysis chips (typically 0.02% of the genome), or partial or full genome sequencing. Once the genotypes are known, the individual's genotype can be compared with the published literature to determine likelihood of trait expression and disease risk.

Automated sequencers have increased the speed and reduced the cost of sequencing, making it possible to offer genetic testing to consumers.

Use of Personal Genomics in Predictive and Precision Medicine

Predictive medicine is the use of the information produced by personal genomics techniques when deciding what medical treatments are appropriate for a particular individual. Precision medicine is focused on "a new taxonomy of human disease based on molecular biology"

Examples of the use of predictive and precision medicine include inherited medical genomics, cancer genomics and pharmacogenomics. In pharmacogenomics genetic information can be used to select the most appropriate drug to prescribe to a patient. The drug should be chosen to maximize the probability of obtaining the desired result in the patient and minimize the probability that the patient will experience side effects. Genetic information may allow physicians to tailor therapy to a given patient, in order to increase drug efficacy and minimize side effects. As of Oct 2012 there are 167 examples of drug gene pairs for which this information is currently useful in clinical practice and this number has been growing rapidly.

Disease risk may be calculated based on genetic markers and genome-wide association studies for common medical conditions, which are multifactorial and include environmental components in the assessment. Diseases which are individually rare (less than 200,000 people affected in the USA) are nevertheless collectively common (affecting roughly 8-10% of the US population). Over 2500 of these diseases (including a few more common ones) have predictive genetics of sufficiently high clinical impact that they are recommended as medical genetic tests available for single genes (and in whole genome sequencing) and growing at about 200 new genetic diseases per year.

Cost of Sequencing an Individual's Genome

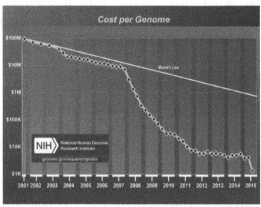

Typical cost of sequencing a human-sized genome, on a logarithmic scale. Note the drastic trend faster than Moore's law beginning in January 2008 as post-Sanger sequencing came online at sequencing centers.

The cost of sequencing a human genome is dropping rapidly, due to the continual development of new, faster, cheaper DNA sequencing technologies such as "next generation DNA sequencing".

The National Human Genome Research Institute, part of the U.S. National Institutes of Health, set a target to be able to sequence a human-sized genome for US$100,000 by 2009 and US$1,000 by 2014.

There are 6 billion base pairs in the diploid human genome. Statistical analysis reveals that a coverage of approximately ten times is required to get coverage of both alleles in 90% human genome from 25 base pair reads with shotgun sequencing. This means a total of 60 billion base pairs that must be sequenced. An Applied Biosystems SOLiD, Illumina or Helicos sequencing machine can sequence 2 to 10 billion base pairs in each $8,000 to $18,000 run. The cost must also take into account personnel costs, data processing costs, legal, communications and other costs. One way to assess this is via commercial offerings. The first such whole diploid genome sequencing (6 billion bp, 3 billion from each parent) was from Knome and their price dropped from $350,000 in 2008 to $99,000 in 2009. This inspects 3000-fold more bases of the genome than SNP chip-based genotyping, identifying both novel and known sequence variants, some relevant to personal health or ancestry. In June 2009, Illumina announced the launch of its own Personal Full Genome Sequencing Service at a depth of 30X for $48,000 per genome. In 2010, they cut the price to $19,500.

In 2009, Complete Genomics of Mountain View announced that it would provide full genome sequencing for $5,000, from June 2009. This will only be available to institutions, not individuals. Prices are expected to drop further over the next few years through economies of scale and increased competition. As of 2014, full exome sequencing was offered by Gentle for less than $2,000, including personal counseling along with the results.

The decreasing cost in general of genomic mapping has permitted genealogical sites to offer it as a service, to the extent that one may submit one's genome to crowd sourced scientific endeavours such as DNA.land at the New York Genome Center, an example both of the economies of scale and of citizen science.

Projects and Services Already Available

- Sequencing.com provides free, unlimited data storage for all genetic data in high-security data centers and software applications to analyze the data based on their patent-pending Real-Time Personalization™ technology. The company invented an open API that translates genetic code into software code so that third-party developers without any training in genetics can integrate genetic code into their own apps. The company also runs the not-for-profit Altruist Endeavor, which is an open data initiative consisting of a free, publicly accessible online repository of anonymous genetic data in order to enable genetic research.

- The Genographic Project is a project of the National Geographic Society and IBM to collect DNA samples to map historical human migration patterns. Launched in 2005, with more than 650,000 public participants as of December 2015, it helped to create the direct-to-consumer (DTC) genetic testing industry.

- The Personal Genome Project (PGP) is a long term, large cohort study based at Harvard Medical School which aims to sequence and publicize the complete genomes and medical records of 100,000 volunteers, in order to enable research into personal genomics and personalized medicine.

- SNPedia is a wiki that collects and shares information about the consequences of DNA variations, and through the associated program Promethease, anyone who has obtained DNA data about themselves (from any company) can get a free, independent report containing risk assessments and related information.

- deCODEme.com charged $1100 to carry out genotyping of approximately 1 million SNPs and provided risk estimates for 47 diseases as well as ancestry analyses. However, sales of genetic scans direct to consumer through deCODEme have now been discontinued.

- Navigenics began offering SNP-based genomic risk assessments as of April 2008. Navigenics is medically focused and emphasizes a clinician's and genetic counselor's role in interpreting results. Affymetrix Genome-Wide Human SNP Array 6.0, which genotypes 900,000 SNPs. Navigenics' service has now been discontinued.

- Pathway Genomics analyzes over 100 genetic markers to identify genetic risk for common health conditions such as melanoma, prostate cancer and rheumatoid arthritis.

- LifeNome provides an analysis of over 6500 genetic variations to assess predisposition likelihood for over 800 complex wellness traits across nutrition and dieting, fitness, skin care, preventive well-being, aging, allergies and sensitivities and other wellness traits.

- UBiome is a bacterial genomics company who offer microbiome sequencing to the public based in San Francisco, California.

- 23andMe founded in 2006 allows people to send their saliva in a testing kit to have their DNA screened for genes associated with certain inherited conditions, such as cystic fibrosis or sickle cell anaemia, and other genetic markers relating to parts of their lives and ancestry. Its saliva-based direct-to-consumer personal genome test was named Invention of the Year by *Time* magazine in 2008. The company is now backed by Google.

- Illumina, Oxford Nanopore Technologies, Sequenom, Pacific Biosciences, Complete Genomics, and 454 Life Sciences are commercializing full genome sequencing but do not provide genetic analysis or counselling.

- DNALifeStyleCoach is a service by Titanovo that offers SNPs genotyping and results interpretation in areas of nutrigenetics, sports genetics, anti-aging and psychogenetics.

- Gene by Gene provides Whole Genome Sequencing from $6995 to $7595, and other variants.

- Life Technologies

- Mapmygenome offers several SNP and NGS panels for personal genomics.

- Full Genomes Corporation offers whole genome sequencing and y chromosome sequencing for personal genomics.

Ethical Issues

Genetic discrimination is discriminating on the basis of information obtained from an individual's genome. Genetic non-discrimination laws have been enacted in some US states and at the federal level, by the Genetic Information Nondiscrimination Act (GINA). The GINA legislation prevents discrimination by health insurers and employers, but does not apply to life insurance or long-term care insurance. Given the ethical concerns about presymptomatic genetic testing of minors, it is likely that personal genomics will first be applied to adults who can provide consent to undergo such testing, although genome sequencing is already proving valuable for children if any symptoms are present.

Patients will need to be educated on interpreting their results and what they should be rationally taking from the experience. It is not only the average person who needs to be educated in the dimensions of their own genomic sequence but also professionals, including physicians and science journalists, who must be provided with the knowledge required to inform and educate their patients and the public Examples of such efforts include the Personal Genetics Education Project (pgEd) and the Smithsonian collaboration with NHGRI

Other Issues

Full sequencing of the genome can identify polymorphisms that are so rare that no conclusions may be drawn about their impact, creating uncertainty in the analysis of individual genomes, particularly in the context of clinical care. Czech medical geneticist Eva Machácková writes: "In some cases it is difficult to distinguish if the detected sequence variant is a causal mutation or a neutral (polymorphic) variation without any effect on phenotype. The interpretation of rare sequence variants of unknown significance detected in disease-causing genes becomes an increasingly important problem."

There is a heavy debate as to how relevant the results of personal genome kits are and whether or not the ramifications of knowing one's predisposition to a disease is worth the potential psychological stress. There are also three potential problems associated with the validity of personal genome kits. The first issue is the test's validity. Handling errors of the sample increases the likelihood for errors which could affect the test results and interpretation. The second affects the clinical validity, which could affect the test's ability to detect or predict associated disorders. The third problem is the clinical utility of personal genome kits and associated risks, and the benefits of introducing them into clinical practices.

Doctors are currently conducting tests for which some are not correctly trained to interpret the results. Many are unaware of how SNPs respond to one another. This results in presenting the client with potentially misleading and worrisome results which could strain the already overloaded health care system. This may antagonize the individual to make uneducated decisions such as unhealthy lifestyle choices and family planning modifications. Moreover, negative results which may potentially be inaccurate, theoretically decrease the quality of life and mental health of the individual (such as increased depression and extensive anxiety).

There is also controversy regarding the concerns with companies testing individual DNA. There are issues such as "leaking" information, the right to privacy and what responsibility the company has to ensure this does not happen. Regulation rules are not clearly laid out. What is still not determined is who legally owns the genome information: the company or the individual whose genome has been read. There have been published examples of personal genome information being exploited. Additional privacy concerns, related to, e.g., genetic discrimination, loss of anonymity, and psychological impacts, have been increasingly pointed out by the academic community as well as government agencies.

Conversely, sequencing one's genome would allow for more personalized medical treatments using pharmacogenomics; the use of genetic information to select appropriate drugs. Treatments can be catered to the individual and the certain genetic predispositions they may have (such as personalized chemotherapy).

Popular Culture

The 1997 science fiction film GATTACA presents a near-future society where personal genomics is readily available to anyone, and explores its societal impact.

Oncogenomics

Oncogenomics is a sub-field of genomics that characterizes cancer-associated genes. It focuses on genomic, epigenomic and transcript alterations in cancer.

Cancer is a genetic disease caused by accumulation of DNA mutations and epigenetic alterations leading to unrestrained cell proliferation and neoplasm formation. The goal of oncogenomics is to identify new oncogenes or tumor suppressor genes that may provide new insights into cancer diagnosis, predicting clinical outcome of cancers and new targets for cancer therapies. The success of targeted cancer therapies such as Gleevec, Herceptin and Avastin raised the hope for oncogenomics to elucidate new targets for cancer treatment.

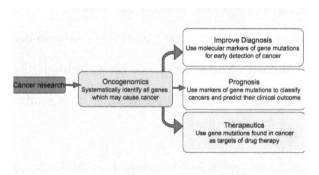

Overall goals of oncogenomics

Besides understanding the underlying genetic mechanisms that initiate or drive cancer progression, oncogenomics targets personalized cancer treatment. Cancer develops due to DNA mutations and epigenetic alterations that accumulate randomly. Identifying and targeting the mutations in an individual patient may lead to increased treatment efficacy.

The completion of the Human Genome Project facilitated the field of oncogenomics and increased the abilities of researchers to find oncogenes. Sequencing technologies and global methylation profiling techniques have been applied to the study of oncogenomics.

History

The genomics era began in the 1990s, with the generation of DNA sequences of many organisms. In the 21st century, the completion of the Human Genome Project enabled the study of functional genomics and examining tumor genomes. Cancer is a main focus.

The epigenomics era largely began more recently, about 2000. One major source of epigenetic change is altered methylation of CpG islands at the promoter region of genes. A number of recently devised methods can assess the DNA methylation status in cancers versus normal tissues. Some methods assess methylation of CpGs located in different classes of loci, including CpG islands, shores, and shelves as well as promoters, gene bodies, and intergenic regions. Cancer is also a major focus of epigenetic studies.

Access to whole cancer genome sequencing is important to cancer (or cancer genome) research because:

- Mutations are the immediate cause of cancer and define the tumor phenotype.

- Access to cancerous and normal tissue samples from the same patient and the fact that most cancer mutations represent somatic events, allow the identification of cancer-specific mutations.

- Cancer mutations are cumulative and sometimes are related to disease stage. Metastasis and drug resistance are distinguishable.

Access to methylation profiling is important to cancer research because:

- Epi-drivers, along with Mut-drivers, can act as immediate causes of cancers

- Cancer epimutations are cumulative and sometimes related to disease stage

Whole Genome Sequencing

The first cancer genome was sequenced in 2008. This study sequenced a typical acute myeloid leukaemia (AML) genome and its normal counterpart genome obtained from the same patient. The comparison revealed ten mutated genes. Two were already thought to contribute to tumor progression: an internal tandem duplication of the FLT3 receptor tyrosine kinase gene, which activates kinase signaling and is associated with a poor prognosis and a four base insertion in exon 12 of the NPM1 gene (NPMc). These mutations are found in 25-30% of AML tumors and are thought to contribute to disease progression rather than to cause it directly.

The remaining 8 were new mutations and all were single base changes: Four were in families that are strongly associated with cancer pathogenesis (PTPRT, CDH24, PCLKC and SLC15A1). The other four had no previous association with cancer pathogenesis. They did have potential functions in metabolic pathways that suggested mechanisms by which they could act to promote cancer (KNDC1, GPR124, EB12, GRINC1B)

These genes are involved in pathways known to contribute to cancer pathogenesis, but before this study most would not have been candidates for targeted gene therapy. This analysis validated the approach of whole cancer genome sequencing in identifying somatic mutations and the importance of parallel sequencing of normal and tumor cell genomes.

In 2011, the genome of an exceptional bladder cancer patient whose tumor had been eliminated by the drug everolimus was sequenced, revealing mutations in two genes, *TSC1* and *NF2*. The mutations disregulated mTOR, the protein inhibited by everolimus, allowing it to reproduce without limit. As a result, in 2015, the Exceptional Responders Initiative was created at the National Cancer Institute. The initiative allows such exceptional patients (who have responded positively for at least six months to a cancer drug that usually fails) to have their genomes sequenced to identify the relevant mutations. Once identified, other patients could be screened for those mutations and then be given the drug. In 2016 To that end, a nationwide cancer drug trial began in 2015, involving up to twenty-four hundred centers. Patients with appropriate mutations are matched with one of more than forty drugs.

In 2014 the Center for Molecular Oncology rolled out the MSK-IMPACT test, a screening tool that looks for mutations in 341 cancer-associated genes. By 2015 more than five thousand patients had been screened. Patients with appropriate mutations are eligible to enroll in clinical trials that provide targeted therapy.

Technologies

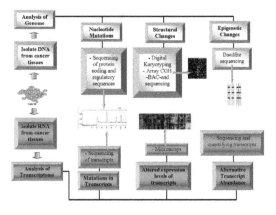

Current technologies being used in Oncogenomics.

Genomics technologies include:

Genome Sequencing

- *DNA sequencing*: Pyrosequencing-based sequencers offer a relatively low-cost method to generate sequence data.

- *Array Comparative Genome Hybridization*: This technique measures the DNA copy number differences between normal and cancer genomes. It uses the fluorescence intensity from fluorescent-labeled samples, which are hybridized to known probes on a microarray.

- *Representational oligonucleotide microarray analysis*: Detects copy number variation using amplified restriction-digested genomic fragments that are hybridized to human oligonucleotides, achieving a resolution between 30 and 35 kbit/s.

- *Digital Karyotyping*: Detects copy number variation using genomics tags obtained via restriction enzyme digests. These tags are then linked to into ditags, concatenated, cloned, sequenced and mapped back to the reference genome to evaluate tag density.

- *Bacterial Artificial Chromosome (BAC)-end sequencing (end-sequence profiling)*: Identifies chromosomal breakpoints by generating a BAC library from a cancer genome and sequencing their ends. The BAC clones that contain chromosome aberrations have end sequences that do not map to a similar region of the reference genome, thus identifying a chromosomal breakpoint.

Transcriptomes

- *Microarrays*: Assess transcript abundance. Useful in classification, prognosis, raise the possibility of differential treatment approaches and aid identification of mutations in the proteins' coding regions. The relative abundance of alternative transcripts has become an important feature of cancer research. Particular alternative transcript forms correlate with specific cancer types.

Bioinformatics and Functional Analysis of Oncogenes

Bioinformatics technologies allow the statistical analysis of genomic data. The functional characteristics of oncogenes has yet to be established. Potential functions include their transformational capabilities relating to tumour formation and specific roles at each stage of cancer development.

Operomics

Operomics aims to integrate genomics, transcriptomics and proteomics to understand the molecular mechanisms that underlie the cancer development.

Comparative Oncogenomics

Comparative oncogenomics uses cross-species comparisons to identify oncogenes. This research involves studying cancer genomes, transcriptomes and proteomes in model organisms such as mice, identifying potential oncogenes and referring back to human cancer samples to see whether homologues of these oncogenes are important in causing human cancers. Genetic alterations in mouse models are similar to those found in human cancers. These models are generated by methods including retroviral insertion mutagenesis or graft transplantation of cancerous cells.

Source of Carcinogenic Driver Mutations

As pointed out by Gao et al., the stability and integrity of the human genome are maintained by the DNA damage repair (DDR) system. Un-repaired DNA damage is a major cause of mutations that drive carcinogenesis. If DNA repair is deficient, DNA damage tends to accumulate. Such excess DNA damage can increase mutational errors during DNA replication due to error-prone translesion synthesis. Excess DNA damage can also increase epigenetic alterations due to errors during DNA repair. Such mutations and epigenetic alterations can give rise to cancer.

DDR genes are often repressed in human cancer by epigenetic mechanisms. Such repression may involve DNA methylation of promoter regions or repression of DDR genes by a microRNA. Epigenetic repression of DDR genes occurs more frequently than gene mutation in many types of cancer. Thus, epigenetic repression often plays a more important role than mutation in reducing expression of DDR genes. This reduced expression of DDR genes is likely an important driver of carcinogenesis.

Synthetic Lethality

Synthetic lethality arises when a combination of deficiencies in the expression of two or more genes leads to cell death, whereas a deficiency in only one of these genes does not. The deficiencies can arise through mutations, epigenetic alterations or inhibitors of one of the genes.

Some oncogenes are essential for survival of all cells (not only cancer cells). Thus, drugs that knock out these oncogenes (and thereby kill cancer cells) may also damage normal cells, inducing significant illness. However, other genes may be essential to cancer cells but not to healthy cells.

Treatments based on the principle of synthetic lethality have prolonged the survival of cancer patients, and show promise for future advances in reversal of carcinogenesis. A major type of synthetic lethality operates on the DNA repair defect that often initiates a cancer, and is still present in the tumor cells. Some examples are given here.

BRCA1 or BRCA2 expression is deficient in a majority of high-grade breast and ovarian cancers, usually due to epigenetic methylation of its promoter or epigenetic repression by an over-expressed microRNA. BRCA1 and BRCA2 are important components of the major pathway for homologous recombinational repair of double-strand breaks. If one or the other is deficient, it increases the risk of cancer, especially breast or ovarian cancer. A back-up DNA repair pathway, for some of the damages usually repaired by BRCA1 and BRCA2, depends on PARP1. Thus, many ovarian cancers respond to an FDA-approved treatment with a PARP inhibitor, causing synthetic lethality to cancer cells deficient in BRCA1 or BRCA2. This treatment is also being evaluated for breast cancer and numerous other cancers in Phase III clinical trials in 2016.

There are two pathways for homologous recombinational repair of double-strand breaks. The major pathway depends on BRCA1, PALB2 and BRCA2 while an alternative pathway depends on RAD52. Pre-clinical studies, involving epigenetically reduced or mutated BRCA-deficient cells (in culture or injected into mice), show that inhibition of RAD52 is synthetically lethal with BRCA-deficiency.

Mutations in genes employed in DNA mismatch repair (MMR) cause a high mutation rate. In tumors, such frequent subsequent mutations often generate "non-self" immunogenic antigens. A human Phase II clinical trial, with 41 patients, evaluated one synthetic lethal approach for tumors with or without MMR defects. The product of gene *PD-1* ordinarily represses cytotoxic immune responses. Inhibition of this gene allows a greater immune response. When cancer patients with a defect in MMR in their tumors were exposed to an inhibitor of PD-1, 67% - 78% of patients experienced immune-related progression-free survival. In contrast, for patients without defective MMR, addition of PD-1 inhibitor generated only 11% of patients with immune-related progression-free survival. Thus inhibition of PD-1 is primarily synthetically lethal with MMR defects.

ARID1A, a chromatin modifier, is required for non-homologous end joining, a major pathway that repairs double-strand breaks in DNA, and also has transcription regulatory roles. ARID1A mutations are one of the 12 most common carcinogenic mutations. Mutation or epigenetically decreased expression of ARID1A has been found in 17 types of cancer. Pre-clinical studies in cells and in mice show that synthetic lethality for ARID1A deficiency occurs by either inhibition of the methyltransferase activity of EZH2, or with addition of the kinase inhibitor dasatinib.

Another approach is to individually knock out each gene in a genome and observe the effect on normal and cancerous cells. If the knockout of an otherwise nonessential gene has little or no effect on healthy cells, but is lethal to cancerous cells containing a mutated oncogene, then the system-wide suppression of the suppressed gene can destroy cancerous cells while leaving healthy ones relatively undamaged. The technique was used to identify PARP-1 inhibitors to treat BRCA1/BRCA2-associated cancers. In this case, the combined presence of PARP-1 inhibition and of the cancer-associated mutations in BRCA genes is lethal only to the cancerous cells.

Databases for Cancer Research

The Cancer Genome Project is an initiative to map out all somatic mutations in cancer. The project systematically sequences the exons and flanking splice junctions of the genomes of primary tumors and cancerous cell lines. COSMIC software displays the data generated from these experiments. As of February 2008, the CGP had identified 4,746 genes and 2,985 mutations in 1,848 tumours.

The Cancer Genome Anatomy Project includes information of research on cancer genomes, transcriptomes and proteomes.

Progenetix is an oncogenomic reference database, presenting cytogenetic and molecular-cytogenetic tumor data.

Oncomine has compiled data from cancer transcriptome profiles.

The integrative oncogenomics database IntOGen and the Gitools datasets integrate multidimensional human oncogenomic data classified by tumor type. The first version of IntOGen focused on the role of deregulated gene expression and CNV in cancer. A later version emphasized mutational cancer driver genes across 28 tumor types,. All releases of IntOGen data are made available at the IntOGen database.

The International Cancer Genome Consortium is the biggest project to collect human cancer genome data. The data is accessible through the ICGC website. The BioExpress® Oncology Suite contains gene expression data from primary, metastatic and benign tumor samples and normal samples, including matched adjacent controls. The suite includes hematological malignancy samples for many well-known cancers.

Specific databases for model animals include the Retrovirus Tagged Cancer Gene Database (RTCGD) that compiled research on retroviral and transposon insertional mutagenesis in mouse tumors.

Gene Families

Mutational analysis of entire gene families revealed that genes of the same family have similar functions, as predicted by similar coding sequences and protein domains. Two such classes are the kinase family, involved in adding phosphate groups to proteins and the phosphatase family, involved with removing phosphate groups from proteins. These families were first examined because of their apparent role in transducing cellular signals of cell growth or death. In particular, more than 50% of colorectal cancers carry a mutation in a kinase or phosphatase gene. Phosphatidylinositold 3-kinases (PIK3CA) gene encodes for lipid kinases that commonly contain mutations in colorectal, breast, gastric, lung and various other cancers. Drug therapies can inhibit PIK3CA. Another example is the BRAF gene, one of the first to be implicated in melanomas. BRAF encodes a serine/threonine kinase that is involved in the RAS-RAF-MAPK growth signaling pathway. Mutations in BRAF cause constitutive phosphorylation and activity in 59% of melanomas. Before BRAF, the genetic mechanism of melanoma development was unknown and therefore prognosis for patients was poor.

Mitochondrial DNA

Mitochondrial DNA (mtDNA) mutations are linked the formation of tumors. Four types of mtDNA mutations have been identified:

Point Mutations

Point mutations have been observed in the coding and non-coding region of the mtD-NA contained in cancer cells. In individuals with bladder, head/neck and lung cancers, the point mutations within the coding region show signs of resembling each other. This suggests that when a healthy cell transforms into a tumor cell (a neoplastic transformation) the mitochondria seem to become homogenous. Abundant point mutations located within the non-coding region, D-loop, of the cancerous mitochondria suggest that mutations within this region might be an important characteristic in some cancers.

Deletions

This type of mutation is sporadically detected due to its small size (< 1kb). The appearance of certain specific mtDNA mutations (264-bp deletion and 66-bp deletion in the complex 1 subunit gene ND1) in multiple types of cancer provide some evidence that small mtDNA deletions might appear at the beginning of tumorigenesis. It also suggests that the amount of mitochondria containing these deletions increases as the tumor progresses. An exception is a relatively large deletion that appears in many cancers (known as the "common deletion"), but more mtDNA large scale deletions have been found in normal cells compared to tumor cells. This may be due to a seemingly adaptive process of tumor cells to eliminate any mitochondria that contain these large scale deletions (the "common deletion" is > 4kb).

Insertions

Two small mtDNA insertions of ~260 and ~520 bp can be present in breast cancer, gastric cancer, hepatocellular carcinoma (HCC) and colon cancer and in normal cells. No correlation between these insertions and cancer are established.

Copy Number Mutations

The characterization of mtDNA via real-time polymerase chain reaction assays shows the presence of quantitative alteration of mtDNA copy number in many cancers. Increase in copy number is expected to occur because of oxidative stress. On the other hand, decrease is thought to be caused by somatic point mutations in the replication origin site of the H-strand and/or the D310 homopolymeric c-stretch in the D-loop region, mutations in the p53 (tumor suppressor gene) mediated pathway and/or inefficient enzyme activity due to POLG mutations. Any increase/decrease in copy number then remains constant within tumor cells. The fact that the amount of mtDNA is constant in tumor cells suggests that the amount of mtDNA is controlled by a much more complicated system in tumor cells, rather than simply altered as a consequence of abnormal cell proliferation. The role of mtDNA content in human cancers apparently varies for particular tumor types or sites.

Mutations in mitochondrial DNA in various cancers							
Cancer Type	Location of Point mutations				Nucleotide Position of Deletions	Increase of mtDNA copy #	Decrease of mtDNA copy #
	D-Loop	mR-NAs	tR-NAs	rR-NAs			
Bladder	X	X		X	15,642-15,662		
Breast	X	X	X	X	8470-13,447 and 8482-13459		X
Head and neck	X	X	X	X	8470-13,447 and 8482-13459	X	
Oral	X	X			8470-13,447 and 8482-13459		
Hepatocellular carcinoma (HCC)	X	X	X	X	306-556 and 3894-3960		X
Esophageal	X	X		X	8470-13,447 and 8482-13459	X	
Gastric	X	X	X		298-348		X
Prostate	X			X	8470-13,447 and 8482-13459	X	

57.7% (500/867) contained somatic point putations and of the 1172 mutations surveyed 37.8% (443/1127) were located in the D-loop control region, 13.1% (154/1172) were located in the tRNA or rRNA genes and 49.1% (575/1127) were found in the mRNA genes needed for producing complexes required for mitochondrial respiration.

Diagnostic Applications

Some anticancer drugs target mtDNA and have shown positive results in killing tumor cells. Research has used mitochondrial mutations as biomarkers for cancer cell therapy. It is easier to target mutation within mitochondrial DNA versus nuclear DNA because the mitochondrial genome is much smaller and easier to screen for specific mutations. MtDNA content alterations found in blood samples might be able to serve as a screening marker for predicting future cancer susceptibility as well as tracking malignant tumor progression. Along with these potential helpful characteristics of mtDNA, it is not under the control of the cell cycle and is important for maintaining ATP generation and mitochondrial homeostasis. These characteristics make targeting mtDNA a practical therapeutic strategy.

Cancer Biomarkers

Several biomarkers can be useful in cancer staging, prognosis and treatment. They can range from single-nucleotide polymorphisms (SNPs), chromosomal aberrations, changes in DNA copy number, microsatellite instability, promoter region methylation, or even high or low protein levels.

Comparative Genomics

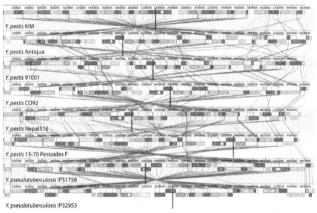

Whole genome alignment is a typical method in comparative genomics. This alignment of eight *Yersinia* bacteria genomes reveals 78 locally collinear blocks conserved among all eight taxa. Each chromosome has been laid out horizontally and homologous blocks in each genome are shown as identically colored regions linked across genomes. Regions that are inverted relative to *Y. pestis* KIM are shifted below a genome's center axis.

Comparative genomics is a field of biological research in which the genomic features of different organisms are compared. The genomic features may include the DNA sequence, genes, gene order, regulatory sequences, and other genomic structural landmarks. In this branch of genomics, whole or large parts of genomes resulting from genome projects are compared to study basic biological similarities and differences as well as evolutionary relationships between organisms. The major principle of comparative genomics is that common features of two organisms will often be encoded within the DNA that is evolutionarily conserved between them. Therefore, comparative genomic approaches start with making some form of alignment of genome sequences and looking for orthologous sequences (sequences that share a common ancestry) in the aligned genomes and checking to what extent those sequences are conserved. Based on these, genome and molecular evolution are inferred and this may in turn be put in the context of, for example, phenotypic evolution or population genetics.

Virtually started as soon as the whole genomes of two organisms became available (that is, the genomes of the bacteria *Haemophilus influenzae* and *Mycoplasma genitalium*) in 1995, comparative genomics is now a standard component of the analysis of every new genome sequence. With the explosion in the number of genome project due to the advancements in DNA sequencing technologies, particularly the next-generation sequencing methods in late 2000s, this field has become more sophisticated, making it possible to deal with many genomes in a single study. Comparative genomics has revealed high levels of similarity between closely related organisms, such as humans and chimpanzees, and, more surprisingly, similarity between seemingly distantly related organisms, such as humans and the yeast *Saccharomyces cerevisiae*. It has also showed the extreme diversity of the gene composition in different evolutionary lineages.

History

Comparative genomics has a root in the comparison of virus genomes in the early 1980s. For example, small RNA viruses infecting animals (picornaviruses) and those infecting plants (cowpea mosaic virus) were compared and turned out to share significant sequence similarity and, in part, the order of their genes. In 1986, the first comparative genomic study at a larger scale was published, comparing the genomes of varicella-zoster virus and Epstein-Barr virus that contained more than 100 genes each.

The first complete genome sequence of a cellular organism, that of *Haemophilus influenzae* Rd, was published in 1995. The second genome sequencing paper was of the small parasitic bacterium *Mycoplasma genitalium* published in the same year. Starting from this paper, reports on new genomes inevitably became comparative-genomic studies.

The first high-resolution whole genome comparison system was developed in 1998 by Art Delcher, Simon Kasif and Steven Salzberg and applied to the comparison of entire highly related microbial organisms with their collaborators at the Institute for Genomic Research (TIGR). The system is called MUMMER and was described in a publication in Nucleic Acids Research in 1999. The system helps researchers to identify large rearrangements, single base mutations, reversals, tandem repeat expansions and other polymorphisms. In bacteria, MUMMER enables the identification of polymorphisms that are responsible for virulence, pathogenicity, and anti-biotic resistance. The system was also applied to the Minimal Organism Project at TIGR and subsequently to many other comparative genomics projects.

Saccharomyces cerevisiae, the baker's yeast, was the first eukaryote to have its complete genome sequence published in 1996. After the publication of the roundworm *Caenorhabditis elegans* genome in 1998 and together with the fruit fly *Drosophila melanogaster* genome in 2000, Gerald M. Rubin and his team published a paper titled "Comparative Genomics of the Eukaryotes", in which they compared the genomes of the eukaryotes *D. melanogaster*, *C. elegans*, and *S. cerevisiae*, as well as the prokaryote *H. influenzae*. At the same time, Bonnie Berger, Eric Lander, and their team published a paper on whole-genome comparison of human and mouse.

With the publication of the large genomes of vertebrates in the 2000s, including human, the Japanese pufferfish *Takifugu rubripes*, and mouse, precomputed results of large genome comparisons have been released for downloading or for visualization in a genome browser. Instead of undertaking their own analyses, most biologists can access these large cross-species comparisons and avoid the impracticality caused by the size of the genomes.

Next-generation sequencing methods, which were first introduced in 2007, have produced an enormous amount of genomic data and have allowed researchers to generate multiple (prokaryotic) draft genome sequences at once. These methods can also quickly uncover single-nucleotide polymorphisms, insertions and deletions by mapping unassembled reads against a well annotated reference genome, and thus provide a list of possible gene differences that may be the basis for any functional variation among strains.

Evolutionary Principles

One character of biology is evolution, evolutionary theory is also the theoretical foundation of comparative genomics, and at the same time the results of comparative genomics unprecedentedly enriched and developed the theory of evolution. When two or more of the genome sequence are compared, you can get the evolutionary relationships of the sequences in a phylogenetic tree. Based on a variety of biological genome data and the study of vertical and horizontal evolution processes, one can understand vital parts of the gene structure and its regulatory function. But in a genome about 1.5% ~ 14.5% of the genes are related to the "lateral migration phenomenon", namely the transfer of a gene between populations which can exist at the same time. Thus, the differences in sequences have nothing to do with evolution.

Similarity of related genomes is the basis of comparative genomics. If two creatures have a recent common ancestor, the differences between the two species genomes are evolved from the ancestors' genome. The closer the relationship between two organisms, the higher the similiarities between their genomes. If there is close relationship between them, then their genome will display a linear behaviour (synteny), namely some or all of the genetic sequences are conserved. Thus, the genome sequences can be used to identify gene function, by analyzing their homology (sequence similarity) to genes of known function.

Orthologous sequences are related sequences in different species: a gene exists in the original species, the species divided into two species, so genes in new species are orthologous to the sequence in the original species. Paralogous sequences are separated by gene cloning (gene duplication): if a particular gene in the genome is copied, then the copy of the two sequences is paralogous to the original gene. A pair of orthologous sequences is called orthologous pairs (orthologs), a pair of paralogous sequence is called collateral pairs (paralogs). Orthologous pairs usually have the same or similar function, which is not necessarily the case for collateral pairs. In collateral pairs, the sequences tend to evolve into having different functions.

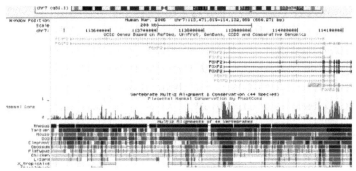

Human FOXP2 gene and evolutionary conservation is shown in and multiple alignment (at bottom of figure) in this image from the UCSC Genome Browser. Note that conservation tends to cluster around coding regions (exons).

Comparative genomics exploits both similarities and differences in the proteins, RNA, and regulatory regions of different organisms to infer how selection has acted upon these elements. Those elements that are responsible for similarities between different species should be conserved through time (stabilizing selection), while those elements responsible for differences among species should be divergent (positive selection). Finally, those elements that are unimportant to the evolutionary success of the organism will be unconserved (selection is neutral).

One of the important goals of the field is the identification of the mechanisms of eukaryotic genome evolution. It is however often complicated by the multiplicity of events that have taken place throughout the history of individual lineages, leaving only distorted and superimposed traces in the genome of each living organism. For this reason comparative genomics studies of small model organisms (for example the model Caenorhabditis elegans and closely related Caenorhabditis briggsae) are of great importance to advance our understanding of general mechanisms of evolution.

Methods

Computational approaches to genome comparison have recently become a common research topic in computer science. A public collection of case studies and demonstrations is growing, ranging from whole genome comparisons to gene expression analysis. This has increased the introduction of different ideas, including concepts from systems and control, information theory, strings analysis and data mining. It is anticipated that computational approaches will become and remain a standard topic for research and teaching, while multiple courses will begin training students to be fluent in both topics.

Tools

Computational tools for analyzing sequences and complete genomes are developed quickly due to the availability of large amount of genomic data. At the same time, comparative analysis tools are progressed and improved. In the challenges about these analyses, it is very important to visualize the comparative results.

Visualization of sequence conservation is a tough task of comparative sequence analysis. As we know, it is highly inefficient to examine the alignment of long genomic regions manually. Internet-based genome browsers provide many useful tools for investigating genomic sequences due to integrating all sequence-based biological information on genomic regions. When we extract large amount of relevant biological data, they can be very easy to use and less time-consuming.

- UCSC Browser: This site contains the reference sequence and working draft assemblies for a large collection of genomes.

- Ensembl: The Ensembl project produces genome databases for vertebrates and other eukaryotic species, and makes this information freely available online.

- MapView: The Map Viewer provides a wide variety of genome mapping and sequencing data.

- VISTA is a comprehensive suite of programs and databases for comparative analysis of genomic sequences. It was built to visualize the results of comparative analysis based on DNA alignments. The presentation of comparative data generated by VISTA can easily suit both small and large scale of data.

An advantage of using online tools is that these websites are being developed and updated constantly. There are many new settings and content can be used online to improve efficiency.

Applications

Agriculture

Agriculture is a field that reaps the benefits of comparative genomics. Identifying the loci of advantageous genes is a key step in breeding crops that are optimized for greater yield, cost-efficiency, quality, and disease resistance. For example, one genome wide association study conducted on 517 rice landraces revealed 80 loci associated with several categories of agronomic performance, such as grain weight, amylose content, and drought tolerance. Many of the loci were previously uncharacterized. Not only is this methodology powerful, it is also quick. Previous methods of identifying loci associated with agronomic performance required several generations of carefully monitored breeding of parent strains, a time consuming effort that is unnecessary for comparative genomic studies.

Medicine

The medical field also benefits from the study of comparative genomics. Vaccinology in particular has experienced useful advances in technology due to genomic approaches to problems. In an approach known as reverse vaccinology, researchers can discover candidate antigens for vaccine development by analyzing the genome of a pathogen or a family of pathogens. Applying a comparative genomics approach by analyzing the genomes of several related pathogens can lead to the development of vaccines that are multiprotective. A team of researchers employed such an approach to create a universal vaccine for Group B Streptococcus, a group of bacteria responsible for severe neonatal infection. Comparative genomics can also be used to generate specificity for vaccines against pathogens that are closely related to commensal microorganisms. For example, researchers used comparative genomic analysis of commensal and pathogenic strains of E. coli to identify pathogen specific genes as a basis for finding antigens that result in immune response against pathogenic strains but not commensal ones.

Research

Comparative genomics also opens up new avenues in other areas of research. As DNA sequencing technology has become more accessible, the number of sequenced genomes has grown. With the increasing reservoir of available genomic data, the potency of comparative genomic inference has grown as well. A notable case of this increased potency is found in recent primate research. Comparative genomic methods have allowed researchers to gather information about genetic variation, differential gene expression, and evolutionary dynamics in primates that were indiscernible using previous data and methods. The Great Ape Genome Project used comparative genomic methods to investigate genetic variation with reference to the six great ape species, finding healthy levels of variation in their gene pool despite shrinking population size. Another study showed that patterns of DNA methylation, which are a known regulation mechanism for gene expression, differ in the prefrontal cortex of humans versus chimps, and implicated this difference in the evolutionary divergence of the two species.

Genome Project

Genome projects are scientific endeavours that ultimately aim to determine the complete genome sequence of an organism (be it an animal, a plant, a fungus, a bacterium, an archaean, a protist or a virus) and to annotate protein-coding genes and other important genome-encoded features. The genome sequence of an organism includes the collective DNA sequences of each chromosome in the organism. For a bacterium containing a single chromosome, a genome project will aim to map the sequence of that chromosome. For the human species, whose genome includes 22 pairs of autosomes and 2 sex chromosomes, a complete genome sequence will involve 46 separate chromosome sequences.

When printed, the human genome sequence fills around 100 huge books of close print

The Human Genome Project was a landmark genome project that is already having a major impact on research across the life sciences, with potential for spurring numerous medical and commercial developments.

Genome Assembly

Genome assembly refers to the process of taking a large number of short DNA sequences and putting them back together to create a representation of the original chromosomes from which the DNA originated. In a shotgun sequencing project, all the DNA from a source (usually a single organism, anything from a bacterium to a mammal) is first fractured into millions of small pieces. These pieces are then "read" by automated sequencing machines, which can read up to 1000 nucleotides or bases at a time. (The four bases are adenine, guanine, cytosine, and thymine, represented as AGCT.) A genome assembly algorithm works by taking all the pieces and aligning them to one another, and detecting all places where two of the short sequences, or *reads*, overlap. These overlapping reads can be merged, and the process continues.

Genome assembly is a very difficult computational problem, made more difficult because many genomes contain large numbers of identical sequences, known as repeats. These repeats can be thousands of nucleotides long, and some occur in thousands of different locations, especially in the large genomes of plants and animals.

The resulting (draft) genome sequence is produced by combining the information sequenced contigs and then employing linking information to create scaffolds. Scaffolds are positioned along the physical map of the chromosomes creating a "golden path".

Assembly Software

Originally, most large-scale DNA sequencing centers developed their own software for assembling the sequences that they produced. However, this has changed as the software has grown more complex and as the number of sequencing centers has increased. An example of such assembler *Short Oligonucleotide Analysis Package* developed by

BGI for de novo assembly of human-sized genomes, alignment, SNP detection, resequencing, indel finding, and structural variation analysis.

Genome Annotation

Since the 1980s, molecular biology and bioinformatics have created the need for DNA annotation. DNA annotation or genome annotation is the process of identifying attaching biological information to sequences, and particularly in identifying the locations of genes and determining what those genes do.

When is a Genome Project Finished?

When sequencing a genome, there are usually regions that are difficult to sequence (often regions with highly repetitive DNA). Thus, 'completed' genome sequences are rarely ever complete, and terms such as 'working draft' or 'essentially complete' have been used to more accurately describe the status of such genome projects. Even when every base pair of a genome sequence has been determined, there are still likely to be errors present because DNA sequencing is not a completely accurate process. It could also be argued that a complete genome project should include the sequences of mitochondria and (for plants) chloroplasts as these organelles have their own genomes.

It is often reported that the goal of sequencing a genome is to obtain information about the complete set of genes in that particular genome sequence. The proportion of a genome that encodes for genes may be very small (particularly in eukaryotes such as humans, where coding DNA may only account for a few percent of the entire sequence). However, it is not always possible (or desirable) to only sequence the coding regions separately. Also, as scientists understand more about the role of this noncoding DNA (often referred to as junk DNA), it will become more important to have a complete genome sequence as a background to understanding the genetics and biology of any given organism.

In many ways genome projects do not confine themselves to only determining a DNA sequence of an organism. Such projects may also include gene prediction to find out where the genes are in a genome, and what those genes do. There may also be related projects to sequence ESTs or mRNAs to help find out where the genes actually are.

Historical and Technological Perspectives

Historically, when sequencing eukaryotic genomes (such as the worm *Caenorhabditis elegans*) it was common to first map the genome to provide a series of landmarks across the genome. Rather than sequence a chromosome in one go, it would be sequenced piece by piece (with the prior knowledge of approximately where that piece is located on the larger chromosome). Changes in technology and in particular improvements to the processing power of computers, means that genomes can now be 'shotgun sequenced' in one go (there are caveats to this approach though when compared to the traditional approach).

Improvements in DNA sequencing technology has meant that the cost of sequencing a new genome sequence has steadily fallen (in terms of cost per base pair) and newer technology has also meant that genomes can be sequenced far more quickly.

When research agencies decide what new genomes to sequence, the emphasis has been on species which are either high importance as model organism or have a relevance to human health (e.g. pathogenic bacteria or vectors of disease such as mosquitos) or species which have commercial importance (e.g. livestock and crop plants). Secondary emphasis is placed on species whose genomes will help answer important questions in molecular evolution (e.g. the common chimpanzee).

In the future, it is likely that it will become even cheaper and quicker to sequence a genome. This will allow for complete genome sequences to be determined from many different individuals of the same species. For humans, this will allow us to better understand aspects of human genetic diversity.

Example Genome Projects

L1 Dominette 01449, the Hereford who serves as the subject of the Bovine Genome Project

Many organisms have genome projects that have either been completed or will be completed shortly, including:

- Humans, Homo sapiens

- Humans, Homo sapiens

- Palaeo-Eskimo, an ancient-human

- Neanderthal, "*Homo neanderthalensis*" (partial)

- Common chimpanzee *Pan troglodytes*

- Domestic Cow

- Bovine Genome

- Honey Bee Genome Sequencing Consortium

- Horse genome

- Human microbiome project

- International Grape Genome Program

- International HapMap Project

- Tomato 150+ genome resequencing project

- 100K Genome Project

- Genomics England

Genome-wide Association Study

In genetics, a genome-wide association study (GWA study, or GWAS), also known as whole genome association study (WGA study, or WGAS), is an examination of a genome-wide set of genetic variants in different individuals to see if any variant is associated with a trait. GWASs typically focus on associations between single-nucleotide polymorphisms (SNPs) and traits like major human diseases, but can equally be applied to any other organism.

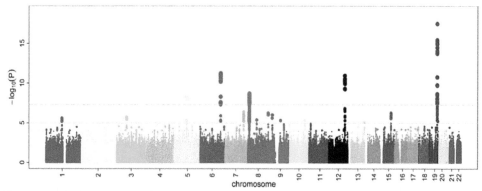

An illustration of a Manhattan plot depicting several strongly associated risk loci. Each dot represents a SNP, with the X-axis showing genomic location and Y-axis showing association level. This example is taken from a GWA study investigating microcirculation, so the tops indicates genetic variants that more often are found in individuals with constrictions in small blood vessels.

In the case of GWAS applied to human data, these studies compare the DNA of participants having varying phenotypes for a particular trait or disease. Participants in a

GWAS study may be people with a disease (cases) and similar people without (controls), or they may be people with different phenotypes for a particular trait, for example blood pressure. This approach is known as phenotype-first, in which the participants are classified first by their clinical manifestation(s), as opposed to genotype-first. Each person gives a sample of DNA, from which millions of genetic variants are read using SNP arrays. If one type of the variant (one allele) is more frequent in people with the disease, the variant is said to be *associated* with the disease. The associated SNPs are then considered to mark a region of the human genome that may influence the risk of disease. In contrast to methods that specifically test one or a few genetic regions, the GWA studies investigate the entire genome. The approach is therefore said to be *non-candidate-driven* in contrast to *gene-specific candidate-driven studies*. GWA studies identify SNPs and other variants in DNA associated with a disease, but they cannot on their own specify which genes are causal.

The first successful GWAS was published in 2005. It investigated patients with age-related macular degeneration and found two SNPs with significantly altered allele frequency compared to healthy controls. As of 2011, hundreds or thousands of individuals are tested, over 1,200 human GWA studies have examined over 200 diseases and traits, and almost 4,000 SNP associations have been found. Several GWA studies have received criticism for omitting important quality control steps, rendering the findings invalid, but modern publications address these issues. However, the methodology itself still has opponents.

Background

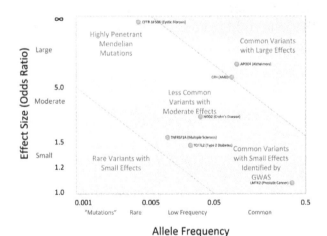

GWA studies typically identify common variants with small effect sizes (*lower right*).

Any two human genomes differ in millions of different ways. There are small variations in the individual nucleotides of the genomes (SNPs) as well as many larger variations, such as deletions, insertions and copy number variations. Any of these may cause alterations in an individual's traits, or phenotype, which can be anything from disease risk to physical properties such as height. Around the year 2000, prior to the introduction of GWA studies, the primary method of investigation was through inheritance studies of genetic linkage in families. This approach had proven highly useful towards single gene disorders. However, for common and complex diseases the results of genetic linkage studies proved hard to reproduce. A suggested alternative to linkage studies was the genetic association study. This study type asks if the allele of a genetic variant is found more often than expected in individuals with the phenotype of interest (e.g. with the disease being studied). Early calculations on statistical power indicated that this approach could be better than linkage studies at detecting weak genetic effects.

In addition to the conceptual framework several additional factors enabled the GWA studies. One was the advent of biobanks, which are repositories of human genetic material that greatly reduced the cost and difficulty of collecting sufficient numbers of biological specimens for study. Another was the International HapMap Project, which, from 2003 identified a majority of the common SNPs interrogated in a GWA study. The haploblock structure identified by HapMap project also allowed the focus on the subset of SNPs that would describe most of the variation. Also the development of the methods to genotype all these SNPs using genotyping arrays was an important prerequisite.

Methods

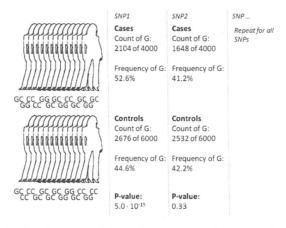

Example calculation illustrating the methodology of a case-control GWA study. The allele count of each measured SNP is evaluated—in this case with a chi-squared test—to identify variants associated with the trait in question. The numbers in this example are taken from a 2007 study of coronary artery disease (CAD) that showed that the individuals with the G-allele of SNP1 ($rs1333049$) were overrepresented amongst CAD-patients.

The most common approach of GWA studies is the case-control setup, which compares two large groups of individuals, one healthy control group and one case group affected by a disease. All individuals in each group are genotyped for the majority of common known SNPs. The exact number of SNPs depends on the genotyping technology, but are typically one million or more. For each of these SNPs it is then investigated if the allele frequency is significantly altered between the case and the control group. In such setups, the fundamental unit for reporting effect sizes is the odds ratio. The odds ratio is the ratio of two odds, which in the context of GWA studies are the odds of disease for individuals having a specific allele and the odds of disease for individuals who do not have that same allele. When the allele frequency in the case group is much higher than in the control group, the odds ratio is higher than 1, and vice versa for lower allele frequency. Additionally, a P-value for the significance of the odds ratio is typically calculated using a simple chi-squared test. Finding odds ratios that are significantly different from 1 is the objective of the GWA study because this shows that a SNP is associated with disease.

There are several variations to this case-control approach. A common alternative to case-control GWA studies is the analysis of quantitative phenotypic data, e.g. height or biomarker concentrations or even gene expression. Likewise, alternative statistics designed for dominance or recessive penetrance patterns can be used. Calculations are typically done using bioinformatics software such as SNPTEST and PLINK, which also include support for many of these alternative statistics. Earlier GWAS focused on the effect of individual SNPs. However, the empirical evidence shows that complex interactions among two or more SNPs, epistasis, might contribute to complex diseases. Moreover, the researchers tries to integrate GWA data with other biological data such as protein protein interaction network to extract more informative results.

A key step in the majority of GWA studies is the imputation of genotypes at SNPs not on the genotype chip used in the study. This process greatly increases the number of SNPs that can be tested for association, increases the power of the study, and facilitates meta-analysis of GWAS across distinct cohorts. Genotype imputation is carried out by statistical methods that combine the GWAS data together with a reference panel of haplotypes. These methods take advantage of sharing of haplotypes between individuals over short stretches of sequence to impute alleles. Existing software packages for genotype imputation include IMPUTE2 and MaCH.

In addition to the calculation of association, it is common to take into account any variables that could potentially confound the results. Sex and age are common examples of confounding variables. Moreover, it is also known that many genetic variations are associated with the geographical and historical populations in which the mutations first arose. Because of this association, studies must take account of the geographical and ethnical background of participants by controlling for what is called population stratification.

After odds ratios and P-values have been calculated for all SNPs, a common approach is to create a Manhattan plot. In the context of GWA studies, this plot shows the negative logarithm of the P-value as a function of genomic location. Thus the SNPs with the most significant association stands out on the plot, usually as stacks of points because of haploblock structure. Importantly, the P-value threshold for significance is corrected for multiple testing issues. The exact threshold varies by study, but the conventional threshold is 5×10^{-8} to be significant in the face of hundreds of thousands to millions of tested SNPs. GWA studies typically perform the first analysis in a discovery cohort, followed by validation of the most significant SNPs in an independent validation cohort.

Results

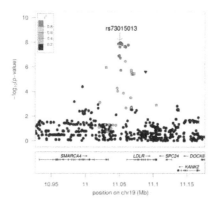

Regional association plot, showing individual SNPs in the LDL receptor region and their association to LDL-cholesterol levels. This type of plot is similar to the Manhattan plot in the lead section, but for a more limited section of the genome. The haploblock structure is visualized with colour scale and the association level is given by the left Y-axis. The dot representing the rs73015013 SNP (in the top-middle) has a high Y-axis location because this SNP explains some of the variation in LDL-cholesterol.

Attempts have been made at creating comprehensive catalogues of SNPs that have been identified from GWA studies. As of 2009, SNPs associated with diseases are numbered in the thousands.

The first GWA study, conducted in 2005, compared 96 patients with age-related macular degeneration (ARMD) with 50 healthy controls. It identified two SNPs with significantly altered allele frequency between the two groups. These SNPs were located in the gene encoding complement factor H, which was an unexpected finding in the research of ARMD. The findings from these first GWA studies have subsequently prompted further functional research towards therapeutical manipulation of the complement system in ARMD. Another landmark publication in the history of GWA studies was the Wellcome Trust Case Control Consortium (WTCCC) study, the largest GWA study ever conducted at the time of its publication in 2007. The WTCCC included 14,000 cases of seven common diseases (~2,000 individuals for each of coronary heart disease, type 1 diabetes, type 2 diabetes, rheumatoid arthritis, Crohn's disease, bipolar disorder, and hypertension) and 3,000 shared controls. This study was successful in uncovering many new disease genes underlying these diseases.

Since these first landmark GWA studies, there have been two general trends. One has been towards larger and larger sample sizes. At the end of 2011, the largest sample sizes were in the range of 200,000 individuals. The reason is the drive towards reliably detecting risk-SNPs that have smaller odds ratios and lower allele frequency. Another trend has been towards the use of more narrowly defined phenotypes, such as blood lipids, proinsulin or similar biomarkers. These are called *intermediate phenotypes*, and their analyses may be of value to functional research into biomarkers.

A central point of debate on GWA studies has been that most of the SNP variations found by GWA studies are associated with only a small increased risk of the disease, and have only a small predictive value. The median odds ratio is 1.33 per risk-SNP, with only a few showing odds ratios above 3.0. These magnitudes are considered small because they do not explain much of the heritable variation. This heritable variation is known from heritability studies based on monozygotic twins. For example, it is known that 80–90% of height is heritable. Of these 80-90%, however, the GWA studies only account for a minority.

Clinical Applications

A challenge for future successful GWA study is to apply the findings in a way that accelerates drug and diagnostics development, including better integration of genetic studies into the drug-development process and a focus on the role of genetic variation in maintaining health as a blueprint for designing new drugs and diagnostics. Several studies have looked into the use of risk-SNP markers as a means of directly improving the accuracy of prognosis. Some have found that the accuracy of prognosis improves, while others report only minor benefits from this use. Generally, a problem with this direct approach is the small magnitudes of the effects observed. A small effect ultimately translates into a poor separation of cases and controls and thus only a small improvement of prognosis accuracy. An alternative application is therefore the potential for GWA studies to elucidate pathophysiology.

One such success is related to identifying the genetic variant associated with response to anti-hepatitis C virus treatment. For genotype 1 hepatitis C treated with Pegylated interferon-alpha-2a or Pegylated interferon-alpha-2b combined with ribavirin, a GWA study has shown that SNPs near the human IL28B gene, encoding interferon lambda 3, are associated with significant differences in response to the treatment. A later report demonstrated that the same genetic variants are also associated with the natural clearance of the genotype 1 hepatitis C virus. These major findings facilitated the development of personalized medicine and allowed physicians to customize medical decisions based on the patient's genotype.

The goal of elucidating pathophysiology has also led to increased interest in the association between risk-SNPs and the gene expression of nearby genes, the so-called expression quantitative trait loci (eQTL) studies. The reason is that GWAS studies identify risk-SNPs, but not risk-genes, and specification of genes is one step closer towards actionable drug targets. As a result, major GWA studies of 2011 typically included extensive eQTL analysis. One of the strongest eQTL effects observed for a GWA-identified risk SNP is the SORT1 locus. Functional follow up studies of this locus using small interfering RNA and gene knock-out mice have shed light on the metabolism of low-density lipoproteins, which have important clinical implications for cardiovascular disease.

Limitations

GWA studies have several issues and limitations that can be taken care of through proper quality control and study setup. Lack of well defined case and control groups, insufficient sample size, control for multiple testing and control for population stratification are common problems. Particularly the statistical issue of multiple testing wherein it has been noted that "the GWA approach can be problematic because the massive number of statistical tests performed presents an unprecedented potential for false-positive results". Ignoring these correctible issues has been cited as contributing to a general sense of problems with the GWA methodology. In addition to easily correctible problems such as these, some more subtle but important issues have surfaced. A high-profile GWA study that investigated individuals with very long life spans to identify SNPs associated with longevity is an example of this. The publication came under scrutiny because of a discrepancy between the type of genotyping array in the case and control group, which caused several SNPs to be falsely highlighted as associated with longevity. The study was subsequently retracted.

In addition to these preventable issues, GWA studies have attracted more fundamental criticism, mainly because of their assumption that common genetic variation plays a large role in explaining the heritable variation of common disease. This aspect of GWA studies has attracted the criticism that, although it could not have been known prospectively, GWA studies were ultimately not worth the expenditure. Alternative strategies suggested involve linkage analysis.More recently, the rapidly decreasing price of complete genome sequencing have also provided a realistic alternative to genotyping array-based GWA studies. It can be discussed if the use of this new technique is still referred to as a GWA study, but high-throughput sequencing does have potential to side-step some of the shortcomings of non-sequencing GWA.

Fine-mapping

Genotyping arrays designed for GWAS rely on linkage disequilibrium to provide coverage of the entire genome by genotyping a subset of variants. Because of this, the reported associated variants are unlikely to be the actual causal variants. Associated regions can contain hundreds of variants spanning large regions and encompassing many different genes, making the biological interpretation of GWAS loci more difficult. Fine-mapping is a process to refine these lists of associated variants to a credible set most likely to include the causal variant.

Fine-mapping requires all variants in the associated region to have been genotyped or imputed (dense coverage), very stringent quality control resulting in high-quality genotypes, and large sample sizes sufficient in separating out highly correlated signals. There are several different methods to perform fine-mapping, and all methods produce a posterior probability that a variant in that locus is causal. Because the requirements are often difficult to satisfy, there are still limited examples of these methods being more generally applied.

References

- Bergman NH, ed. (2007). Comparative Genomics: Volumes 1 and 2. Totowa (NJ): Humana Press. ISBN 978-193411-537-4. PMID 21250292.

- Pevsner J (2009). Bioinformatics and functional genomics (2nd ed.). Hoboken, N.J: Wiley-Blackwell. ISBN 9780470085851.

- Culver KW, Labow MA (2002-11-08). "Genomics". In Robinson R. Genetics. Macmillan Science Library. Macmillan Reference USA. ISBN 0028656067.

- McElheny V (2010). Drawing the map of life : inside the Human Genome Project. New York NY: Basic Books. ISBN 9780465043330.

- Barnes B, Dupré J (2008). Genomes and what to make of them. Chicago: University of Chicago Press. ISBN 978-0-226-17295-8.

- Keith JM, ed. (2008). "Bioinformatics". Methods in Molecular Biology. 453. doi:10.1007/978-1-60327-429-6. ISBN 978-1-60327-428-9.

- Francis RC (2011). Epigenetics : the ultimate mystery of inheritance. New York: W.W. Norton. ISBN 9780393070057.

- Marco D, ed. (2011). Metagenomics: Current Innovations and Future Trends. Caister Academic Press. ISBN 978-1-904455-87-5.

- McGrath S, van Sinderen D, eds. (2007). Bacteriophage: Genetics and Molecular Biology (1st ed.). Caister Academic Press. ISBN 978-1-904455-14-1.

- Herrero A, Flores E, eds. (2008). The Cyanobacteria: Molecular Biology, Genomics and Evolution (1st ed.). Caister Academic Press. ISBN 978-1-904455-15-8.

- Church GM, Regis E (2012). Regenesis : how synthetic biology will reinvent nature and ourselves. New York: Basic Books. ISBN 9780465021758.

Computational Biology: An Integrated Study

Computational biology involves the application of the theoretical methods and data analytical methods to the study of biology and social systems. This involves subjects such as computer science, statistics, chemistry, molecular biology, ecology and visualization. This chapter will provide an integrated understanding of computational biology.

Computational Biology

Computational biology involves the development and application of data-analytical and theoretical methods, mathematical modeling and computational simulation techniques to the study of biological, behavioral, and social systems. The field is broadly defined and includes foundations in computer science, applied mathematics, animation, statistics, biochemistry, chemistry, biophysics, molecular biology, genetics, genomics, ecology, evolution, anatomy, neuroscience, and visualization.

Computational biology is different from biological computation, which is a subfield of computer science and computer engineering using bioengineering and biology to build computers, but is similar to bioinformatics, which is an interdisciplinary science using computers to store and process biological data.

Introduction

Computational Biology, sometimes referred to as bioinformatics, is the science of using biological data to develop algorithms and relations among various biological systems. Prior to the advent of computational biology, biologists were unable to have access to large amounts of data. Researchers were able to develop analytical methods for interpreting biological information, but were unable to share them quickly among colleagues.

Bioinformatics began to develop in the early 1970s. It was considered the science of analyzing informatics processes of various biological systems. At this time, research in artificial intelligence was using network models of the human brain in order to generate new algorithms. This use of biological data to develop other fields pushed biological researchers to revisit the idea of using computers to evaluate and compare large data sets. By 1982, information was being shared amongst researchers through the use of punch cards. The amount of data being shared began to grow exponentially by the end of the 1980s. This required the development of new computational methods in order to quickly analyze and interpret relevant information.

Since the late 1990s, computational biology has become an important part of developing emerging technologies for the field of biology. The terms computational biology and evolutionary computation have a similar name, but are not to be confused. Unlike computational biology, evolutionary computation is not concerned with modeling and analyzing biological data. It instead creates algorithms based on the ideas of evolution across species. Sometimes referred to as genetic algorithms, the research of this field can be applied to computational biology. While evolutionary computation is not inherently a part of computational biology, Computational evolutionary biology is a subfield of it.

Computational biology has been used to help sequence the human genome, create accurate models of the human brain, and assist in modeling biological systems.

Subfields

Computational Biomodeling

Computational biomodeling is a field concerned with building computer models of biological systems. Computational biomodeling aims to develop and use visual simulations in order to assess the complexity of biological systems. This is accomplished through the use of specialized algorithms, and visualization software. These models allow for prediction of how systems will react under different environments. This is useful for determining if a system is robust. A robust biological system is one that "maintain their state and functions against external and internal perturbations", which is essential for a biological system to survive. Computational biomodeling generates a large archive of such data, allowing for analysis from multiple users. While current techniques focus on small biological systems, researchers are working on approaches that will allow for larger networks to be analyzed and modeled. A majority of researchers believe that this will be essential in developing modern medical approaches to creating new drugs and gene therapy. A useful modelling approach is to use Petri nets via tools such as esyN

Computational Genomics (Computational Genetics)

Computational genomics is a field within genomics which studies the genomes of cells and organisms. It is often referred to as Computational and Statistical Genetics. The Human Genome Project is one example of computational genomics. This project looks to sequence the entire human genome into a set of data. Once fully implemented, this could allow for doctors to analyze the genome of an individual patient. This opens the possibility of personalized medicine, prescribing treatments based on an individual's pre-existing genetic patterns. This project has created many similar programs. Researchers are looking to sequence the genomes of animals, plants, bacteria, and all other types of life.

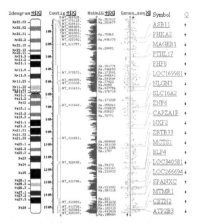

A partially sequenced genome.

One of the main ways that genomes are compared is by homology. Homology is the study of biological structures and nucleotide sequences in different organisms that come from a common ancestor. Research suggests that between 80 and 90% of genes in newly sequenced prokaryotic genomes can be identified this way.

This field is still in development. An untouched project in the development of computational genomics is the analysis of intergenic regions. Studies show that roughly 97% of the human genome consists of these regions. Researchers in computational genomics are working on understanding the functions of non-coding regions of the human genome through the development of computational and statistical methods and via large consortia projects such as ENCODE (The Encyclopedia of DNA Elements) and the Roadmap Epigenomics Project.

Computational Neuroscience

Computational neuroscience is the study of brain function in terms of the information processing properties of the structures that make up the nervous system. It is a subset of the field of neuroscience, and looks to analyze brain data to create practical applications. It looks to model the brain in order to examine specific types aspects of the neurological system. Various types of models of the brain include:

- Realistic Brain Models: These models look to represent every aspect of the brain, including as much detail at the cellular level as possible. Realistic models provide the most information about the brain, but also have the largest margin for error. More variables in a brain model create the possibility for more error to occur. These models do not account for parts of the cellular structure that scientists do not know about. Realistic brain models are the most computationally heavy and the most expensive to implement.

- Simplifying Brain Models: These models look to limit the scope of a model in order to assess a specific physical property of the neurological system. This allows for the intensive computational problems to be solved, and reduces the amount of potential error from a realistic brain model.

It is the work of computational neuroscientists to improve the algorithms and data structures currently used to increase the speed of such calculations.

Computational Pharmacology

Computational pharmacology (from a computational biology perspective) is "the study of the effects of genomic data to find links between specific genotypes and diseases and then screening drug data". The pharmaceutical industry requires a shift in methods to analyze drug data. Pharmacologists were able to use Microsoft Excel to compare chemical and genomic data related to the effectiveness of drugs. However, the industry has reached what is referred to as the Excel barricade. This arises from the limited number of cells accessible on a spreadsheet. This development led to the need for computational pharmacology. Scientists and researchers develop computational methods to analyze these massive data sets. This allows for an efficient comparison between the notable data points and allows for more accurate drugs to be developed.

Analysts project that if major medications fail due to patents, that computational biology will be necessary to replace current drugs on the market. Doctoral students in computational biology are being encouraged to pursue careers in industry rather than take Post-Doctoral positions. This is a direct result of major pharmaceutical companies needing more qualified analysts of the large data sets required for producing new drugs.

Computational Evolutionary Biology

Computational biology has assisted the field of evolutionary biology in many capacities. This includes:

- Using DNA data to reconstruct the tree of life with computational phylogenetics

- Fitting population genetics models (either forward time or backward time) to DNA data to make inferences about demographic or selective history

- Building population genetics models of evolutionary systems from first principles in order to predict what is likely to evolve.

Cancer Computational Biology

Cancer computational biology is a field that aims to determine the future mutations in cancer through an algorithmic approach to analyzing data. Research in this field has led to the use of high-throughput measurement. High throughput measurement allows for the gathering of millions of data points using robotics and other sensing devices. This data is collected from DNA, RNA, and other biological structures. Areas of focus include determining the characteristics of tumors, analyzing molecules that are deterministic in causing cancer, and understanding how the human genome relates to the causation of tumors and cancer.

Software and Tools

Computational Biologists use a wide range of software. These range from command line programs to graphical and web-based programs.

Open Source Software

Open source software provides a platform to develop computational biological methods. Specifically, open source means that anybody can access software developed in research. PLOS cites four main reasons for the use of open source software including:

- Reproducibility: This allows for researchers to use the exact methods used to calculate the relations between biological data.

- Faster Development: developers and researchers do not have to reinvent existing code for minor tasks. Instead they can use pre-existing programs to save time on the development and implementation of larger projects.

- Increased quality: Having input from multiple researchers studying the same topic provides a layer of assurance that errors will not be in the code.

- Long-term availability: Open source programs are not tied to any businesses or patents. This allows for them to be posted to multiple web pages and ensure that they are available in the future.

Conferences

There are several large conferences that are concerned with computational biology. Some notable examples are Intelligent Systems for Molecular Biology (ISMB), European Conference on Computational Biology (ECCB) and Research in Computational Molecular Biology (RECOMB).

Related Fields

Computational biology, bioinformatics and mathematical biology are all interdisciplinary approaches to the life sciences that draw from quantitative disciplines such as mathematics and information science. The NIH describes computational/mathematical biology as the use of computational/mathematical approaches to address theoretical and experimental questions in biology and, by contrast, bioinformatics as the application of information science to understand complex life-sciences data.

Specifically, the NIH defines

Computational biology: The development and application of data-analytical and theo-retical methods, mathematical modeling and computational simulation techniques to the study of biological, behavioral, and social systems.

Bioinformatics: Research, development, or application of computational tools and ap-proaches for expanding the use of biological, medical, behavioral or health data, in-cluding those to acquire, store, organize, archive, analyze, or visualize such data.

While each field is distinct, there may be significant overlap at their interface.

Gene Prediction

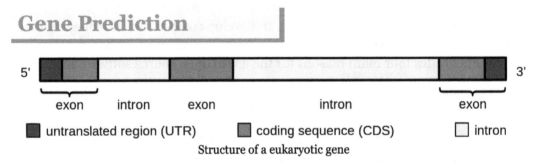

Structure of a eukaryotic gene

In computational biology gene prediction or gene finding refers to the process of iden-tifying the regions of genomic DNA that encode genes. This includes protein-coding genes as well as RNA genes, but may also include prediction of other functional ele-ments such as regulatory regions. Gene finding is one of the first and most important steps in understanding the genome of a species once it has been sequenced.

In its earliest days, "gene finding" was based on painstaking experimentation on liv-ing cells and organisms. Statistical analysis of the rates of homologous recombination of several different genes could determine their order on a certain chromosome, and information from many such experiments could be combined to create a genetic map specifying the rough location of known genes relative to each other. Today, with com-prehensive genome sequence and powerful computational resources at the disposal of the research community, gene finding has been redefined as a largely computational problem.

Determining that a sequence is functional should be distinguished from determining the function of the gene or its product. Predicting the function of a gene and confirm-ing that the gene prediction is accurate still demands *in vivo* experimentation through gene knockout and other assays, although frontiers of bioinformatics research are mak-ing it increasingly possible to predict the function of a gene based on its sequence alone.

Gene prediction is one of the key steps in genome annotation, following sequence as-sembly, the filtering of non-coding regions and repeat masking.

Gene prediction is closely related to the so-called 'target search problem' investigating how DNA-binding proteins (transcription factors) locate specific binding sites within the genome. Many aspects of structural gene prediction are based on current understanding of underlying biochemical processes in the cell such as gene transcription, translation, protein–protein interactions and regulation processes, which are subject of active research in the various omics fields such as transcriptomics, proteomics, metabolomics, and more generally structural and functional genomics.

Empirical Methods

In empirical (similarity, homology or evidence-based) gene finding systems, the target genome is searched for sequences that are similar to extrinsic evidence in the form of the known expressed sequence tags, messenger RNA (mRNA), protein products, and homologous or orthologous sequences. Given an mRNA sequence, it is trivial to derive a unique genomic DNA sequence from which it had to have been transcribed. Given a protein sequence, a family of possible coding DNA sequences can be derived by reverse translation of the genetic code. Once candidate DNA sequences have been determined, it is a relatively straightforward algorithmic problem to efficiently search a target genome for matches, complete or partial, and exact or inexact. Given a sequence, local alignment algorithms such as BLAST, FASTA and Smith-Waterman look for regions of similarity between the target sequence and possible candidate matches. Matches can be complete or partial, and exact or inexact. The success of this approach is limited by the contents and accuracy of the sequence database.

A high degree of similarity to a known messenger RNA or protein product is strong evidence that a region of a target genome is a protein-coding gene. However, to apply this approach systemically requires extensive sequencing of mRNA and protein products. Not only is this expensive, but in complex organisms, only a subset of all genes in the organism's genome are expressed at any given time, meaning that extrinsic evidence for many genes is not readily accessible in any single cell culture. Thus, to collect extrinsic evidence for most or all of the genes in a complex organism requires the study of many hundreds or thousands of cell types, which presents further difficulties. For example, some human genes may be expressed only during development as an embryo or fetus, which might be difficult to study for ethical reasons.

Despite these difficulties, extensive transcript and protein sequence databases have been generated for human as well as other important model organisms in biology, such as mice and yeast. For example, the RefSeq database contains transcript and protein sequence from many different species, and the Ensembl system comprehensively maps this evidence to human and several other genomes. It is, however, likely that these databases are both incomplete and contain small but significant amounts of erroneous data.

New high-throughput transcriptome sequencing technologies such as RNA-Seq and ChIP-sequencing open opportunities for incorporating additional extrinsic evidence into gene prediction and validation, and allow structurally rich and more accurate alternative to previous methods of measuring gene expression such as expressed sequence tag or DNA microarray.

Major challenges involved in gene prediction involve dealing with sequencing errors in raw DNA data, dependence on the quality of the sequence assembly, handling short reads, Frameshift mutations, overlapping genes and incomplete genes.

In prokaryotes it's essential to consider horizontal gene transfer when searching for gene sequence homology. An additional important factor underused in current gene detection tools is existence of gene clusters—operons in both prokaryotes and eukaryotes. Most popular gene detectors treat each gene in isolation, independent of others, which is not biologically accurate.

Ab Initio Methods

Ab Initio gene prediction is an intrinsic method based on gene content and signal detection. Because of the inherent expense and difficulty in obtaining extrinsic evidence for many genes, it is also necessary to resort to *ab initio* gene finding, in which the genomic DNA sequence alone is systematically searched for certain tell-tale signs of protein-coding genes. These signs can be broadly categorized as either *signals*, specific sequences that indicate the presence of a gene nearby, or *content*, statistical properties of the protein-coding sequence itself. *Ab initio* gene finding might be more accurately characterized as gene *prediction*, since extrinsic evidence is generally required to conclusively establish that a putative gene is functional.

In the genomes of prokaryotes, genes have specific and relatively well-understood promoter sequences (signals), such as the Pribnow box and transcription factor binding sites, which are easy to systematically identify. Also, the sequence coding for a protein occurs as one contiguous open reading frame (ORF), which is typically many hundred or thousands of base pairs long. The statistics of stop codons are such that even finding an open reading frame of this length is a fairly informative sign. (Since 3 of the 64 possible codons in the genetic code are stop codons, one would expect a stop codon approximately every 20–25 codons, or 60–75 base pairs, in a random sequence.) Furthermore, protein-coding DNA has certain periodicities and other statistical properties that are easy to detect in sequence of this length. These characteristics make prokaryotic gene finding relatively straightforward, and well-designed systems are able to achieve high levels of accuracy.

Ab initio gene finding in eukaryotes, especially complex organisms like humans, is considerably more challenging for several reasons. First, the promoter and other regulatory signals in these genomes are more complex and less well-understood than in prokaryotes, making them more difficult to reliably recognize. Two classic examples of signals identified by eukaryotic gene finders are CpG islands and binding sites for a poly(A) tail.

Second, splicing mechanisms employed by eukaryotic cells mean that a particular protein-coding sequence in the genome is divided into several parts (exons), separated by non-coding sequences (introns). (Splice sites are themselves another signal that eukaryotic gene finders are often designed to identify.) A typical protein-coding gene in humans might be divided into a dozen exons, each less than two hundred base pairs in length, and some as short as twenty to thirty. It is therefore much more difficult to detect periodicities and other known content properties of protein-coding DNA in eukaryotes.

Advanced gene finders for both prokaryotic and eukaryotic genomes typically use complex probabilistic models, such as hidden Markov models (HMMs) to combine information from a variety of different signal and content measurements. The GLIMMER system is a widely used and highly accurate gene finder for prokaryotes. GeneMark is another popular approach. Eukaryotic *ab initio* gene finders, by comparison, have achieved only limited success; notable examples are the GENSCAN and geneid programs. The SNAP gene finder is HMM-based like Genscan, and attempts to be more adaptable to different organisms, addressing problems related to using a gene finder on a genome sequence that it was not trained against. A few recent approaches like mSplicer, CONTRAST, or mGene also use machine learning techniques like support vector machines for successful gene prediction. They build a discriminative model using hidden Markov support vector machines or conditional random fields to learn an accurate gene prediction scoring function.

Ab Initio methods have been benchmarked, with some approaching 100% sensitivity, however as the sensitivity increases, accuracy suffers as a result of increased false positives.

Other Signals

Among the derived signals used for prediction are statistics resulting from the sub-sequence statistics like k-mer statistics, Isochore (genetics) or Compositional domain GC composition/uniformity/entropy, sequence and frame length, Intron/Exon/Donor/Acceptor/Promoter and Ribosomal binding site vocabulary, Fractal dimension, Fourier transform of a pseudo-number-coded DNA, Z-curve parameters and certain run features.

It has been suggested that signals other than those directly detectable in sequences may improve gene prediction. For example, the role of secondary structure in the identification of regulatory motifs has been reported. In addition, it has been suggested that RNA secondary structure prediction helps splice site prediction.

Neural Networks

Neural networks are computational models that excel at machine learning and pattern recognition. Neural networks must be trained with example data before being able to generalise for experimental data, and tested against benchmark data. Neural networks are able to come up with approximate solutions to problems that are hard to solve algorithmically, provided there is sufficient training data. When applied to gene prediction, neural networks can be used alongside other *ab initio* methods to predict or identify biological features such as splice sites. One approach involves using a sliding window, which traverses the sequence data in an overlapping manner. The output at each position is a score based on whether the network thinks the window contains a donor splice site or an acceptor splice site. Larger windows offer more accuracy but also require more computational power. A neural network is an example of a signal sensor as its goal is to identify a functional site in the genome.

Combined Approaches

Programs such as Maker combine extrinsic and *ab initio* approaches by mapping protein and EST data to the genome to validate *ab initio* predictions. Augustus, which may be used as part of the Maker pipeline, can also incorporate hints in the form of EST alignments or protein profiles to increase the accuracy of the gene prediction.

Comparative Genomics Approaches

As the entire genomes of many different species are sequenced, a promising direction in current research on gene finding is a comparative genomics approach.

This is based on the principle that the forces of natural selection cause genes and other functional elements to undergo mutation at a slower rate than the rest of the genome, since mutations in functional elements are more likely to negatively impact the organism than mutations elsewhere. Genes can thus be detected by comparing the genomes of related species to detect this evolutionary pressure for conservation. This approach was first applied to the mouse and human genomes, using programs such as SLAM, SGP and TWINSCAN/N-SCAN and CONTRAST.

Multiple Informants

TWINSCAN examined only human-mouse synteny to look for orthologous genes. Programs such as N-SCAN and CONTRAST allowed the incorporation of alignments from multiple organisms, or in the case of N-SCAN, a single alternate organism from the target. The use of multiple informants can lead to significant improvements in accuracy.

CONTRAST is composed of two elements. The first is a smaller classifier, identifying donor splice sites and acceptor splice sites as well as start and stop codons. The second element involves constructing a full model using machine learning. Breaking the problem into two means that smaller targeted data sets can be used to train the classifiers, and that classifier can operate independently and be trained with smaller windows.

The full model can use the independent classifier, and not have to waste computational time or model complexity re-classifying intron-exon boundaries. The paper in which CONTRAST is introduced proposes that their method (and those of TWINSCAN, etc.) be classified as *de novo* gene assembly, using alternate genomes, and identifying it as distinct from *ab initio*, which uses a target 'informant' genomes.

Comparative gene finding can also be used to project high quality annotations from one genome to another. Notable examples include Projector, GeneWise and GeneMapper. Such techniques now play a central role in the annotation of all genomes.

Pseudogene Prediction

Pseudogenes are close relatives of genes, sharing very high sequence homology, but being unable to code for the same protein product. Whilst once relegated as byproducts of gene sequencing, increasingly, as regulatory roles are being uncovered, they are becoming predictive targets in their own right. Pseudogene prediction utilises existing sequence similarity and ab initio methods, whilst adding additional filtering and methods of identifying pseudogene characteristics.

Sequence similarity methods can be customised for pseudogene prediction using additional filtering to find candidate pseudogenes. This could use disablement detection, which looks for nonsense or frameshift mutations that would truncate or collapse an otherwise functional coding sequence. Additionally, translating DNA into proteins sequences can be more effective than just straight DNA homology.

Content sensors can be filtered according to the differences in statistical properties between pseudogenes and genes, such as a reduced count of CpG islands in pseudogenes, or the differences in G-C content between pseudogenes and their neighbours. Signal sensors also can be honed to pseudogenes, looking for the absence of introns or polyadenine tails.

Metagenomic Gene Prediction

Metagenomics is the study of genetic material recovered from the environment, resulting in sequence information from a pool of organisms. Predicting genes is useful for comparative metagenomics.

Metagenomics tools also fall into the basic categories of using either sequence similarity approaches (MEGAN4) and ab initio techniques (GLIMMER-MG).

Glimmer-MG is an extension to GLIMMER that relies mostly on an ab initio approach for gene finding and by using training sets from related organisms. The prediction strategy is augmented by classification and clustering gene data sets prior to applying ab initio gene prediction methods. The data is clustered by species. This classification method leverages techniques from metagenomic phylogenetic classification. An example of software for this purpose is, Phymm, which uses interpolated markov models—and PhymmBL, which integrates BLAST into the classification routines.

MEGAN4 uses a sequence similarity approach, using local alignment against databases of known sequences, but also attempts to classify using additional information on functional roles, biological pathways and enzymes. As in single organism gene prediction, sequence similarity approaches are limited by the size of the database.

FragGeneScan and MetaGeneAnnotator are popular gene prediction programs based on Hidden Markov model. These predictors account for sequencing errors, partial genes and work for short reads.

Modelling Biological Systems

Modelling biological systems is a significant task of systems biology and mathematical biology. Computational systems biology aims to develop and use efficient algorithms, data structures, visualization and communication tools with the goal of computer modelling of biological systems. It involves the use of computer simulations of biological systems, including cellular subsystems (such as the networks of metabolites and enzymes which comprise metabolism, signal transduction pathways and gene regulatory networks), to both analyze and visualize the complex connections of these cellular processes.

Artificial life or virtual evolution attempts to understand evolutionary processes via the computer simulation of simple (artificial) life forms.

Overview

It is understood that an unexpected emergent property of a complex system is a result of the interplay of the cause-and-effect among simpler, integrated parts. Biological systems manifest many important examples of emergent properties in the complex interplay of components. Traditional study of biological systems requires reductive methods in which quantities of data are gathered by category, such as concentration over time in response to a certain stimulus. Computers are critical to analysis and modelling of these data. The goal is to create accurate real-time models of a system's response to environmental and internal stimuli, such as a model of a cancer cell in order to find weaknesses in its signalling pathways, or modelling of ion channel mutations to see effects on cardiomyocytes and in turn, the function of a beating heart.

Standards

By far the most widely accepted standard format for storing and exchanging models in the field is the Systems Biology Markup Language (SBML) The SBML.org website includes a guide to many important software packages used in computational systems biology. Other markup languages with different emphases include BioPAX and CellML.

Particular Tasks

Cellular Model

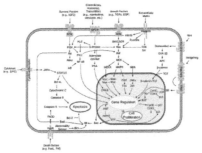

Part of the Cell Cycle

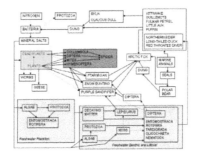

Summerhayes and Elton's 1923 food web of Bear Island (*Arrows represent an organism being consumed by another organism*).

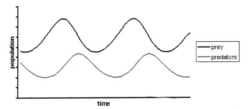

A sample time-series of the Lotka–Volterra model. Note that the two populations exhibit cyclic behaviour.

Creating a cellular model has been a particularly challenging task of systems biology and mathematical biology. It involves the use of computer simulations of the many cellular subsystems such as the networks of metabolites and enzymes which comprise metabolism, signal transduction pathways and gene regulatory networks to both analyze and visualize the complex connections of these cellular processes.

The complex network of biochemical reaction/transport processes and their spatial organization make the development of a predictive model of a living cell a grand challenge for the 21st century, listed as such by the National Science Foundation (NSF) in 2006.

A whole cell computational model for the bacterium *Mycoplasma genitalium*, including all its 525 genes, gene products, and their interactions, was built by scientists from Stanford University and the J. Craig Venter Institute and published on 20 July 2012 in Cell.

A dynamic computer model of intracellular signaling was the basis for Merrimack Pharmaceuticals to discover the target for their cancer medicine MM-111.

Membrane computing is the task of modelling specifically a cell membrane.

Multi-cellular Organism Simulation

An open source simulation of C. elegans at the cellular level is being pursued by the OpenWorm community. So far the physics engine Gepetto has been built and models of the neural connectome and a muscle cell have been created in the NeuroML format.

Protein Folding

Protein structure prediction is the prediction of the three-dimensional structure of a protein from its amino acid sequence—that is, the prediction of a protein's tertiary structure from its primary structure. It is one of the most important goals pursued by bioinformatics and theoretical chemistry. Protein structure prediction is of high importance in medicine (for example, in drug design) and biotechnology (for example, in the design of novel enzymes). Every two years, the performance of current methods is assessed in the CASP experiment.

Human Biological Systems

Brain Model

The Blue Brain Project is an attempt to create a synthetic brain by reverse-engineering the mammalian brain down to the molecular level. The aim of the project, founded in May 2005 by the Brain and Mind Institute of the *École Polytechnique* in Lausanne, Switzerland, is to study the brain's architectural and functional principles. The project is headed by the Institute's director, Henry Markram. Using a Blue Gene supercomputer running Michael Hines's NEURON software, the simulation does not consist simply of an artificial neural network, but involves a partially biologically realistic model of neurons. It is hoped by its proponents that it will eventually shed light on the nature of consciousness. There are a number of sub-projects, including the Cajal Blue Brain, coordinated by the Supercomputing and Visualization Center of Madrid (CeSViMa), and others run by universities and independent laboratories in the UK, U.S., and Israel. The Human Brain Project builds on the work of the Blue Brain Project. It is one of six pilot projects in the Future Emerging Technologies Research Program of the European Commission, competing for a billion euro funding.

Model of the Immune System

The last decade has seen the emergence of a growing number of simulations of the immune system.

Virtual Liver

The Virtual Liver project is a 43 million euro research program funded by the German Government, made up of seventy research group distributed across Germany. The goal is to produce a virtual liver, a dynamic mathematical model that represents human liver physiology, morphology and function.

Tree Model

Electronic trees (e-trees) usually use L-systems to simulate growth. L-systems are very important in the field of complexity science and A-life. A universally accepted system for describing changes in plant morphology at the cellular or modular level has yet to be devised. The most widely implemented tree generating algorithms are described in the papers "Creation and Rendering of Realistic Trees", and Real-Time Tree Rendering

Ecological Models

Ecosystem models are mathematical representations of ecosystems. Typically they simplify complex foodwebs down to their major components or trophic levels, and quantify these as either numbers of organisms, biomass or the inventory/concentration of some pertinent chemical element (for instance, carbon or a nutrient species such as nitrogen or phosphorus).

Models in Ecotoxicology

The purpose of models in ecotoxicology is the understanding, simulation and prediction of effects caused by toxicants in the environment. Most current models describe effects on one of many different levels of biological organization (e.g. organisms or populations). A challenge is the development of models that predict effects across biological scales. Ecotoxicology and models discusses some types of ecotoxicological models and provides links to many others.

Modelling of Infectious Disease

It is possible to model the progress of most infectious diseases mathematically to discover the likely outcome of an epidemic or to help manage them by vaccination. This field tries to find parameters for various infectious diseases and to use those parameters to make useful calculations about the effects of a mass vaccination programme.

Computational Genomics

Computational genomics (often referred to as Computational Genetics) refers to the use of computational and statistical analysis to decipher biology from genome sequences and related data, including both DNA and RNA sequence as well as other "post-genomic" data (i.e., experimental data obtained with technologies that require the genome sequence, such as genomic DNA microarrays). These, in combination with computational and statistical approaches to understanding the function of the genes and statistical association analysis, this field is also often referred to as Computational and Statistical Genetics/genomics. As such, computational genomics may be regarded as a subset of bioinformatics and computational biology, but with a focus on using whole genomes (rather than individual genes) to understand the principles of how the DNA of a species controls its biology at the molecular level and beyond. With the current abundance of massive biological datasets, computational studies have become one of the most important means to biological discovery.

History

The roots of computational genomics are shared with those of bioinformatics. During the 1960s, Margaret Dayhoff and others at the National Biomedical Research Foundation assembled databases of homologous protein sequences for evolutionary study. Their research developed a phylogenetic tree that determined the evolutionary changes that were required for a particular protein to change into another protein based on the underlying amino acid sequences. This led them to create a scoring matrix that assessed the likelihood of one protein being related to another.

Beginning in the 1980s, databases of genome sequences began to be recorded, but this presented new challenges in the form of searching and comparing the databases of gene information. Unlike text-searching algorithms that are used on websites such as Google or Wikipedia, searching for sections of genetic similarity requires one to find strings that are not simply identical, but similar. This led to the development of the Needleman-Wunsch algorithm, which is a dynamic programming algorithm for comparing sets of amino acid sequences with each other by using scoring matrices derived from the earlier research by Dayhoff. Later, the BLAST algorithm was developed for performing fast, optimized searches of gene sequence databases. BLAST and its derivatives are probably the most widely used algorithms for this purpose.

The emergence of the phrase "computational genomics" coincides with the availability of complete sequenced genomes in the mid-to-late 1990s. The first meeting of the Annual Conference on Computational Genomics was organized by scientists from The Institute for Genomic Research (TIGR) in 1998, providing a forum for this speciality and effectively distinguishing this area of science from the more general fields of Genomics or Computational Biology. The first use of this term in scientific literature, according to MEDLINE abstracts, was just one year earlier in Nucleic Acids Research. The final Computational Genomics conference was held in 2006, featuring a keynote talk by Nobel Laureate Barry Marshall, co-discoverer of the link between Helicobacter pylori and stomach ulcers. As of 2014, the leading conferences in the field include Intelligent Systems for Molecular Biology (ISMB) and RECOMB.

The development of computer-assisted mathematics (using products such as Mathematica or Matlab) has helped engineers, mathematicians and computer scientists to start operating in this domain, and a public collection of case studies and demonstrations is growing, ranging from whole genome comparisons to gene expression analysis. This has increased the introduction of different ideas, including concepts from systems and control, information theory, strings analysis and data mining. It is anticipated that computational approaches will become and remain a standard topic for research and teaching, while students fluent in both topics start being formed in the multiple courses created in the past few years.

Contributions of Computational Genomics Research to Biology

Contributions of computational genomics research to biology include:

- discovering subtle patterns in genomic sequences

- proposing cellular signalling networks

- proposing mechanisms of genome evolution

- predict precise locations of all human genes using comparative genomics techniques with several mammalian and vertebrate species

- predict conserved genomic regions that are related to early embryonic development

- discover potential links between repeated sequence motifs and tissue-specific gene expression

- measure regions of genomes that have undergone unusually rapid evolution

Latest Development (from 2012)

First Computer Model of an Organism

Researchers at Stanford University created the first software simulation of an entire organism. The smallest free-living organism, *Mycoplasma genitalium*, has 525 genes which are fully mapped. With data from more than 900 scientific papers reported on the bacterium, researchers developed the software model using the object-oriented programming approach. A series of modules mimic the various functions of the cell and then are integrated together into a whole simulated organism. The simulation runs on a single CPU, recreates the complete life span of the cell at the molecular level, reproducing the interactions of molecules in cell processes including metabolism and cell division.

The 'silicon cell' will act as computerized laboratories that could perform experiments which are difficult to do on an actual organism, or could carry out procedures much faster. The applications will include faster screening of new compounds, understanding of basic cellular principles and behavior.

Computational and Statistical Genetics

The interdisciplinary research field of Computational and Statistical Genetics uses the latest approaches in genomics, quantitative genetics, computational sciences, bioinformatics and statistics to develop and apply computationally efficient and statistically robust methods to sort through increasingly rich and massive genome wide data sets to identify complex genetic patterns, gene functionalities and interactions, disease and phenotype associations involving the genomes of various organisms. This field is also often referred to as computational genomics. This is an important discipline within the umbrella field computational biology.

Haplotype Phasing

During the last two decades, there has been a great interest in understanding the genetic and genomic makeup of various species, including humans primarily aided by the different genome sequencing technologies to read the genomes that has been rapidly developing. However, these technologies are still limited, and computational and statistical methods are a must to detect and process errors and put together the pieces of partial information from the sequencing and genotyping technologies.

A haplotype is defined the sequence of nucleotides (A,G,T,C) along a single chromosome. In humans, we have 23 pairs of chromosomes. Another example is maize which is also a diploid with 10 pairs of chromosomes. However, with current technology, it is difficult to separate the two chromosomes within a pair and the assays produce the combined haplotype, called the genotype information at each nucleotide. The objective of haplotype phasing is to find the phase of the two haplotypes given the combined genotype information. Knowledge of the haplotypes is extremely important and not only gives us a complete picture of an individuals genome, but also aids other computational genomic processes such as Imputation among many significant biological motivations.

For diploid organisms such as humans and maize, each organism has two copies of a chromosome - one each from the two parents. The two copies are highly similar to each other. A haplotype is the sequence of nucleotides in a chromosome. the haplotype phasing problem is focused on the nucleotides where the two homologous chromosomes differ. Computationally, for a genomic region with K differing nucleotide sites, there are $2^K - 1$ possible haplotypes, so the phasing problem focuses on efficiently finding the most probable haplotypes given an observed genotype.

Prediction of SNP Genotypes by Imputation

Although the genome of a higher organism (eukaryotes) contains millions of single nucleotide polymorphisms (SNPs), genotyping arrays are pre- determined to detect only a handful of such markers. The missing markers are predicted using imputation analysis. Imputation of un-genotyped markers has now become an essential part of genetic and genomic studies. It utilizes the knowledge of linkage disequilibrium (LD) from haplotypes in a known reference panel (for example, HapMap and the 1000 Genomes Projects) to predict genotypes at the missing or un-genotyped markers. The process allows the scientists to accurately perform analysis of both the genotyped polymorphic markers and the un-genotyped markers that are predicted computationally. It has been shown that downstream studies benefit a lot from imputation analysis in the form of improved the power to detect disease-associated loci. Another crucial contribution of imputation is that it also facilitates combining genetic and genomic studies that used different genotyping platforms for their experiments. For example. although 415 million common and rare genetic variants exist in the human genome,the current genotyping arrays such as Affymetrix and Illumina microarrays can only assay up to 2.5 million SNPs. Therefore, imputation analysis is an important research direction and it is important to identify methods and platforms to impute high quality genotype data using existing genotypes and reference panels from publicly available resources, such as the International HapMap Project and the 1000 Genomes Project. For humans, the analysis has successfully generated predicted genotypes in many races including Europeans and African Americans.

A number of different methods exist for genotype imputation. The three most widely used imputation methods are - Mach, Impute and Beagle. All three methods utilize hidden markov models as the underlying basis for estimating the distribution of the haplotype frequencies. Mach and Impute2 are more computationally intensive compared with Beagle. Both Impute and Mach are based on different implementations of the product of the conditionals or PAC model. Beagle groups the reference panel haplotypes into clusters at each SNP to form localized haplotype-cluster model that allows it to dynamically vary the number of clusters at each SNP making it computationally faster than Mach and Impute2.

Genome-wide Association Analysis

Over the past few years, genome-wide association studies (GWAS) have become a powerful tool for investigating the genetic basis of common diseases and has improved our understanding of the genetic basis of many complex traits. Traditional single SNP (single-nucleotide polymorphism) GWAS is the most commonly used method to find trait associated DNA sequence variants - associations between variants and one or more phenotypes of interest are investigated by studying individuals with different phenotypes and examining their genotypes at the position of each SNP individually. The SNPs for which one variant is statistically more common in individuals belonging to one phenotypic group are then reported as being associated with the phenotype. However, most complex common diseases involve small population-level contributions from multiple genomic loci. To detect such small effects as genome-wide significant, traditional GWAS rely on increased sample size e.g. to detect an effect which accounts for 0.1% of total variance, traditional GWAS needs to sample almost 30,000 individuals. Although the development of high throughput SNP genotyping technologies has lowered the cost and improved the efficiency of genotyping. Performing such a large scale study still costs considerable money and time. Recently, association analysis methods utilizing gene-based tests have been proposed that are based on the fact that variations in protein-coding and adjacent regulatory regions are more likely to have functional relevance. These methods have the advantage that they can account for multiple independent functional variants within a gene, with the potential to greatly increase the power to identify disease/trait associated genes. Also, imputation of ungenotyped markers using known reference panels(e.g. HapMap and the 1000 Genomes Project) predicts genotypes at the missing or untyped markers thereby allowing one to accurately evaluate the evidence for association at genetic markers that are not directly genotyped (in addition to the typed markers) and has been shown to improve the power of GWAS to detect disease associated loci.

Statistical Disease Related Interaction Analysis

In this era of large amount of genetic and genomic data, accurate representation and identification of statistical interactions in biological/genetic/genomic data constitutes a vital basis for designing interventions and curative solutions for many complex diseases. Variations in human genome have been long known to make us susceptible to many diseases. We are hurtling towards the era of personal genomics and personalized medicine that require accurate predictions of disease risk posed by predisposing genetic factors. Computational and statistical methods for identifying these genetic variations, and building these into intelligent models for diseaseassociation and interaction analysis studies genome-wide are a dire necessity across many disease areas. The principal challenges are: (1) most complex diseases involve small or weak contributions from multiple genetic factors that explain only a minuscule fraction of the population variation attributed to genetic factors. (2) Biological data is inherently extremely noisy, so the underlying complexities of biological systems (such as linkage disequilibrium and genetic heterogeneity) need to be incorporated into the statistical models for disease association studies. The chances of developing many common diseases such as cancer, autoimmune diseases and cardiovascular diseases involves complex interactions between multiple genes and several endogenous and exogenous environmental agents or covariates. Many previous disease association studies could not produce significant results because of the lack of incorporation of statistical interactions in their mathematical models explaining the disease outcome. Consequently much of the genetic risks underlying several diseases and disorders remain unknown. Computational methods such as to model and identify the genetic/genomic variations underlying disease risks has a great potential to improve prediction of disease outcomes, understand the interactions and design better therapeutic methods based on them.

Computational Phylogenetics

Computational phylogenetics is the application of computational algorithms, methods, and programs to phylogenetic analyses. The goal is to assemble a phylogenetic tree representing a hypothesis about the evolutionary ancestry of a set of genes, species, or other taxa. For example, these techniques have been used to explore the family tree of hominid species and the relationships between specific genes shared by many types of organisms. Traditional phylogenetics relies on morphological data obtained by measuring and quantifying the phenotypic properties of representative organisms, while the more recent field of molecular phylogenetics uses nucleotide sequences encoding genes or amino acid sequences encoding proteins as the basis for classification. Many forms of molecular phylogenetics are closely related to and make extensive use of sequence alignment in constructing and refining phylogenetic trees, which are used to classify the evolutionary relationships between homologous genes represented in the genomes of divergent species. The phylogenetic trees constructed by computational methods are unlikely to perfectly reproduce the evolutionary tree that represents the historical relationships between the species being analyzed. The historical species tree may also differ from the historical tree of an individual homologous gene shared by those species.

Producing a phylogenetic tree requires a measure of homology among the characteristics shared by the taxa being compared. In morphological studies, this requires explicit decisions about which physical characteristics to measure and how to use them to encode distinct states corresponding to the input taxa. In molecular studies, a primary problem is in producing a multiple sequence alignment (MSA) between the genes or amino acid sequences of interest. Progressive sequence alignment methods produce a phylogenetic tree by necessity because they incorporate new sequences into the calculated alignment in order of genetic distance.

Types of Phylogenetic Trees and Networks

Phylogenetic trees generated by computational phylogenetics can be either *rooted* or *unrooted* depending on the input data and the algorithm used. A rooted tree is a directed graph that explicitly identifies a most recent common ancestor (MRCA), usually an imputed sequence that is not represented in the input. Genetic distance measures can be used to plot a tree with the input sequences as leaf nodes and their distances from the root proportional to their genetic distance from the hypothesized MRCA. Identification of a root usually requires the inclusion in the input data of at least one "out-group" known to be only distantly related to the sequences of interest.

By contrast, unrooted trees plot the distances and relationships between input sequences without making assumptions regarding their descent. An unrooted tree can always be produced from a rooted tree, but a root cannot usually be placed on an unrooted tree without additional data on divergence rates, such as the assumption of the molecular clock hypothesis.

The set of all possible phylogenetic trees for a given group of input sequences can be conceptualized as a discretely defined multidimensional "tree space" through which search paths can be traced by optimization algorithms. Although counting the total number of trees for a nontrivial number of input sequences can be complicated by variations in the definition of a tree topology, it is always true that there are more rooted than unrooted trees for a given number of inputs and choice of parameters.

Both rooted and unrooted phylogenetic trees can be further generalized to rooted or unrooted phylogenetic networks, which allow for the modeling of evolutionary phenomena such as hybridization or horizontal gene transfer.

Coding Characters and Defining Homology

Morphological Analysis

The basic problem in morphological phylogenetics is the assembly of a matrix representing a mapping from each of the taxa being compared to representative measurements for each of the phenotypic characteristics being used as a classifier. The types of phenotypic data used to construct this matrix depend on the taxa being compared; for individual species, they may involve measurements of average body size, lengths or sizes of particular bones or other physical features, or even behavioral manifestations. Of course, since not every possible phenotypic characteristic could be measured and encoded for analysis, the selection of which features to measure is a major inherent obstacle to the method. The decision of which traits to use as a basis for the matrix necessarily represents a hypothesis about which traits of a species or higher taxon are evolutionarily relevant. Morphological studies can be confounded by examples of convergent evolution of phenotypes. A major challenge in constructing useful classes is the high likelihood of inter-taxon overlap in the distribution of the phenotype's variation. The inclusion of extinct taxa in morphological analysis is often difficult due to absence of or incomplete fossil records, but has been shown to have a significant effect on the trees produced; in one study only the inclusion of extinct species of apes produced a morphologically derived tree that was consistent with that produced from molecular data.

Some phenotypic classifications, particularly those used when analyzing very diverse groups of taxa, are discrete and unambiguous; classifying organisms as possessing or lacking a tail, for example, is straightforward in the majority of cases, as is counting features such as eyes or vertebrae. However, the most appropriate representation of continuously varying phenotypic measurements is a controversial problem without a general solution. A common method is simply to sort the measurements of interest into two or more classes, rendering continuous observed variation as discretely classifiable (e.g., all examples with humerus bones longer than a given cutoff are scored as members of one state, and all members whose humerus bones are shorter than the cutoff are scored as members of a second state). This results in an easily manipulated data set but has been criticized for poor reporting of the basis for the class definitions and for sacrificing information compared to methods that use a continuous weighted distribution of measurements.

Because morphological data is extremely labor-intensive to collect, whether from literature sources or from field observations, reuse of previously compiled data matrices is not uncommon, although this may propagate flaws in the original matrix into multiple derivative analyses.

Molecular Analysis

The problem of character coding is very different in molecular analyses, as the characters in biological sequence data are immediate and discretely defined - distinct nucleotides in DNA or RNA sequences and distinct amino acids in protein sequences. However, defining homology can be challenging due to the inherent difficulties of multiple sequence alignment. For a given gapped MSA, several rooted phylogenetic trees can be constructed that vary in their interpretations of which changes are "mutations" versus ancestral characters, and which events are insertion mutations or deletion mutations. For example, given only a pairwise alignment with a gap region, it is impossible to determine whether one sequence bears an insertion mutation or the other carries a deletion. The problem is magnified in MSAs with unaligned and nonoverlapping gaps. In practice, sizable regions of a calculated alignment may be discounted in phylogenetic tree construction to avoid integrating noisy data into the tree calculation.

Distance-matrix Methods

Distance-matrix methods of phylogenetic analysis explicitly rely on a measure of "genetic distance" between the sequences being classified, and therefore they require an MSA as an input. Distance is often defined as the fraction of mismatches at aligned positions, with gaps either ignored or counted as mismatches. Distance methods attempt to construct an all-to-all matrix from the sequence query set describing the distance between each sequence pair. From this is constructed a phylogenetic tree that places closely related sequences under the same interior node and whose branch lengths closely reproduce the observed distances between sequences. Distance-matrix methods may produce either rooted or unrooted trees, depending on the algorithm used to calculate them. They are frequently used as the basis for progressive and iterative types of multiple sequence alignments. The main disadvantage of distance-matrix methods is their inability to efficiently use information about local high-variation regions that appear across multiple subtrees.

Neighbor-joining

Neighbor-joining methods apply general cluster analysis techniques to sequence analysis using genetic distance as a clustering metric. The simple neighbor-joining method produces unrooted trees, but it does not assume a constant rate of evolution (i.e., a molecular clock) across lineages. Its relative, UPGMA (Unweighted Pair Group Method with Arithmetic mean) produces rooted trees and requires a constant-rate assumption - that is, it assumes an ultrametric tree in which the distances from the root to every branch tip are equal.

Fitch-Margoliash Method

The Fitch-Margoliash method uses a weighted least squares method for clustering based on genetic distance. Closely related sequences are given more weight in the tree construction process to correct for the increased inaccuracy in measuring distances between distantly related sequences. The distances used as input to the algorithm must be normalized to prevent large artifacts in computing relationships between closely related and distantly related groups. The distances calculated by this method must be linear; the linearity criterion for distances requires that the expected values of the branch lengths for two individual branches must equal the expected value of the sum of the two branch distances - a property that applies to biological sequences only when they have been corrected for the possibility of back mutations at individual sites. This correction is done through the use of a substitution matrix such as that derived from the Jukes-Cantor model of DNA evolution. The distance correction is only necessary in practice when the evolution rates differ among branches. Another modification of the algorithm can be helpful, especially in case of concentrated distances (please report to concentration of measure phenomenon and curse of dimensionality): that modification, described in, has been shown to improve the efficiency of the algorithm and its robustness.

The least-squares criterion applied to these distances is more accurate but less efficient than the neighbor-joining methods. An additional improvement that corrects for correlations between distances that arise from many closely related sequences in the data set can also be applied at increased computational cost. Finding the optimal least-squares tree with any correction factor is NP-complete, so heuristic search methods like those used in maximum-parsimony analysis are applied to the search through tree space.

Using Outgroups

Independent information about the relationship between sequences or groups can be used to help reduce the tree search space and root unrooted trees. Standard usage of distance-matrix methods involves the inclusion of at least one outgroup sequence known to be only distantly related to the sequences of interest in the query set. This usage can be seen as a type of experimental control. If the outgroup has been appropriately chosen, it will have a much greater genetic distance and thus a longer branch length than any other sequence, and it will appear near the root of a rooted tree. Choosing an appropriate outgroup requires the selection of a sequence that is moderately related to the sequences of interest; too close a relationship defeats the purpose of the outgroup and too distant adds noise to the analysis. Care should also be taken to avoid situations in which the species from which the sequences were taken are distantly related, but the gene encoded by the sequences is highly conserved across lineages. Horizontal gene transfer, especially between otherwise divergent bacteria, can also confound outgroup usage.

Maximum Parsimony

Maximum parsimony (MP) is a method of identifying the potential phylogenetic tree that requires the smallest total number of evolutionary events to explain the observed sequence data. Some ways of scoring trees also include a "cost" associated with particular types of evolutionary events and attempt to locate the tree with the smallest total cost. This is a useful approach in cases where not every possible type of event is equally likely - for example, when particular nucleotides or amino acids are known to be more mutable than others.

The most naive way of identifying the most parsimonious tree is simple enumeration - considering each possible tree in succession and searching for the tree with the smallest score. However, this is only possible for a relatively small number of sequences or species because the problem of identifying the most parsimonious tree is known to be NP-hard; consequently a number of heuristic search methods for optimization have been developed to locate a highly parsimonious tree, if not the best in the set. Most such methods involve a steepest descent-style minimization mechanism operating on a tree rearrangement criterion.

Branch and Bound

The branch and bound algorithm is a general method used to increase the efficiency of searches for near-optimal solutions of NP-hard problems first applied to phylogenetics in the early 1980s. Branch and bound is particularly well suited to phylogenetic tree construction because it inherently requires dividing a problem into a tree structure as it subdivides the problem space into smaller regions. As its name implies, it requires as input both a branching rule (in the case of phylogenetics, the addition of the next species or sequence to the tree) and a bound (a rule that excludes certain regions of the search space from consideration, thereby assuming that the optimal solution cannot occupy that region). Identifying a good bound is the most challenging aspect of the algorithm's application to phylogenetics. A simple way of defining the bound is a maximum number of assumed evolutionary changes allowed per tree. A set of criteria known as Zharkikh's rules severely limit the search space by defining characteristics shared by all candidate "most parsimonious" trees. The two most basic rules require the elimination of all but one redundant sequence (for cases where multiple observations have produced identical data) and the elimination of character sites at which two or more states do not occur in at least two species. Under ideal conditions these rules and their associated algorithm would completely define a tree.

Sankoff-Morel-Cedergren Algorithm

The Sankoff-Morel-Cedergren algorithm was among the first published methods to simultaneously produce an MSA and a phylogenetic tree for nucleotide sequences. The method uses a maximum parsimony calculation in conjunction with a scoring function that penalizes gaps and mismatches, thereby favoring the tree that introduces a minimal number of such events (an alternative view holds that the trees to be favored are those that maximize the amount of sequence similarity that can be interpreted as homology, a point of view that may lead to different optimal trees). The imputed sequences at the interior nodes of the tree are scored and summed over all the nodes in each possible tree. The lowest-scoring tree sum provides both an optimal tree and an optimal MSA given the scoring function. Because the method is highly computationally intensive, an approximate method in which initial guesses for the interior alignments are refined one node at a time. Both the full and the approximate version are in practice calculated by dynamic programming.

MALIGN and POY

More recent phylogenetic tree/MSA methods use heuristics to isolate high-scoring, but not necessarily optimal, trees. The MALIGN method uses a maximum-parsimony technique to compute a multiple alignment by maximizing a cladogram score, and its companion POY uses an iterative method that couples the optimization of the phylogenetic tree with improvements in the corresponding MSA. However, the use of these methods in constructing evolutionary hypotheses has been criticized as biased due to the deliberate construction of trees reflecting minimal evolutionary events. This, in turn, has been countered by the view that such methods should be seen as heuristic approaches to find the trees that maximize the amount of sequence similarity that can be interpreted as homology.

Maximum Likelihood

The maximum likelihood method uses standard statistical techniques for inferring probability distributions to assign probabilities to particular possible phylogenetic trees. The method requires a substitution model to assess the probability of particular mutations; roughly, a tree that requires more mutations at interior nodes to explain the observed phylogeny will be assessed as having a lower probability. This is broadly similar to the maximum-parsimony method, but maximum likelihood allows additional statistical flexibility by permitting varying rates of evolution across both lineages and sites. In fact, the method requires that evolution at different sites and along different lineages must be statistically independent. Maximum likelihood is thus well suited to the analysis of distantly related sequences, but it is believed to be computationally intractable to compute due to its NP-hardness.

The "pruning" algorithm, a variant of dynamic programming, is often used to reduce the search space by efficiently calculating the likelihood of subtrees. The method calculates the likelihood for each site in a "linear" manner, starting at a node whose only descendants are leaves (that is, the tips of the tree) and working backwards toward the "bottom" node in nested sets. However, the trees produced by the method are only rooted if the substitution model is irreversible, which is not generally true of biological systems. The search for the maximum-likelihood tree also includes a branch length optimization component that is difficult to improve upon algorithmically; general global optimization tools such as the Newton-Raphson method are often used.

Bayesian Inference

Bayesian inference can be used to produce phylogenetic trees in a manner closely related to the maximum likelihood methods. Bayesian methods assume a prior probability distribution of the possible trees, which may simply be the probability of any one tree among all the possible trees that could be generated from the data, or may be a more sophisticated estimate derived from the assumption that divergence events such as speciation occur as stochastic processes. The choice of prior distribution is a point of contention among users of Bayesian-inference phylogenetics methods.

Implementations of Bayesian methods generally use Markov chain Monte Carlo sampling algorithms, although the choice of move set varies; selections used in Bayesian phylogenetics include circularly permuting leaf nodes of a proposed tree at each step and swapping descendant subtrees of a random internal node between two related trees. The use of Bayesian methods in phylogenetics has been controversial, largely due to incomplete specification of the choice of move set, acceptance criterion, and prior distribution in published work. Bayesian methods are generally held to be superior to parsimony-based methods; they can be more prone to long-branch attraction than maximum likelihood techniques, although they are better able to accommodate missing data.

Whereas likelihood methods find the tree that maximizes the probability of the data, a Bayesian approach recovers a tree that represents the most likely clades, by drawing on the posterior distribution. However, estimates of the posterior probability of clades (measuring their 'support') can be quite wide of the mark, especially in clades that aren't overwhelmingly likely. As such, other methods have been put forwards to estimate posterior probability.

Model Selection

Molecular phylogenetics methods rely on a defined substitution model that encodes a hypothesis about the relative rates of mutation at various sites along the gene or amino acid sequences being studied. At their simplest, substitution models aim to correct for differences in the rates of transitions and transversions in nucleotide sequences. The use of substitution models is necessitated by the fact that the genetic distance between two sequences increases linearly only for a short time after the two sequences diverge from each other (alternatively, the distance is linear only shortly before coalescence). The longer the amount of time after divergence, the more likely it becomes that two mutations occur at the same nucleotide site. Simple genetic distance calculations will thus undercount the number of mutation events that have occurred in evolutionary history. The extent of this undercount increases with increasing time since divergence, which can lead to the phenomenon of long branch attraction, or the misassignment of two distantly related but convergently evolving sequences as closely related. The maximum parsimony method is particularly susceptible to this problem due to its explicit search for a tree representing a minimum number of distinct evolutionary events.

Types of Models

All substitution models assign a set of weights to each possible change of state represented in the sequence. The most common model types are implicitly reversible because they assign the same weight to, for example, a G>C nucleotide mutation as to a C>G mutation. The simplest possible model, the Jukes-Cantor model, assigns an equal probability to every possible change of state for a given nucleotide base. The rate of change between any two distinct nucleotides will be one-third of the overall substitution rate. More advanced models distinguish between transitions and transversions. The most general possible time-reversible model, called the GTR model, has six mutation rate parameters. An even more generalized model known as the general 12-parameter model breaks time-reversibility, at the cost of much additional complexity in calculating genetic distances that are consistent among multiple lineages. One possible variation on this theme adjusts the rates so that overall GC content - an important measure of DNA double helix stability - varies over time.

Models may also allow for the variation of rates with positions in the input sequence. The most obvious example of such variation follows from the arrangement of nucleotides in protein-coding genes into three-base codons. If the location of the open reading frame (ORF) is known, rates of mutation can be adjusted for position of a given site within a codon, since it is known that wobble base pairing can allow for higher mutation rates in the third nucleotide of a given codon without affecting the codon's meaning in the genetic code. A less hypothesis-driven example that does not rely on ORF identification simply assigns to each site a rate randomly drawn from a predetermined distribution, often the gamma distribution or log-normal distribution. Finally, a more conservative estimate of rate variations known as the covarion method allows autocorrelated variations in rates, so that the mutation rate of a given site is correlated across sites and lineages.

Choosing the Best Model

The selection of an appropriate model is critical for the production of good phyloge-netic analyses, both because underparameterized or overly restrictive models may pro-duce aberrant behavior when their underlying assumptions are violated, and because overly complex or overparameterized models are computationally expensive and the parameters may be overfit. The most common method of model selection is the likeli-hood ratio test (LRT), which produces a likelihood estimate that can be interpreted as a measure of "goodness of fit" between the model and the input data. However, care must be taken in using these results, since a more complex model with more parameters will always have a higher likelihood than a simplified version of the same model, which can lead to the naive selection of models that are overly complex. For this reason model selection computer programs will choose the simplest model that is not significantly worse than more complex substitution models. A significant disadvantage of the LRT is the necessity of making a series of pairwise comparisons between models; it has been shown that the order in which the models are compared has a major effect on the one that is eventually selected.

An alternative model selection method is the Akaike information criterion (AIC), for-mally an estimate of the Kullback–Leibler divergence between the true model and the model being tested. It can be interpreted as a likelihood estimate with a correction factor to penalize overparameterized models. The AIC is calculated on an individual model rather than a pair, so it is independent of the order in which models are assessed. A related alternative, the Bayesian information criterion (BIC), has a similar basic in-terpretation but penalizes complex models more heavily.

A comprehensive step-by-step protocol on constructing phylogenetic tree, including DNA/Amino Acid contiguous sequence assembly, multiple sequence alignment, mod-el-test (testing best-fitting substitution models) and phylogeny reconstruction using Maximum Likelihood and Bayesian Inference, is available at Nature Protocol

An non traditional way of evaluating the Pylogenetic Tree is to compare it with clus-tering result. One can use a Multidimensional Scaling technique, so called Interpola-tive Joining to do dimensionality reduction to visualize the clustering result for the sequences in 3D, and then map the phylogenetic tree onto the clustering result. A better tree usually has a higher correlation with the clustering result.

Evaluating Tree Support

As with all statistical analysis, the estimation of phylogenies from character data re-quires an evaluation of confidence. A number of methods exist to test the amount of support for a phylogenetic tree, either by evaluating the support for each sub-tree in the phylogeny (nodal support) or evaluating whether the phylogeny is significantly differ-ent from other possible trees (alternative tree hypothesis tests).

Nodal Support

The most common method for assessing tree support is to evaluate the statistical support for each node on the tree. Typically, a node with very low support is not considered valid in further analysis, and visually may be collapsed into a polytomy to indicate that relationships within a clade are unresolved.

Consensus Tree

Many methods for assessing nodal support involve consideration of multiple phylogenies. The consensus tree summarizes the nodes that are shared among a set of trees. In a *strict consensus,* only nodes found in every tree are shown, and the rest are collapsed into an unresolved polytomy. Less conservative methods, such as the *majority-rule consensus* tree, consider nodes that are supported by a given percentage of trees under consideration (such as at least 50%).

For example, in maximum parsimony analysis, there may be many trees with the same parsimony score. A strict consensus tree would show which nodes are found in all equally parsimonious trees, and which nodes differ. Consensus trees are also used to evaluate support on phylogenies reconstructed with Bayesian inference.

Bootstrapping and Jackknifing

In statistics, the bootstrap is a method for inferring the variability of data that has an unknown distribution using pseudoreplications of the original data. For example, given a set of 100 data points, a pseudoreplicate is a data set of the same size (100 points) randomly sampled from the original data, with replacement. That is, each original data point may be represented more than once in the pseudoreplicate, or not at all. Statistical support involves evaluation of whether the original data has similar properties to a large set of pseudoreplicates.

In phylogenetics, bootstrapping is conducted using the columns of the character matrix. Each pseudoreplicate contains the same number of species (rows) and characters (columns) randomly sampled from the original matrix, with replacement. A phylogeny is reconstructed from each pseudoreplicate, with the same methods used to reconstruct the phylogeny from the original data. For each node on the phylogeny, the nodal support is the percentage of pseudoreplicates containing that node.

The statistical rigor of the bootstrap test has been empirically evaluated using viral populations with known evolutionary histories, finding that 70% bootstrap support corresponds to a 95% probability that the clade exists. However, this was tested under ideal conditions (e.g. no change in evolutionary rates, symmetric phylogenies). In practice, values above 70% are generally supported and left to the researcher or reader to evaluate confidence. Nodes with support lower than 70% are typically considered unresolved.

Jackknifing in phylogenetics is a similar procedure, except the columns of the matrix are sampled without replacement. Pseudoreplicates are generated by randomly sub-sampling the data—for example, a "10% jackknife" would involve randomly sampling 10% of the matrix many times to evaluate nodal support.

Posterior Probability

Reconstruction of phylogenies using Bayesian inference generates a posterior distribution of highly probable trees given the data and evolutionary model, rather than a single "best" tree. The trees in the posterior distribution generally have many different topologies. Most Bayesian inference methods utilize a Markov-chain Monte Carlo iteration, and the initial steps of this chain are not considered reliable reconstructions of the phylogeny. Trees generated early in the chain are usually discarded as burn-in. The most common method of evaluating nodal support in a Bayesian phylogenetic analysis is to calculate the percentage of trees in the posterior distribution (post-burn-in) which contain the node.

The statistical support for a node in Bayesian inference is expected to reflect the probability that a clade really exists given the data and evolutionary model. Therefore, the threshold for accepting a node as supported is generally higher than for bootstrapping.

Step Counting Methods

Bremer support counts the number of extra steps needed to contradict a clade.

Shortcomings

These measures each have their weaknesses. For example, smaller or larger clades tend to attract larger support values than mid-sized clades, simply as a result of the number of taxa in them.

Bootstrap support can provide high estimates of node support as a result of noise in the data rather than the true existence of a clade.

Limitations and Workarounds

Ultimately, there is no way to measure whether a particular phylogenetic hypothesis is accurate or not, unless the true relationships among the taxa being examined are already known (which may happen with bacteria or viruses under laboratory conditions). The best result an empirical phylogeneticist can hope to attain is a tree with branches that are well supported by the available evidence. Several potential pitfalls have been identified:

Homoplasy

Certain characters are more likely to evolve convergently than others; logically, such characters should be given less weight in the reconstruction of a tree. Weights in the form of a model of evolution can be inferred from sets of molecular data, so that maximum likelihood or Bayesian methods can be used to analyze them. For molecular sequences, this problem is exacerbated when the taxa under study have diverged substantially. As time since the divergence of two taxa increase, so does the probability of multiple substitutions on the same site, or back mutations, all of which result in homoplasies. For morphological data, unfortunately, the only objective way to determine convergence is by the construction of a tree – a somewhat circular method. Even so, weighting homoplasious characters does indeed lead to better-supported trees. Further refinement can be brought by weighting changes in one direction higher than changes in another; for instance, the presence of thoracic wings almost guarantees placement among the pterygote insects because, although wings are often lost secondarily, there is no evidence that they have been gained more than once.

Horizontal Gene Transfer

In general, organisms can inherit genes in two ways: vertical gene transfer and horizontal gene transfer. Vertical gene transfer is the passage of genes from parent to offspring, and horizontal (also called lateral) gene transfer occurs when genes jump between unrelated organisms, a common phenomenon especially in prokaryotes; a good example of this is the acquired antibiotic resistance as a result of gene exchange between various bacteria leading to multi-drug-resistant bacterial species. There have also been well-documented cases of horizontal gene transfer between eukaryotes.

Horizontal gene transfer has complicated the determination of phylogenies of organisms, and inconsistencies in phylogeny have been reported among specific groups of organisms depending on the genes used to construct evolutionary trees. The only way to determine which genes have been acquired vertically and which horizontally is to parsimoniously assume that the largest set of genes that have been inherited together have been inherited vertically; this requires analyzing a large number of genes.

Hybrids, Speciation, Introgressions and Incomplete Lineage Sorting

The basic assumption underlying the mathematical model of cladistics is a situation where species split neatly in bifurcating fashion. While such an assumption may hold on a larger scale, speciation is often much less orderly. Research since the cladistic method was introduced has shown that hybrid speciation, once thought rare, is in fact quite common, particularly in plants. Also paraphyletic speciation is common, making the assumption of a bifurcating pattern unsuitable, leading to phylogenetic networks rather than trees. Introgression can also move genes between otherwise distinct species and sometimes even genera, complicating phylogenetic analysis based on genes. This phenomenon can contribute to "incomplete lineage sorting" and is thought to be a common phenomenon across a number of groups. In species level analysis this can be dealt with by larger sampling or better whole genome analysis. Often the problem is avoided by restricting the analysis to fewer, not closely related specimen.

Taxon Sampling

Owing to the development of advanced sequencing techniques in molecular biology, it has become feasible to gather large amounts of data (DNA or amino acid sequences) to infer phylogenetic hypotheses. For example, it is not rare to find studies with character matrices based on whole mitochondrial genomes (~16,000 nucleotides, in many animals). However, simulations have shown that it is more important to increase the number of taxa in the matrix than to increase the number of characters, because the more taxa there are, the more accurate and more robust is the resulting phylogenetic tree. This may be partly due to the breaking up of long branches.

Phylogenetic Signal

Another important factor that affects the accuracy of tree reconstruction is whether the data analyzed actually contain a useful phylogenetic signal, a term that is used generally to denote whether a character evolves slowly enough to have the same state in closely related taxa as opposed to varying randomly. Tests for phylogenetic signal exist.

Continuous Characters

Morphological characters that sample a continuum may contain phylogenetic signal, but are hard to code as discrete characters. Several methods have been used, one of which is gap coding, and there are variations on gap coding. In the original form of gap coding:

group means for a character are first ordered by size. The pooled within-group standard deviation is calculated ... and differences between adjacent means ... are compared relative to this standard deviation. Any pair of adjacent means is considered different and given different integer scores ... if the means are separated by a "gap" greater than the within-group standard deviation ... times some arbitrary constant.

If more taxa are added to the analysis, the gaps between taxa may become so small that all information is lost. Generalized gap coding works around that problem by comparing individual pairs of taxa rather than considering one set that contains all of the taxa.

Missing Data

In general, the more data that are available when constructing a tree, the more accurate and reliable the resulting tree will be. Missing data are no more detrimental than simply having fewer data, although the impact is greatest when most of the missing data are in a small number of taxa. Concentrating the missing data across a small number of characters produces a more robust tree.

The Role of Fossils

Because many characters involve embryological, or soft-tissue or molecular characters that (at best) hardly ever fossilize, and the interpretation of fossils is more ambiguous than that of living taxa, extinct taxa almost invariably have higher proportions of missing data than living ones. However, despite these limitations, the inclusion of fossils is invaluable, as they can provide information in sparse areas of trees, breaking up long branches and constraining intermediate character states; thus, fossil taxa contribute as much to tree resolution as modern taxa. Fossils can also constrain the age of lineages and thus demonstrate how consistent a tree is with the stratigraphic record; stratocladistics incorporates age information into data matrices for phylogenetic analyses.

References

- Favrin, Bean (2 September 2014). "esyN: Network Building, Sharing and Publishing.". PLOS ONE. 9: e106035. doi:10.1371/journal.pone.0106035. PMC 4152123 . PMID 25181461.

- Redding, Sy; Greene, Eric C. (May 2013). "How do proteins locate specific targets in DNA?". Chemical Physics Letters. 570: 1–11. doi:10.1016/j.cplett.2013.03.035.

- McDonagh, CF (2012) Antitumor Activity of a Novel Bispecific Antibody That Targets the ErbB2/ErbB3 Oncogenic Unit and Inhibits Heregulin-Induced Activation of ErbB3. Molecular Cancer Therapeutics.

- "A beginner's guide to eukaryotic genome annotation". Nature Reviews Genetics. 13: 329–342. May 2012. doi:10.1038/nrg3174.

- "NIH working definition of bioinformatics and computational biology" (PDF). Biomedical Information Science and Technology Initiative. 17 July 2000. Retrieved 18 August 2012.

- Hogeweg, Paulien (7 March 2011). "The Roots of Bioinformatics in Theoretical Biology". PLOS Computational Biology. 3. 7: e1002021. doi:10.1371/journal.pcbi.1002021.

Types of Bioinformatics Software

The software used in bioinformatics range from simple tools to complex graphical programs. The types of bioinformatics softwares elucidated in the following section are Biopython, bioconductor, BioPerl, BioJava, BioRuby and EMBOSS. Bioinformatics software is best understood in confluence with the major topics listed in the following chapter.

Biopython

The Biopython Project is an open-source collection of non-commercial Python tools for computational biology and bioinformatics, created by an international association of developers. It contains classes to represent biological sequences and sequence annotations, and it is able to read and write to a variety of file formats. It also allows for a programmatic means of accessing online databases of biological information, such as those at NCBI. Separate modules extend Biopython's capabilities to sequence alignment, protein structure, population genetics, phylogenetics, sequence motifs, and machine learning. Biopython is one of a number of Bio* projects designed to reduce code duplication in computational biology.

History

Biopython development began in 1999 and it was first released in July 2000. It was developed during a similar time frame and with analogous goals to other projects that added bioinformatics capabilities to their respective programming languages, including BioPerl, BioRuby and BioJava. Early developers on the project included Jeff Chang, Andrew Dalke and Brad Chapman, though over 100 people have made contributions to date. In 2007, a similar Python project, namely PyCogent, was established.

The initial scope of Biopython involved accessing, indexing and processing biological sequence files. While this is still a major focus, over the following years added modules have extended its functionality to cover additional areas of biology.

As of version 1.62, Biopython supports running on Python 3 as well as Python 2.

Design

Wherever possible, Biopython follows the conventions used by the Python programming language to make it easier for users familiar with Python. For example, Seq and SeqRecord objects can be manipulated via slicing, in a manner similar to Python's strings and lists. It is also designed to be functionally similar to other Bio* projects, such as BioPerl.

Biopython is able to read and write most common file formats for each of its functional areas, and its license is permissive and compatible with most other software licenses, which allow Biopython to be used in a variety of software projects.

Key Features and Examples

Sequences

A core concept in Biopython is the biological sequence, and this is represented by the Seq class. A Biopython Seq object is similar to a Python string in many respects: it supports the Python slice notation, can be concatenated with other sequences and is immutable. In addition, it includes sequence-specific methods and specifies the particular biological alphabet used.

```
>>> # This script creates a DNA sequence and performs some typical manipulations

>>> from Bio.Seq import Seq

>>> from Bio.Alphabet import IUPAC

>>> dna_sequence = Seq('AGGCTTCTCGTA', IUPAC.unambiguous_dna)

>>> dna_sequence

Seq('AGGCTTCTCGTA', IUPACUnambiguousDNA())

>>> dna_sequence[2:7]

Seq('GCTTC', IUPACUnambiguousDNA())

>>> dna_sequence.reverse_complement()

Seq('TACGAGAAGCCT', IUPACUnambiguousDNA())

>>> rna_sequence = dna_sequence.transcribe()

>>> rna_sequence

Seq('AGGCUUCUCGUA', IUPACUnambiguousRNA())

>>> rna_sequence.translate()

Seq('RLLV', IUPACProtein())
```

Sequence Annotation

The SeqRecord class describes sequences, along with information such as name, description and features in the form of SeqFeature objects. Each SeqFeature object specifies the type of the feature and its location. Feature types can be 'gene', 'CDS' (coding sequence), 'repeat_region', 'mobile_element' or others, and the position of features in the sequence can be exact or approximate.

```
>>> # This script loads an annotated sequence from file and views some of its contents.

>>> from Bio import SeqIO

>>> seq_record = SeqIO.read('pTC2.gb', 'genbank')

>>> seq_record.name

'NC_019375'

>>> seq_record.description

'Providencia stuartii plasmid pTC2, complete sequence.'

>>> seq_record.features

SeqFeature(FeatureLocation(ExactPosition(4516), ExactPosition(5336), strand=1), type='mobile_element')

>>> seq_record.seq

Seq('GGATTGAATATAACCGACGTGACTGTTACATTTAGGTGGCTAAACCCGT-CAAGC...GCC', IUPACAmbiguousDNA())
```

Input and Output

Biopython can read and write to a number of common sequence formats, including FASTA, FASTQ, GenBank, Clustal, PHYLIP and NEXUS. When reading files, descriptive information in the file is used to populate the members of Biopython classes, such as SeqRecord. This allows records of one file format to be converted into others.

Very large sequence files can exceed a computer's memory resources, so Biopython provides various options for accessing records in large files. They can be loaded entirely into memory in Python data structures, such as lists or dictionaries, providing fast access at the cost of memory usage. Alternatively, the files can be read from disk as needed, with slower performance but lower memory requirements.

```
>>> # This script loads a file containing multiple sequences and saves each one in a different format.

>>> from Bio import SeqIO

>>> genomes = SeqIO.parse('salmonella.gb', 'genbank')
```

```
>>> for genome in genomes:

...    SeqIO.write(genome, genome.id + '.fasta', 'fasta')
```

Accessing Online Databases

Through the Bio.Entrez module, users of Biopython can download biological data from NCBI databases. Each of the functions provided by the Entrez search engine is available through functions in this module, including searching for and downloading records.

```
>>> # This script downloads genomes from the NCBI Nucleotide database and saves
them in a FASTA file.

>>> from Bio import Entrez

>>> from Bio import SeqIO

>>> output_file = open('all_records.fasta', "w")

>>> Entrez.email = 'my_email@example.com'

>>> records_to_download = ['FO834906.1', 'FO203501.1']

>>> for record_id in records_to_download:

...    handle = Entrez.efetch(db='nucleotide', id=record_id, rettype='gb')

...    seqRecord = SeqIO.read(handle, format='gb')

...    handle.close()

...    output_file.write(seqRecord.format('fasta'))
```

Phylogeny

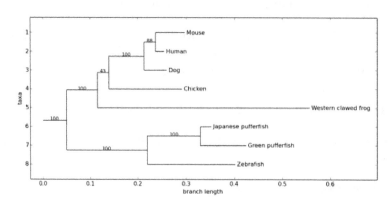

Figure: A rooted phylogenetic tree created by Bio.Phylo showing the relationship between different organisms' Apaf-1 homologs

Figure: The same tree as above, drawn unrooted using Graphviz via Bio.Phylo

The Bio.Phylo module provides tools for working with and visualising phylogenetic trees. A variety of file formats are supported for reading and writing, including Newick, NEXUS and phyloXML. Common tree manipulations and traversals are supported via the Tree and Clade objects. Examples include converting and collating tree files, extracting subsets from a tree, changing a tree's root, and analysing branch features such as length or score.

Rooted trees can be drawn in ASCII or using matplotlib, and the Graphviz library can be used to create unrooted layouts.

Genome Diagrams

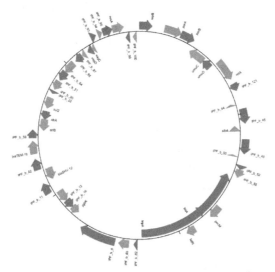

Figure: A diagram of the genes on the pKPS77 plasmid, visualised using the GenomeDiagram module in Biopython

The GenomeDiagram module provides methods of visualising sequences within Biopython. Sequences can be drawn in a linear or circular form, and many output formats are supported, including PDF and PNG. Diagrams are created by making tracks and then adding sequence features to those tracks. By looping over a sequence's features and using their attributes to decide if and how they are added to the diagram's tracks, one can exercise much control over the appearance of the final diagram. Cross-links can be drawn between different tracks, allowing one to compare multiple sequences in a single diagram.

Macromolecular Structure

The Bio.PDB module can load molecular structures from PDB and mmCIF files, and was added to Biopython in 2003. The Structure object is central to this module, and it organises macromolecular structure in a hierarchical fashion: Structure objects contain Model objects which contain Chain objects which contain Residue objects which contain Atom objects. Disordered residues and atoms get their own classes, DisorderedResidue and DisorderedAtom, that describe their uncertain positions.

Using Bio.PDB, one can navigate through individual components of a macromolecular structure file, such as examining each atom in a protein. Common analyses can be carried out, such as measuring distances or angles, comparing residues and calculating residue depth.

Population Genetics

The Bio.PopGen module adds support to Biopython for Genepop, a software package for statistical analysis of population genetics. This allows for analyses of Hardy–Weinberg equilibrium, linkage disequilibrium and other features of a population's allele frequencies.

This module can also carry out population genetic simulations using coalescent theory with the fastsimcoal2 program.

Wrappers for Command Line Tools

Many of Biopython's modules contain command line wrappers for commonly used tools, allowing these tools to be used from within Biopython. These wrappers include BLAST, Clustal, PhyML, EMBOSS and SAMtools. Users can subclass a generic wrapper class to add support for any other command line tool.

Bioconductor

Bioconductor is a free, open source and open development software project for the analysis and comprehension of genomic data generated by wet lab experiments in molecular biology.

Bioconductor is based primarily on the statistical R programming language, but does contain contributions in other programming languages. It has two releases each year that follow the semiannual releases of R. At any one time there is a release version, which corresponds to the released version of R, and a development version, which corresponds to the development version of R. Most users will find the release version appropriate for their needs. In addition there are a large number of genome annotation packages available that are mainly, but not solely, oriented towards different types of microarrays.

The project was started in the Fall of 2001 and is overseen by the Bioconductor core team, based primarily at the Fred Hutchinson Cancer Research Center, with other members coming from international institutions.

Packages

Most Bioconductor components are distributed as R packages, which are add-on modules for R. Initially most of the Bioconductor software packages focused on the analysis of single channel Affymetrix and two or more channel cDNA/Oligo microarrays. As the project has matured, the functional scope of the software packages broadened to include the analysis of all types of genomic data, such as SAGE, sequence, or SNP data.

Goals

The broad goals of the projects are to:

- Provide widespread access to a broad range of powerful statistical and graphical methods for the analysis of genomic data.

- Facilitate the inclusion of biological metadata in the analysis of genomic data, e.g. literature data from PubMed, annotation data from LocusLink/Entrez.

- Provide a common software platform that enables the rapid development and deployment of plug-able, scalable, and interoperable software.

- Further scientific understanding by producing high-quality documentation and reproducible research.

- Train researchers on computational and statistical methods for the analysis of genomic data.

Main Features

- The R Project for Statistical Computing. R and the R package system provides a broad range of advantages to the Bioconductor project including:

   o It contains a high-level interpreted language in which one can easily and quickly prototype new computational methods.

- o It includes a well established system for packaging together software components and documentation.

- o It can address the diversity and complexity of computational biology and bioinformatics problems in a common object-oriented framework.

- o It provides access to on-line computational biology and bioinformatics data sources.

- o It supports a rich set of statistical simulation and modeling activities.

- o It contains cutting edge data and model visualization capabilities.

- o It has been the basis for pathbreaking research in parallel statistical computing.

- o It is under very active development by a dedicated team of researchers with a strong commitment to good documentation and software design.

- Documentation and reproducible research. Each Bioconductor package contains at least one vignette, which is a document that provides a textual, task-oriented description of the package's functionality. These vignettes come in several forms. Many are simple "How-to"s that are designed to demonstrate how a particular task can be accomplished with that package's software. Others provide a more thorough overview of the package or might even discuss general issues related to the package. In the future, the Bioconductor project is looking towards providing vignettes that are not specifically tied to a package, but rather are demonstrating more complex concepts. As with all aspects of the Bioconductor project, users are encouraged to participate in this effort.

- Statistical and graphical methods. The Bioconductor project aims to provide access to a wide range of powerful statistical and graphical methods for the analysis of genomic data. Analysis packages are available for: pre-processing Affymetrix and Illumina, cDNA array data; identifying differentially expressed genes; graph theoretical analyses; plotting genomic data. In addition, the R package system itself provides implementations for a broad range of state-of-the-art statistical and graphical techniques, including linear and non-linear modeling, cluster analysis, prediction, resampling, survival analysis, and time series analysis.

- Genome Annotation. The Bioconductor project provides software for associating microarray and other genomic data in real time to biological metadata from web databases such as GenBank, LocusLink and PubMed (annotate package). Functions are also provided for incorporating the results of statistical analysis in HTML reports with links to annotation WWW resources. Software tools are available for assembling and processing genomic annotation data, from databases such as GenBank, the Gene Ontology Consortium, LocusLink, UniGene, the UCSC Human Genome Project and others with the AnnotationDbi package. Data packages are distributed to provide mappings between different probe identifiers (e.g. Affy IDs, LocusLink, PubMed). Customized annotation libraries can also be assembled.

- Open source. The Bioconductor project has a commitment to full open source discipline, with distribution via a SourceForge.net-like platform. All contributions are expected to exist under an open source license such as Artistic 2.0, GPL2, or BSD. There are many different reasons why open-source software is beneficial to the analysis of microarray data and to computational biology in general. The reasons include:

  o To provide full access to algorithms and their implementation

  o To facilitate software improvements through bug fixing and plug-ins

  o To encourage good scientific computing and statistical practice by providing appropriate tools and instruction

  o To provide a workbench of tools that allow researchers to explore and expand the methods used to analyze biological data

  o To ensure that the international scientific community is the owner of the software tools needed to carry out research

  o To lead and encourage commercial support and development of those tools that are successful

  o To promote reproducible research by providing open and accessible tools with which to carry out that research (reproducible research is distinct from independent verification)

- Open development. Users are encouraged to become developers, either by contributing Bioconductor compliant packages or documentation. Additionally Bioconductor provides a mechanism for linking together different groups with common goals to foster collaboration on software, possibly at the level of shared development.

Milestones

Version	Release Date	Package Count	Dependency
1.0	1 May 2001	15	R 1.5
1.1	9 Nov 2002	20	R 1.6
1.2	29 May 2003	30	R 1.7

1.3	30 Oct 2003	49	R 1.8
1.4	17 May 2004	81	R 1.9
1.5	25 Oct 2004	100	R 2.0
1.6	18 May 2005	123	R 2.1
1.7	14 Oct 2005	141	R 2.2
1.8	27 Apr 2006	172	R 2.3
1.9	4 Oct 2006	188	R 2.4
2.0	26 Apr 2007	214	R 2.5
2.1	8 Oct 2007	233	R 2.6
2.2	1 May 2008	260	R 2.7
2.3	22 Oct 2008	294	R 2.8
2.4	21 Apr 2009	320	R 2.9
2.5	28 Oct 2009	352	R 2.10
2.6	23 Apr 2010	389	R 2.11
2.7	18 Oct 2010	418	R 2.12
2.8	14 Apr 2011	466	R 2.13
2.9	1 Nov 2011	517	R 2.14
2.10	2 Apr 2012	554	R 2.15
2.11	3 Oct 2012	610	R 2.15
2.12	4 Apr 2013	671	R 3.0
2.13	15 Oct 2013	749	R 3.0
2.14	14 Apr 2014	824	R 3.1
3.0	14 Oct 2014	934	R 3.1
3.1	17 Apr 2015	1024	R 3.2
3.2	14 Oct 2015	1104	R 3.2
3.3	4 May 2016	1211	R 3.3
3.4	18 Oct 2016	1296	R 3.3

BioPerl

BioPerl is a collection of Perl modules that facilitate the development of Perl scripts for bioinformatics applications. It has played an integral role in the Human Genome Project.

Background

BioPerl is an active open source software project supported by the Open Bioinformatics Foundation. The first set of Perl codes of Bioperl was created by Tim Hubbard and Jong Bhak at MRC Centre Cambridge where the first genome sequencing was carried out by

Fred Sanger. MRC Centre was one of the hubs and birth places of modern bioinformatics as it had large amount of DNA sequences and 3D protein structures. The name Bioperl was coined jointly by Jong Bhak and Steve Brenner in a small room of Centre for Protein Engineering (CPE) of MRC Centre where Alan Fersht was the director. In that small room, Cyrus Chothia and Tim Hubbard were working with some of their Ph.D. students and colleagues. Tim Hubbard is an expert Perl programmer and he was using th_lib.pl that contained many useful Perl subroutines for bioinformatics. Jong Bhak, being the first Ph.D. student of Tim Hubbard created jong_lib.pl. Jong merged the two Perl subroutine libraries into Bio.pl. One day in 1995, Steve Brenner, a Ph.D. student of Cyrus Chothia visited the room and started to discuss what they would call the perl library after some lengthy (a few months) debate on whether Perl is superior to C for bioinformatics as Steve Brenner had his own C library for bioinformatics. The two Ph.D. students named the net Perl library for biology Bioperl after going through names such as protein perl, protperl, PerlBio, and so on. Steve Brenner organized a Bioperl session in 1995 at ISMB Cambridge although it did not really happen. Bioperl had some users in coming months including Georg Fuellen who organized a training course in Germany. Georg's colleagues and students extended the Bioperl much and this was joined later by other people such as Steve Chervitz who was actively developing Perl codes for his yeast genome DB. The major expansion came when another Cambridge student Ewan Birney joined the wagon after another lengthy debate on if Perl was superior to C for bioinformatics and Ewan and many other people were very active in developing Bioperl.

The first stable release was on 11 June 2002; the most recent stable (in terms of API) release is 1.6.9 from 14 April 2011. There are also developer releases produced periodically. Version series 1.6.0 is considered to be the most stable (in terms of bugs) version of BioPerl and is recommended for everyday use, but the nightly builds are also extremely stable, and many BioPerl users stay current with those.

In order to take advantage of BioPerl, the user needs a basic understanding of the Perl programming language including an understanding of how to use Perl references, modules, objects and methods.

Features

BioPerl provides software modules for many of the typical tasks of bioinformatics programming. These include:

- Accessing nucleotide and peptide sequence data from local and remote databases

- Transforming formats of database/ file records

- Manipulating individual sequences

- Searching for similar sequences

- Creating and manipulating sequence alignments

- Searching for genes and other structures on genomic DNA

- Developing machine readable sequence annotations

Usage

In addition to being used directly by end-users, BioPerl has also provided the base for a wide variety of bioinformatic tools, including amongst others:

- SynBrowse

- GeneComber

- TFBS

- MIMOX

- BioParser

- Degenerate primer design

- Querying the public databases

- Current Comparative Table

New tools and algorithms from external developers are often integrated directly into BioPerl itself:

- Dealing with phylogenetic trees and nested taxa

- FPC Web tools

Related Libraries in Other Programming Languages

Several related bioinformatics libraries implemented in other programming languages exist as part of the Open Bioinformatics Foundation including:

- Biopython

- BioJava

- BioRuby

- BioPHP

- BioJS

- Bioconductor

BioJava

BioJava is an open source project dedicated to providing Java tools for processing biological data. BioJava is a set of library functions written in the Java programming language for manipulating sequences, protein structures, file parsers, CORBA interoperability, DAS, access to AceDB, dynamic programming, and simple statistical routines. BioJava supports a huge range of data, starting from DNA and protein sequences to the level of 3D protein structures. The BioJava libraries are useful for automating many daily and mundane bioinformatics tasks such as to parsing a PDB file, interacting with Jmol and many more. This Application programming interface (API) provides various file parsers, data models and algorithms to facilitate working with the standard data formats and enables rapid application development and analysis. These libraries have also been used in development of various extended analysis tools , for example:

- MUSI: an integrated system for identifying multiple specificity from very large peptide or nucleic acid data sets.

- JEnsembl: a version-aware Java API to Ensembl data systems.

- Expression profiling of signature gene sets with trinucleotide threading

- Resolving the structural features of genomic islands: a machine learning approach

- Utility library for structural bioinformatics

The BioJava project grew out of work by Thomas Down and Matthew Pocock to create an API to simplify development of Java-based Bioinformatics tools. BioJava is an active open source project that has been developed over more than 12 years and by more than 60 developers. BioJava is one of a number of Bio* projects designed to reduce code duplication. Examples of such projects that fall under Bio* apart from BioJava are BioPython, BioPerl, BioRuby, EMBOSS etc.

The latest version of BioJava (3.0.5) is a major update to the previous versions. The new version of BioJava contains several independent modules. The old project has been moved to a separate project called biojava-legacy project.

Features

BioJava provides software modules for many of the typical tasks of bioinformatics programming. These include:

- Accessing nucleotide and peptide sequence data from local and remote databases

- Transforming formats of database/ file records

- Protein structure parsing and manipulation

- Manipulating individual sequences

- Searching for similar sequences

- Creating and manipulating sequence alignments

History and Publications

In the year 2008, BioJava's first Application note was published. It was migrated from its original CVS repository to Git hub on April 2013.

In October 2012, the most recent paper on BioJava was published. As of November 2012 Google Scholar counts more than 130 citations.

Modules

Over the last 2 years, large parts of the original code base have been rewritten. BioJava 3 is a clear departure from the version 1 series. It now consists of several independent modules built using an automation tool called Apache Maven. These modules provide state-of-the-art tools for protein structure comparison, pairwise and multiple sequence alignments, working with DNA and protein sequences, analysis of amino acid properties, detection of protein modifications and prediction of disordered regions in proteins as well as parsers for common file formats using a biologically meaningful data model. The original code has been moved into a separate BioJava legacy project, which is still available for backwards compatibility.

The following sections will describe several of the new modules and highlight some of the new features that are included in the latest version of BioJava.

Core Module

This module provides Java classes to model amino acid or nucleotide sequences. The classes were designed keeping in mind that they should be familiar to the biologists i.e. the names should make sense to the biologists and at the same time also provide a concrete representation of the steps in going from a gene sequence to a protein sequence for the computer scientists and programmers.

A major change between the legacy BioJava project and BioJava3 lies in the way framework has been designed to take advantage of the recent innovations in Java. A sequence is defined as a generic interface allowing the rest of the modules to create any utility that operates on all sequences. Specific classes for common sequences such as DNA and proteins have been defined in order to improve usability for biologists. The translation engine really leverages this work by allowing conversions between DNA, RNA and amino acid sequences. This engine can handle details such as choosing the codon table, converting start codons to methionine, trimming stop codons, specifying the reading frame and handing ambiguous sequences.

Special attentions has been paid in designing the storage of sequences so as to minimize space requirements. Special design patterns such as the Proxy pattern allowed the developers to create the framework such that sequences can be stored in memory, fetched on demand from a web service such as UniProt or read from a FASTA file as needed. The latter two approaches save memory by not loading sequence data until it is referenced in the application. This concept can be extended to handle very large genomic datasets, such as NCBI GenBank or a proprietary database.

Protein Structure Modules

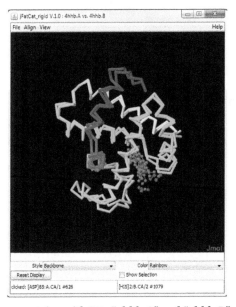

This window shows two proteins with IDs "4hhb.A" and "4hhb.B" aligned against each other. The code is given on the left side. This is produced using BioJava libraries which in turn uses Jmol viewer. The FATCAT rigid algorithm is used here to do the alignment.

The protein structure modules provide tools for representing and manipulating 3D biomolecular structures. It particularly focuses on protein structure comparison. The following algorithms have been implemented and included in BioJava.

- FATCAT algorithm for flexible and rigid body alignment.

- The standard Combinatorial Extension (CE) algorithm.

- A new version of CE that can detect circular permutations in proteins.

These algorithms are used to provide the RCSB Protein Data Bank (PDB) Protein Comparison Tool as well as systematic comparisons of all proteins in the PDB on a weekly basis. Parsers for PDB and mmCIF file formats allow the loading of structure data into a reusable data model. This feature is used by the SIFTS project to map between UniProt sequences and PDB structures. Information from the RCSB PDB can be dynamically fetched without the need to manually download data. For visualization, an interface to the 3D viewer Jmol http://www.jmol.org/ is provided. The team claims that work is underway to improve interaction with the RCSB PDB viewers.

Below is an outline of the code to initialize a window that will display and compare two protein sequences. Please bear in mind that this is just an outline of the code. To make this work one will need to import the correct found in the "org.biojava.bio.structure" package and add also handle exceptions by using a try-catch block.

```
String name1 = "4hhb.A";

String name2 = "4hhb.B";

AtomCache cache = new AtomCache();

Structure structure1 = null;

Structure structure2 = null;

StructureAlignment algorithm =

StructureAlignmentFactory.getAlgorithm(FatCatRigid.algorithmName);

structure1 = cache.getStructure(name1);

structure2 = cache.getStructure(name2);

Atom [ ] ca1 = StructureTools.getAtomCAArray(structure1);

Atom [ ] ca2 = StructureTools.getAtomCAArray(structure2);

FatCatParameters params = new FatCatParameters();

AFPChain afpChain = algorithm.align(ca1,ca2,params);

afpChain.setName1(name1);

afpChain.setName2(name2);

StructureAlignmentDisplay.display(afpChain, ca1, ca2);
```

The code aligns the two protein sequences "4hhb.A" and "4hhb.B" based on the FAT-CAT rigid algorithm.

Genome and Sequencing Modules

This module is focused on the creation of gene sequence objects from the core module.

This is realised by supporting the parsing of the following popular standard file formats generated by open source gene prediction applications:

- GTF files generated by GeneMark

- GFF2 files generated by GeneID

- GFF3 files generated by Glimmer

Then the gene sequence objects are written out as a GFF3 format and is imported into GMOD. These file formats are well defined but what gets written in the file is very flexible.

The following code example takes a 454scaffold file that was used by genemark to predict genes and returns a collection of ChromosomeSequences. Each chromosome sequence maps to a named entry in the fasta file and would contain N gene sequences. The gene sequences can be +/- strand with frame shifts and multiple transcriptions.

Passing the collection of ChromosomeSequences to GeneFeatureHelper.getProteinSequences would return all protein sequences. You can then write the protein sequences to a fasta file.

LinkedHashMap<String, ChromosomeSequence> chromosomeSequenceList =

        GeneFeatureHelper.loadFastaAddGeneFeaturesFromGeneMarkGTF(new File("454Scaffolds.fna"), new File("genemark_hmm.gtf"));

LinkedHashMap<String, ProteinSequence> proteinSequenceList = GeneFeatureHelper.getProteinSequences(chromosomeSequenceList.values());

FastaWriterHelper.writeProteinSequence(new File("genemark_proteins.faa"), proteinSequenceList.values());

You can also output the gene sequence to a fasta file where the coding regions will be upper case and the non-coding regions will be lower case

LinkedHashMap<String, GeneSequence> geneSequenceHashMap = GeneFeatureHelper.getGeneSequences(chromosomeSequenceList.values());

Collection<GeneSequence> geneSequences = geneSequenceHashMap.values();

FastaWriterHelper.writeGeneSequence(new File("genemark_genes.fna"), geneSequences, true);

You can easily write out a gff3 view of a ChromosomeSequence with the following code.

FileOutputStream fo = new FileOutputStream("genemark.gff3");

GFF3Writer gff3Writer = new GFF3Writer();

gff3Writer.write(fo, chromosomeSequenceList);

fo.close();

For providing input-output support for several common variants of the FASTQ file format from the next generation sequencers, a separate sequencing module is provided. It is called the Sequence Module and is contained in the package org.biojava3.sequencing.io.fastq. For samples on how to use this module please go to this link.

Work is in progress towards providing a complete set of java classes to do conversions between different file formats where the list of supported gene prediction applications and genome browsers will get longer based on end user requests.

Alignment Module

This module contains several classes and methods that allow users to perform pairwise and multiple sequence alignment.

Pairwise sequence alignmentFor optimal global alignment, BioJava implements the Needleman-Wunsch algorithm and for performing local alignments the Smith and Waterman's algorithm has been implemented. The outputs of both local and global alignments are available in standard formats.

An example on how to use the libraries is shown below.

protected void align(String uniProtID_1, String uniProtID_2, PairwiseSequenceAlignerType alignmentType) throws IOException, Exception {

      ProteinSequence proteinSeq1 = FastaReaderHelper.readFastaProteinSequence((new URL(String.format

            ("http://www.uniprot.org/uniprot/%s.fasta",   uniProtID_1))).openStream()).get(uniProtID_1);

      ProteinSequence proteinSeq2 = FastaReaderHelper.readFastaProteinSequence((new URL(String.format

            ("http://www.uniprot.org/uniprot/%s.fasta",   uniProtID_2))).openStream()).get(uniProtID_2);

      SequencePair<ProteinSequence, AminoAcidCompound> result = Alignments.getPairwiseAlignment(proteinSeq1, proteinSeq2,

      alignmentType, new SimpleGapPenalty(), new SimpleSubstitutionMatrix<AminoAcidCompound>());

```
        System.out.println(result.toString());

}
```

An example call to the above function would look something like this:

For Global Alignment

align("Q21691", "Q21495", PairwiseSequenceAlignerType.GLOBAL);

For Local Alignment

align("Q21691", "Q21495", PairwiseSequenceAlignerType.LOCAL);

In addition to these two algorithms, there is an implementation of Guan–Uberbacher algorithm which performs global sequence alignment very efficiently since it only uses linear memory.

For Multiple Sequence Alignment, any of the methods discussed above can be used to progressively perform a multiple sequence alignment.

ModFinder Module

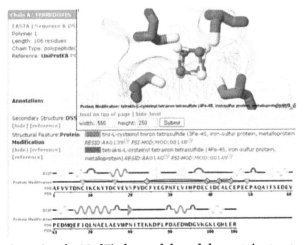

An example application using the ModFinder module and the protein structure module. Protein modifications are mapped onto the sequence and structure of ferredoxin I (PDB ID 1GAO). Two possible iron–sulfur clusters are shown on the protein sequence (3Fe–4S (F3S): orange triangles/lines; 4Fe–4S (SF4): purple diamonds/ lines). The 4Fe–4S cluster is displayed in the Jmol structure window above the sequence display

The ModFinder module provides new methods to identify and classify protein modifications in protein 3D structures. Over 400 different types of protein modifications such as phosphorylation, glycosylation, disulfide bonds metal chelation etc. were collected and curated based on annotations in PSI-MOD, RESID and RCSB PDB. The module also provides an API for detecting protein modifications within protein structures.

Example: Identify and Print all Preloaded Modifications from a Structure

```
Set<ModifiedCompound> identifyAllModfications(Structure struc) {

        ProteinModificationIdentifier parser =

                new ProteinModificationIdentifier();

        parser.identify(struc);

        Set<ModifiedCompound> mcs =

                parser.getIdentifiedModifiedCompound();

        return mcs;

}
```

Example: Identify Phosphorylation Sites in a Structure

```
List<ResidueNumber> identifyPhosphosites(Structure struc) {

        List<ResidueNumber> phosphosites = new ArrayList<ResidueNumber>();

        ProteinModificationIdentifier parser =

                new ProteinModificationIdentifier();

        parser.identify(struc,

                ProteinModificationRegistry.getByKeyword("phosphoprotein"));

        Set<ModifiedCompound> mcs = parser.getIdentifiedModifiedCompound();

        for (ModifiedCompound mc : mcs) {

                Set<StructureGroup> groups = mc.getGroups(true);

                for (StructureGroup group : groups) {

                        phosphosites.add(group.getPDBResidueNumber());

                }

        }

        return phosphosites;

}
```

Demo Code to Run the Above Methods

```java
import org.biojava.bio.structure.ResidueNumber;

import org.biojava.bio.structure.Structure;

import org.biojava.bio.structure.io.PDBFileReader;

import org.biojava3.protmod.structure.ProteinModificationIdentifier;


public static void main(String [ ] args) {
        try {

                PDBFileReader reader = new PDBFileReader();
                reader.setAutoFetch(true);


                // identify all modifications from PDB:1CAD and print them
                String pdbId = "1CAD";
                Structure struc = reader.getStructureById(pdbId);
                Set<ModifiedCompound> mcs = identifyAllModfications(struc);
                for (ModifiedCompound mc : mcs) {
                        System.out.println(mc.toString());
                }


                // identify all phosphosites from PDB:3MVJ and print them
                pdbId = "3MVJ";
                struc = reader.getStructureById(pdbId);
                List<ResidueNumber> psites = identifyPhosphosites(struc);
                for (ResidueNumber psite : psites) {
                        System.out.println(psite.toString());
                }
```

```
    } catch(Exception e) {

            e.printStackTrace();

    }

}
```

There are plans to include additional protein modifications by integrating other resources such as UniProt

Amino Acid Properties Module

This module attempts to provide accurate physio-chemical properties of proteins. The
properties that can calculated using this module are as follows:

- Molecular mass

- Extinction coefficient

- Instability index

- Aliphatic index

- Grand average of hydropathy

- Isoelectric point

- Amino acid composition

The precise molecular weights for common isotopically labelled amino acids are
included in this module. There also exists flexibility to define new amino acid molecules with their molecular weights using simple XML configuration files. This can
be useful where the precise mass is of high importance such as mass spectrometry
experiments.

Protein Disorder Module

The goal of this module is to provide users ways to find disorders in protein molecules.
BioJava includes a Java implementation of the RONN predictor. The latest version of
BioJava(3.0.5) makes use of Java's support for multithreading to improve performance
by up to 3.2 times, on a modern quad-core machine, as compared to the legacy C implementation.

There are two ways to use this module:

- Using library function calls

- Using command line

Making Library Function Calls

The following examples show how to use the module and make function calls to get information about protein disorders. The first two examples make library function calls to calculate the probability of disorder for every residue in the sequence provided.

The third and fourth examples demonstrates how easily one can get the disordered regions of the protein.

Example 1: Calculate the Probability of Disorder for Every Residue in the Sequence

FastaSequence fsequence = new FastaSequence("name", "LLRGRHLMNGTMIMRP-WNFLNDHHFPKFFPHLIEQQAIWLADWWRKKHC" +

"RPLPTRAPTMDQWDHFALIQKHWTANLW-FLTFPFNDKWGWIWFLKDWTPGSADQAQRACTWFFCHGHDTN");

float[]   rawProbabilityScores = Jronn.getDisorderScores(fsequence);

Example 2: Calculate the Probability of Disorder for Every Residue in the Sequence for All Proteins from the FASTA Input File

final List<FastaSequence> sequences = SequenceUtil.readFasta(new FileInput-Stream("src/test/resources/fasta.in"));

Map<FastaSequence, float[]> rawProbabilityScores = Jronn.getDisorderScores(se-quences);

Example 3: Get the Disordered Regions of the Protein for a Single Protein Sequence

FastaSequence fsequence = new FastaSequence("Prot1", "LLRGRHLMNGTMIMRP-WNFLNDHHFPKFFPHLIEQQAIWLADWWRKKHC" +

"RPLPTRAPTMDQWDHFALIQKHWTANLW-FLTFPFNDKWGWIWFLKDWTPGSADQAQRACTWFFCHGHDTN" +

"CQIIFEGRNAPERADPMWTGGLNKHIIAR-GHFFQSNKFHFLERKFCEMAEIERPNFTCRTLDCQKFPWDDP");

Range[] ranges = Jronn.getDisorder(fsequence);

Example 4: Calculate the Disordered Regions for the Proteins from FASTA File

final List<FastaSequence> sequences = SequenceUtil.readFasta(new FileInput-

Stream("src/test/resources/fasta.in"));

Map<FastaSequence, Range [ ] > ranges = Jronn.getDisorder(sequences);

Using Command Line

BioJava module *biojava3-protein-disorder* can be compiled into a single executable JAR file and run using the following command.

java -jar <jar_file_name>

Options Supported by the Command Line Executable

JRONN version 3.1b usage 1 August 2011:

java -jar JRONN_JAR_NAME -i=inputfile <OPTIONS>

Where -i=input file

> Input file can contain one or more FASTA formatted sequences.

All OPTIONS are optional

OPTION DETAILED DESCRIPTION:

> -o full path to the output file, if not specified

> standard out is used

> -d the value of disorder, defaults to 0.5

> -f output format, V for vertical, where the letters

> of the sequence and corresponding disorder values are

> output in two column layout. H for horizontal, where the

> disorder values are provided under the letters of the

> sequence. Letters and values separated by tabulation in

this case. Defaults to V.

-s the file name to write execution statistics to.

-n the number of threads to use. Defaults to the number of

cores available on the computer. n=1 mean sequential

processing. Valid values are 1 < n < (2 x num_of_cores)

Default value will give the best performance.

Examples

Predict disorder values for sequences from input file */home/input.fasta* output the results to the *standard out*. Use default disorder value and utilise all CPUs available on
the computer.

java -jar JRONN.JAR -i=/home/input.fasta

Predict disorder values for sequences from input file */home/input.fasta* output the results in horizontal layout to the */home/jronn.out*, collect execution statistics to */home/
jronn.stat.txt* file and limit the number of threads to two.

java -jar JRONN.JAR -i=/home/input.fasta -o=/home/jronn.out -d=0.6 -n=2 -f=H

The arguments can be provided in any order.

Web Service Access Module

As per the current trends in bioinformatics, web based tools are gaining popularity.
The web service module allows bioinformatics services to be accessed using REST protocols. Currently, two services are implemented: NCBI Blast through the Blast URLAPI
(previously known as QBlast) and the HMMER web service.

Comparisons with Other Alternatives

The need for customized software in the field of bioinformatics has been addressed by
several groups and individuals. Similar to BioJava, open source projects such as BioP-
erl, BioPython and BioRuby all provide tool-kits with multiple functionality that make
it easier to create customized pipelines or analysis.

As the names suggest, the projects mentioned above use different programming languages. All of these APIs offer similar tools so on what criteria should one base their

choice? For programmers who are experienced in only one of these languages, the choice is straightforward. However, for a well-rounded bioinformaticist who knows all of these languages and wants to choose the best language for a job the choice can be made based on the following guidelines given by a software review done on the Bio* tool-kits.

In general, for small programs (<500 lines) that will be used only by a small group or individual, it is hard to beat Perl and BioPerl. These constraints probably cover the needs of 90 per cent of personal bioinformatics programming requirements.

For beginners, and for writing larger programs in the Bio domain, especially those to be shared and supported by others, Python's clarity and brevity make it very attractive.

For those who might be leaning towards a career in bioinformatics and who want to learn only one language, Java has the widest general programming support, very good support in the Bio domain with BioJava, and is now the de facto language of business (the new COBOL, for better or worse).

Apart from these Bio* projects there is another project called STRAP which uses Java and aims for similar goals. The STRAP-toolbox, similar to BioJava is also a Java-toolkit for the design of Bioinformatics programs and scripts. The similarities and differences between BioJava and STRAP are as follows:

Similarities

- Both provide comprehensive collections of methods for protein sequences.

- Both are used by Java programmers for coding Bioinformatics algorithms.

- Both separate implementations and definitions by using java interfaces.

- Both are open source projects.

- Both can read and write many sequence file formats.

Differences

- BioJava is applicable to nucleotide and peptide sequences and can be applied for entire genomes. STRAP cannot cope with single sequences as long as an entire chromosome. Instead STRAP manipulates peptide sequences and 3D- structures of the size of single proteins. Nevertheless, it can hold a high number of sequences and structures in memory. STRAP is designed for protein sequences but can read coding nucleotide files, which are then translated to peptide sequences.

- STRAP is very fast since the graphical user interface must be highly responsive. BioJava is used where speed is less critical.

- BioJava is well designed in terms of type safety, ontology and object design. BioJava uses objects for sequences, annotations and sequence positions. Even single amino acids or nucleotides are object references. To enhance speed, STRAP avoids frequent object instantiations and invocation of non-final object-methods.

  o In BioJava peptide sequences and nucleotide sequences are lists of symbols. The symbols can be retrieved one after the other with an iterator or sub-sequences can be obtained. The advantages are that the entire sequence does not necessarily reside in memory and that programs are less susceptible to programming errors. *Symbol* objects are immutable elements of an alphabet. In STRAP however simple byte arrays are used for sequences and float arrays for coordinates. Besides speed the low memory consumption is an important advantage of basic data types. Classes in Strap expose internal data. Therefore, programmers might commit programming errors like manipulating byte arrays directly instead of using the setter methods. Another disadvantage is that no checks are performed in STRAP whether the characters in sequences are valid with respect to an underlying alphabet.

  o In BioJava sequence positions are realized by the class *Location*. Discontiguous *Location* objects are composed of several contiguous *RangeLocation* objects or *PointLocation* objects. For the class *StrapProtein* however, single residue positions are indicated by integer numbers between 0 and *countResidues()-1*. Multiple positions are given by boolean arrays. True at a given index means selected whereas false means not selected.

- BioJava throws exceptions when methods are invoked with invalid parameters. STRAP avoids the time consuming creation of Throwable objects. Instead, errors in methods are indicated by the return values NaN, -1 or null. From the point of program design however *Throwable* objects are nicer.

- In BioJava a *Sequence* object is either a peptide sequence or a nucleotide sequence. A StrapProtein can hold both at the same time if a coding nucleotide sequence was read and translated into protein. Both, the nucleotide sequence and the peptide sequence are contained in the same StrapProtein object. The coding or non-coding regions can be changed and the peptide sequence alters accordingly.

Projects Using BioJava

The following projects make use of BioJava.

- Metabolic Pathway Builder: Software suite dedicated to the exploration of connections among genes, proteins, reactions and metabolic pathways

- DengueInfo: a Dengue genome information portal that uses BioJava in the middleware and talks to a biosql database.

- Dazzle: A BioJava based DAS server.

- BioSense: A plugin for the InforSense Suite, an analytics software platform by IDBS that unitizes BioJava.

- Bioclipse: A free, open source, workbench for chemo- and bioinformatics with powerful editing and visualization capabilities for molecules, sequences, proteins, spectra etc.

- PROMPT: A free, open source framework and application for the comparison and mapping of protein sets. Uses BioJava for handling most input data formats.

- Cytoscape: An open source bioinformatics software platform for visualizing molecular interaction networks.

- BioWeka: An open source biological data mining application.

- Geneious: A molecular biology toolkit.

- MassSieve: An open source application to analyze mass spec proteomics data.

- Strap: A tool for multiple sequence alignment and sequence based structure alignment.

- Jstacs: A Java framework for statistical analysis and classification of biological sequences

- jLSTM "Long Short-Term Memory" for protein classification

- LaJolla Structural alignment of RNA and proteins using an index structure for fast alignment of thousands of structures. Including an easy to use command line interface. Open source at Sourceforge.

- GenBeans: A rich client platform for bioinformatics primarily focused on molecular biology and sequence analysis.

BioJS

BioJS is an open source project for bioinformatics data on the web. Its goal is to develop an open-source library of JavaScript components to visualise biological data. BioJS develops and maintains small building blocks (components) which can be reused by others. For a discovery of available components, BioJS maintains a registry.

History

The first version of BioJS was released in 2012 by John Gomez. It was developed as a JavaScript library of web components to represent biological data in web applications. Version 2.0 included a complete redesign of the library and was released in 2014 as a Google Summer of Code project by David Dao and Sebastian Wilzbach. Since then over 100 people contributed to the project. Currently more than 150 components are available in the BioJS registry.

Selected List of Components

- DAG Viewer
- DNA Content Viewer
- FeatureViewer
- HeatMapViewer
- Intermine analysis
- Intermine endpoints
- KEGGViewer
- PPI-Interactions
- PsicquicGraph
- Sequence
- wigExplorer
- treeWidget

Institutions Using BioJS

- EBI
- ELife
- InterMine
- Berkeley Lab
- OpenPHACTS
- Rostlab
- TGAC

BioRuby

BioRuby is a collection of Open Source Ruby code, comprising classes for computation molecular biology and bioinformatics. It contains classes for DNA and protein sequence analysis, sequence alignment, biological database parsing, structural biology and other bioinformatics tasks.

BioRuby is released under the GNU GPL version 2 or Ruby licence and is one of a number of Bio* projects, designed to reduce code duplication.

In 2011, the BioRuby project introduced the Biogem software plugin system and are listed on biogems.info, with two or three new plugins added every month.

BioRuby is managed via the bioruby.org website and BioRuby GitHub repository.

History

BioRuby

The BioRuby project was first started in 2000 by Toshiaki Katayama as a Ruby implementation of similar bioinformatics packages such as BioPerl and BioPython. The initial release of version 0.1 has been frequently updated by contributors both informally and at organised "hackathon" events, with the most recent release of version 1.4.3.0001 in May 2013.

In June 2005, BioRuby was funded by IPA as an Exploratory Software Project, culminating with the release of version 1.0.0 in February 2006.

BioRuby has been the focus of a number of Google Summer of Code projects, including;

- 2009: Implementing phyloXML support in BioRuby

- 2010: Ruby 1.9.2 support of BioRuby

- 2010: Implementation of algorithm to infer gene duplications in BioRuby

- 2011: Represent bio-objects and related informatio with images

- 2012: Extend bio-alignment plug-in with Multiple Alignment Format -MAF- parser

Version History

- 0.7.0 December 18, 2005 (438 KB)

- 1.0.0 February 26, 2006 (528 KB)

- 1.4.3.0001 May 24, 2013 (1.42 MB)

Installation

BioRuby is able to be installed onto any instance of Ruby; as Ruby is a highly cross platform language, BioRuby is available on most modern operating systems.

It is required that Ruby be installed prior to BioRuby installation.

Installation of BioRuby

Mac OS X/Unix/Linux

Mac OS X has Ruby and RubyGems installed by default and for Unix/Linux installation of RubyGems is recommended.

If Ruby and RubyGems are installed, BioRuby can be installed using this command via the terminal;

% sudo gem install bio

If you need to install from the source code distribution, obtain the latest package from the archive and in the bioruby source directory, run the following commands;

% su

ruby setup.rb

Windows

Installation via RubyGems is highly recommended; this requires Ruby and RubyGems be installed, then the following command run at the command prompt;

> gem install bio

Usage

BioRuby can be accessed via the terminal, Ruby IDEs or via a BioRubyOnRails implementation. Instructions for the installation and use of BioRubyOnRails can be found at bioruby.

Basic Syntax

The following are examples of basic sequence manipulations using BioRuby. You can find more syntax examples at bioruby.

Basic Sequence Manipulation

String to Bio::Sequence Object

Parsing a string into Bio::Sequence object.

```ruby
#!/usr/bin/env ruby
require 'bio'


# create a DNA sequence object from a String
dna = Bio::Sequence::NA.new("atcggtcggctta")


# create an RNA sequence object from a String
rna = Bio::Sequence::NA.new("auugccuacauaggc")


# create a Protein sequence from a String
aa = Bio::Sequence::AA.new("AGFAVENDSA")


# you can check if the sequence contains illegal characters
# that is not an accepted IUB character for that symbol
# (should prepare a Bio::Sequence::AA#illegal_symbols method also)
puts dna.illegal_bases


# translate and concatenate a DNA sequence to Protein sequence
newseq = aa + dna.translate<br>
puts newseq      # => "AGFAVENDSAIGRL"
```

Bio::Sequence Object to String

This an example that showcases the simplicity of BioRuby. It does not require any method call to convert the sequence object to a string.

Parsing a sequence object into a string.

```ruby
#!/usr/bin/env ruby


# you can use Bio::Sequence object as a String object to print, seamlessly
```

```
dna = Bio::Sequence::NA.new("atgc")

puts dna       # => "atgc"

str = dna.to_s

puts str       # => "atgc"
```

Translation

Translating a DNA or RNA Sequence or SymbolList to Protein

There is no need to convert DNA sequence to RNA sequence or vice versa before its translation in BioRuby. You can simply call a translate method for Bio::Sequence::NA object.

```ruby
#!/usr/bin/env ruby


require 'bio'


# create a DNA sequence
seq = Bio::Sequence::NA.new("atggccattgaatga")


# translate to protein
prot = seq.translate


# prove that it worked
puts seq   # => "atggccattgaatga"
puts prot  # => "MAIE*"
```

Translating a Single Codon to a Single Amino Acid

The general translation example shows how to use the translate method of Bio::Sequence::-NA object but most of what goes on is hidden behind the convenience method. If you only want to translate a single codon into a single amino acid you get exposed to a bit more of the gory detail but you also get a chance to figure out more of what is going on under the hood.

```ruby
#!/usr/bin/env ruby
```

```ruby
require 'bio'


# make a 'codon'
codon = Bio::Sequence::NA.new("uug")


# you can translate the codon as described in the previous section.
puts codon.translate  # => "L"
```

Another way to do this is the following

```ruby
#!/usr/bin/env ruby


require 'bio'


# make a 'codon'
codon = Bio::Sequence::NA.new("uug")


# select the standard codon table
codon_table = Bio::CodonTable


# You need to convert RNA codon to DNA alphabets because the
# CodonTable in BioRuby is implemented as a static Hash with keys
# expressed in DNA alphabets (not RNA alphabets).
codon2 = codon.dna


# get the representation of that codon and translate to amino acid.
amino_acid = codon_table[codon2]
puts amino_acid      # => "L"
```

Sequence I/O

Writing Sequences in Fasta Format

To print out any Bio::Sequence object in FASTA format, All you need is to call is "puts objectName.is_fasta()"

```ruby
#!/usr/bin/env ruby


require 'bio'


# Generates a sample 100bp sequence.

seq1 = Bio::Sequence::NA.new("aatgacccgt" * 10)


# Naming this sequence as "testseq" and print in FASTA format

# (folded by 60 chars per line).

puts seq1.to_fasta("testseq", 60)
```

Reading in a Fasta File

This program opens FASTA format file for reading and iterates on each sequence in the file.

```ruby
#!/usr/bin/env ruby


require 'bio'


file = Bio::FastaFormat.open(ARGV.shift)

file.each do |entry|

# do something on each fasta sequence entry

end
```

This program automatically detects and reads FASTA format files given as its arguments.

```ruby
#!/usr/bin/env ruby
```

```
require 'bio'
```

```
Bio::FlatFile.auto(ARGF) do |ff|
ff.each do |entry|
  # do something on each fasta sequence entry
end
end
```

Similar but specify FASTA format explicitly.

```
#!/usr/bin/env ruby
```

```
require 'bio'
```

```
Bio::FlatFile.open(Bio::FastaFormat, ARGV) do |ff|
 ff.each do |entry|
   # do something on each fasta sequence entry
 end
end
```

Classes and Modules

Major Classes

The below classes have been identified by a group of major code contributors as major classes.

Basic Data Structure

These classes allow you to natively store complicated biological data structure effectively.

Class names	Description
Bio::Sequence::NA, Bio::Sequence::AA	Nucleic and amino acid sequences

Bio::Locations, Bio::Features	Locations / Annotations
Bio::Reference, Bio::PubMed	Literatures
Bio::Pathway, Bio::Relation	Graphs
Bio::Alignment	Alignments

Databases and Sequence File Formats

Accesses online biological databases and reads from common file-formats.

Class names	Description
Bio::GenBank, Bio::EMBL	GenBank / EMBL
Bio::SPTR, Bio::NBRF, Bio::PDB	SwissProt and TrEMBL / PIR / PDB
Bio::FANTOM	FANTOM DB (Functional annotation of mouse)
Bio::KEGG	KEGG database parsers
Bio::GO, Bio::GFF	Bio::PROSITE FASTA format / PROSITE motifs
Bio::FastaFormat, Bio::PROSITE	FASTA format / PROSITE motifs

Wrapper and Parsers for Bioinformatics Tool

These classes allow for easy access to commonly used bioinformatics tools.

Class names	Description
Bio::Blast, Bio::Fasta, Bio::HMMER	Sequence similarity (BLAST / FASTA / HMMER)
Bio::ClustalW, Bio::MAFFT	Multiple sequence alignment (ClustalW / MAFFT)
Bio::PSORT, Bio::TargetP	Protein subcellular localization (PSORT / TargetP)
Bio::SOSUI, Bio::TMHMM	Transmembrane helix prediction (SOSUI / TMHMM)
Bio::GenScan	Gene finding (GenScan)

File, Network and Database I/O

Class names	Description
Bio::Registry	OBDA Registry service
Bio::SQL	OBDA BioSQL RDB schema
Bio::Fetch	OBDA BioFetch via HTTP
Bio::FlatFileIndex	OBDA flat file indexing system
OBDA flat file indexing system	Flat file reader with data format autodetection
Bio::DAS	Distributed Annotation System (DAS)
Bio::KEGG::API	SOAP/WSDL intarface for KEGG

Biogem

Biogem provides a set of tools for bioinformaticians who want to code an application or library that uses or extends BioRuby's core library, as well as share the code as a gem on rubygems.org. Any gem published via the Biogem framework is also listed at biogems.info.

The aim of Biogem is to promote a modular approach to the BioRuby package and simplify the creation of modules by automating process of setting up directory/file scaffolding, a git repository and releasing online package databases.

Biogem makes use of github.com and rubygems.org and requires the setup of unique accounts on these websites.

Popular Biogems

#	Biogem	Description	Version
1	bio	Bioinformatics Library	1.4.3.0001
2	biodiversity	Parser of scientific names	3.1.5
3	Simple Spreadsheet extractor	Basic spreadsheet content extraction using Apache poi	0.13.3
4	Bio gem	Software generator for Ruby	1.36
5	Bio samtools	Binder of samtools for Ruby	2.1.0
6	t2 server	Support for interacting with the taverna 2 server	1.1.0
7	bio ucsc api	The Ruby ucsc api	0.6.2
8	entrez	http request to entrez e-utilities	0.5.8.1
9	bio gadget	Gadget for bioinformatics	0.4.8
10	sequenceserver	Blast search made easy!	0.8.7

Plugins

BioRuby will have a completed plugin system at the 1.5 release.

Bioclipse

The Bioclipse project is a Java-based, open source, visual platform for chemo- and bioinformatics based on the Eclipse Rich Client Platform (RCP). It gained scripting functionality in 2009.

Like any RCP application, Bioclipse uses a plugin architecture that inherits basic functionality and visual interfaces from Eclipse, such as help system, software updates, preferences, cross-platform deployment etc. Via its plugins, Bioclipse provides functionality for chemo- and bioinformatics, and extension points that easily can be extended by other, possibly proprietary, plugins to provide additional functionality.

The first stable release of Bioclipse includes a Chemistry Development Kit (CDK) plugin to provide a chemoinformatic backend, a Jmol plugin for 3D-visualization of molecules, and a BioJava plugin for sequence analysis. Recently, the R platform, using StatET, and OpenTox were added.

Bioclipse is developed as a collaboration between the Proteochemometric Group, Dept. of Pharmaceutical Biosciences, Uppsala University, Sweden, the Christoph Steinbeck Group at the European Bioinformatics Institute, and the Analytical Chemistry Department at Leiden University, but also includes extensions developed at other academic institutes, including the Karolinska Institutet and Maastricht University. The development is backed up by the International Bioclipse Association.

Bioclipse Scripting Language

The Bioclipse Scripting Language (BSL) is a scripting environment, currently based on JavaScript and Groovy. It extends the scripting language with managers that wrap the functionality of third party libraries, as mentioned above. These scripts thus provide means to make analyses in Bioclipse sharable, for example, on MyExperiment.org. Bioclipse defines a number of core data types that managers support, allowing information to be used between these managers.

EMBOSS

EMBOSS is an acronym for European Molecular Biology Open Software Suite. EMBOSS is a free open source software analysis package specially developed for the needs of the molecular biology and bioinformatics user community. The software automatically copes with data in a variety of formats and even allows transparent retrieval of sequence data from the web. Also, as extensive libraries are provided with the package, it is a platform to allow other scientists to develop and release software in true open source spirit. EMBOSS also integrates a range of currently available packages and tools for sequence analysis into a seamless whole.

The 'European' part of the name hints at the wider scope. The core EMBOSS groups are collaborating with many other groups to develop the new applications that the users need. This was done from the beginning with EMBnet, the European Molecular Biology Network. EMBnet has many nodes worldwide most of which are national bioinformatics services. EMBnet has the programming expertise. In September 1998, the first workshop was held, when 30 people from EMBnet went to Hinxton to learn about EMBOSS and to discuss the way forward.

The EMBOSS package contains a variety of applications for sequence alignment, rapid database searching with sequence patterns, protein motif identification (including domain analysis), and much more.

The AJAX and NUCLEUS libraries are released under the GNU Library General Public Licence. EMBOSS applications are released under the GNU General Public Licence.

EMBOSs Application Groups

Group	Description
Acd	Acd file utilities
Alignment consensus	Merging sequences to make a consensus
Alignment differences	Finding differences between sequences
Alignment dot plots	Dot plot sequence comparisons
Alignment global	Global sequence alignment
Alignment local	Local sequence alignment
Alignment multiple	Multiple sequence alignment
Display	Publication-quality display
Edit	Sequence editing
Enzyme kinetics	Enzyme kinetics calculations
Feature tables	Manipulation and display of sequence annotation
HMM	Hidden markov model analysis
Information	Information and general help for users
Menus	Menu interface(s)
Nucleic 2d structure	Nucleic acid secondary structure
Nucleic codon usage	Codon usage analysis
Nucleic composition	Composition of nucleotide sequences
Nucleic CpG islands	CpG island detection and analysis
Nucleic gene finding	Predictions of genes and other genomic features
Nucleic motifs	Nucleic acid motif searches
Nucleic mutation	Nucleic acid sequence mutation
Nucleic primers	Primer prediction
Nucleic profiles	Nucleic acid profile generation and searching
Nucleic repeats	Nucleic acid repeat detection
Nucleic restriction	Restriction enzyme sites in nucleotide sequences
Nucleic RNA folding	RNA folding methods and analysis
Nucleic transcription	Transcription factors, promoters and terminator prediction
Nucleic translation	Translation of nucleotide sequence to protein sequence
Phylogeny consensus	Phylogenetic consensus methods
Phylogeny continuous characters	Phylogenetic continuous character methods
Phylogeny discrete characters	Phylogenetic discrete character methods
Phylogeny distance matrix	Phylogenetic distance matrix methods
Phylogeny gene frequencies	Phylogenetic gene frequency methods
Phylogeny molecular sequence	Phylogenetic molecular sequence methods

Phylogeny tree drawing	Phylogenetic tree drawing methods
Protein 2d structure	Protein secondary structure
Protein 3d structure	Protein tertiary structure
Protein composition	Composition of protein sequences
Protein motifs	Protein motif searches
Protein mutation	Protein sequence mutation
Protein profiles	Protein profile generation and searching
Test	Testing tools, not for general use
Utils database creation	Database installation
Utils database indexing	Database indexing
Utils misc	Utility tools

GenoCAD

GenoCAD is one of the earliest computer assisted design tools for synthetic biology. The software is a bioinformatics tool developed and maintained by GenoFAB. GenoCAD facilitates the design of protein expression vectors, artificial gene networks and other genetic constructs for genetic engineering and is based on the theory of formal languages. GenoCAD can be used online at www.genocad.com.

History

GenoCAD originated as an offshoot of an attempt to formalize functional constraints of genetic constructs using the theory of formal languages. In 2007, the website genocad.org (now retired) was set up as a proof of concept by researchers at Virginia Bioinformatics Institute, Virginia Tech. Using the website, users could design genes by repeatedly replacing high-level genetic constructs with lower level genetic constructs, and eventually with actual DNA sequences.

On August 31, 2009, the National Science Foundation granted a three-year $1,421,725 grant to Dr. Jean Peccoud, an associate professor at the Virginia Bioinformatics Institute at Virginia Tech, for the development of GenoCAD. GenoCAD was and continues to be developed by GenoFAB, a company founded by Peccoud (currently CSO and acting CEO), who was also one of the authors of the originating study.

Source code for GenoCAD was originally released on Sourceforge in December 2009.

GenoCAD version 2.0 was released in November 2011 and included the ability to simulate the behavior of the designed genetic code. This feature was a result of a collaboration with the team behind COPASI.

In April, 2015, Peccoud and colleagues published a library of biological parts, called GenoLIB, that can be incorporated into the GenoCAD platform.

Goals

The four aims of the project are to develop a:

1. computer language to represent the structure of synthetic DNA molecules used in E.coli, yeast, mice, and Arabidopsis thaliana cells

2. compiler capable of translating DNA sequences into mathematical models in order to predict the encoded phenotype

3. collaborative workflow environment which allow to share parts, designs, fabrication resource

4. means to forward the results to the user community through an external advisory board, an annual user conference, and outreach to industry

Features

The main features of GenoCAD can be organized into three main categories.

Workflow of GenoCAD

- Management of genetic sequences: The purpose of this group of features is to help users identify, within large collections of genetic parts, the parts needed for a project and to organize them in project-specific libraries.

    o *Genetic parts*: Parts have a unique identifier, a name and a more general description. They also have a DNA sequence. Parts are associated with a grammar and assigned to a parts category such a promoter, gene, etc.

    o *Parts libraries*: Collections of parts are organized in libraries. In some cases part libraries correspond to parts imported from a single source such as another sequence database. In other cases, libraries correspond to the parts used for a particular design project. Parts can be moved from one library to another through a temporary storage area called the cart (analogous to e-commerce shopping carts).

    o *Searching parts*: Users can search the parts database using the Lucene search engine. Basic and advanced search modes are available. Users can develop complex queries and save them for future reuse.

- o *Importing/Exporting parts*: Parts can be imported and exported individually or as entire libraries using standard file formats (e.g., tab delimited, FASTA, SBML).

- Combining sequences into genetic constructs: The purpose of this group of features is to streamline the process of combining genetic parts into designs compliant with a specific design strategy.

  - o *Point-and-click design tool*: This wizard guides the user through a series of design decisions that determine the design structure and the selection of parts included in the design.

  - o *Design management*: Designs can be saved in the user workspace. Design statuses are regularly updated to warn users of the consequences of editing parts on previously saved designs.

  - o *Exporting designs*: Designs can be exported using standard file formats (e.g., GenBank, tab delimited, FASTA).

  - o *Design safety*: Designs are protected from some types of errors by forcing the user to follow the appropriate design strategy.

  - o *Simulation*: Sequences designed in GenoCAD can be simulated to display chemical production in the resulting cell .

- User workspace: Users can personalize their workspace by adding parts to the GenoCAD database, creating specialized libraries corresponding to specific design projects, and saving designs at different stages of development.

Theoretical Foundation

GenoCAD is rooted in the theory of formal languages; in particular, the design rules describing how to combine different kinds of parts and form context-free grammars.

A context free grammar can be defined by its terminals, variables, start variable and substitution rules. In GenoCAD, the terminals of the grammar are sequences of DNA that perform a particular biological purpose (e.g. a promoter). The variables are less homogeneous: they can represent longer sequences that have multiple functions or can represent a section of DNA that can contain one of multiple different sequences of DNA but perform the same function (e.g. a variable represents the set of promoters). GenoCAD includes built in substitution rules to ensure that the DNA sequence is biologically viable. Users can also define their own sets of rules for other purposes.

Designing a sequence of DNA in GenoCAD is much like creating a derivation in a context free grammar. The user starts with the start variable and repeatedly selects a variable and a substitution for it until only terminals are left.

Alternatives

The most common alternatives to GenoCAD are Proto, GEC and EuGene

Tool	Advantages	Disadvantages
GEC	• Designer only needs to know basic part types and determine constraints	• Does not support SBOL
Eu-Gene	• Interfacing with other simulation and assembly tools	• No graphical user interface • No web based interface
Proto	• Choice of molecules and sequences can be made by other programs • Integration capability with some other languages	• Relatively hard to learn • Results are less efficient

References

- Hahne, F.; Huber, W.; Gentleman, R.; Falcon, S. (2008). Bioconductor Case Studies. Springer. ISBN 978-0-387-77239-4.

- Gentleman, R.; Carey, V.; Huber, W.; Irizarry, R.; Dudoit, S. (2005). Bioinformatics and Computational Biology Solutions Using R and Bioconductor. Springer. ISBN 978-0-387-25146-2.

- Sipser, Michael (2013). Introduction to the Theory of Computation, Third edition. Boston, MA, USA: Cengage Learning. p. 104. ISBN 978-1-133-18779-0.

- Chapman, Brad (11 March 2004), The Biopython Project: Philosophy, functionality and facts (PDF), retrieved 11 September 2014.

- "Klebsiella pneumoniae strain KPS77 plasmid pKPS77, complete sequence". NCBI. Retrieved 10 September 2014.

- Gomez, John; Jimenez, Rafael (2014). "Sequence, a BioJS component for visualising sequences". F1000Research. doi:10.12688/f1000research.3-52.v1. ISSN 2046-1402.

- Schreiber, Fabian (2014). "treeWidget: a BioJS component to visualise phylogenetic trees". F1000Research. doi:10.12688/f1000research.3-49.v1. ISSN 2046-1402.

- Jodi Lewis (September 14, 2009). "National Science Foundation awards $1.4 million for GenoCAD development". Retrieved October 7, 2013.

- Jean Peccoud (June 21, 2013). "GenoCAD: Computer Assisted Design of Synthetic DNA". Retrieved October 7, 2013.

- Habibi, N., Mohd Hashim, S. Z., Rodriguez, C. A., & Samian, M. R. (2013). A Review of CADs, Languages and Data Models for Synthetic Biology. Jurnal Teknologi, 63(1).

- Paterson T, Law A (November 2012). "JEnsembl: a version-aware Java API to Ensembl data systems". Bioinformatics. 28 (21): 2724–31.

Diverse Aspects of Bioinformatics

Bioinformatics has diverse aspects; some of these are structural bioinformatics, modelling biological systems, protein-protein interaction prediction, interactome, flow cytometry bioinformatics etc. The topics discussed in the section are of great importance to broaden the existing knowledge on bioinformatics.

Structural Bioinformatics

Structural bioinformatics is the branch of bioinformatics which is related to the analysis and prediction of the three-dimensional structure of biological macromolecules such as proteins, RNA, and DNA. It deals with generalizations about macromolecular 3D structure such as comparisons of overall folds and local motifs, principles of molecular folding, evolution, and binding interactions, and structure/function relationships, working both from experimentally solved structures and from computational models. The term *structural* has the same meaning as in structural biology, and structural bioinformatics can be seen as a part of computational structural biology.

Modelling Biological Systems

Modelling biological systems is a significant task of systems biology and mathematical biology. Computational systems biology aims to develop and use efficient algorithms, data structures, visualization and communication tools with the goal of computer modelling of biological systems. It involves the use of computer simulations of biological systems, including cellular subsystems (such as the networks of metabolites and enzymes which comprise metabolism, signal transduction pathways and gene regulatory networks), to both analyze and visualize the complex connections of these cellular processes.

Artificial life or virtual evolution attempts to understand evolutionary processes via the computer simulation of simple (artificial) life forms.

Overview

It is understood that an unexpected emergent property of a complex system is a result of the interplay of the cause-and-effect among simpler, integrated parts. Biological systems manifest many important examples of emergent properties in the complex interplay of components. Traditional study of biological systems requires reductive methods in which quantities of data are gathered by category, such as concentration over time in response to a certain stimulus. Computers are critical to analysis and modelling of these data. The goal is to create accurate real-time models of a system's response to environmental and internal stimuli, such as a model of a cancer cell in order to find weaknesses in its signalling pathways, or modelling of ion channel mutations to see effects on cardiomyocytes and in turn, the function of a beating heart.

Standards

By far the most widely accepted standard format for storing and exchanging models in the field is the Systems Biology Markup Language (SBML) The SBML.org website includes a guide to many important software packages used in computational systems biology. Other markup languages with different emphases include BioPAX and CellML.

Particular Tasks

Cellular Model

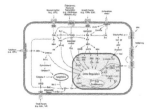

Part of the Cell Cycle

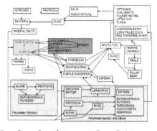

Summerhayes and Elton's 1923 food web of Bear Island (*Arrows represent an organism being consumed by another organism*).

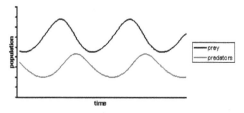

A sample time-series of the Lotka–Volterra model. Note that the two populations exhibit cyclic behaviour.

Creating a cellular model has been a particularly challenging task of systems biology and mathematical biology. It involves the use of computer simulations of the many cellular subsystems such as the networks of metabolites and enzymes which comprise metabolism, signal transduction pathways and gene regulatory networks to both analyze and visualize the complex connections of these cellular processes.

The complex network of biochemical reaction/transport processes and their spatial organization make the development of a predictive model of a living cell a grand challenge for the 21st century, listed as such by the National Science Foundation (NSF) in 2006.

A whole cell computational model for the bacterium *Mycoplasma genitalium*, including all its 525 genes, gene products, and their interactions, was built by scientists from Stanford University and the J. Craig Venter Institute and published on 20 July 2012 in Cell.

A dynamic computer model of intracellular signaling was the basis for Merrimack Pharmaceuticals to discover the target for their cancer medicine MM-111.

Membrane computing is the task of modelling specifically a cell membrane.

Multi-cellular Organism Simulation

An open source simulation of C. elegans at the cellular level is being pursued by the OpenWorm community. So far the physics engine Gepetto has been built and models of the neural connectome and a muscle cell have been created in the NeuroML format.

Protein Folding

Protein structure prediction is the prediction of the three-dimensional structure of a protein from its amino acid sequence—that is, the prediction of a protein's tertiary structure from its primary structure. It is one of the most important goals pursued by bioinformatics and theoretical chemistry. Protein structure prediction is of high importance in medicine (for example, in drug design) and biotechnology (for example, in the design of novel enzymes). Every two years, the performance of current methods is assessed in the CASP experiment.

Human Biological Systems

Brain Model

The Blue Brain Project is an attempt to create a synthetic brain by reverse-engineering the mammalian brain down to the molecular level. The aim of the project, founded in May 2005 by the Brain and Mind Institute of the *École Polytechnique* in Lausanne, Switzerland, is to study the brain's architectural and functional principles. The project is headed by the Institute's director, Henry Markram. Using a Blue

Gene supercomputer running Michael Hines's NEURON software, the simulation does not consist simply of an artificial neural network, but involves a partially biologically realistic model of neurons. It is hoped by its proponents that it will eventually shed light on the nature of consciousness. There are a number of sub-projects, including the Cajal Blue Brain, coordinated by the Supercomputing and Visualization Center of Madrid (CeSViMa), and others run by universities and independent laboratories in the UK, U.S., and Israel. The Human Brain Project builds on the work of the Blue Brain Project. It is one of six pilot projects in the Future Emerging Technologies Research Program of the European Commission, competing for a billion euro funding.

Model of the Immune System

The last decade has seen the emergence of a growing number of simulations of the immune system.

Virtual Liver

The Virtual Liver project is a 43 million euro research program funded by the German Government, made up of seventy research group distributed across Germany. The goal is to produce a virtual liver, a dynamic mathematical model that represents human liver physiology, morphology and function.

Tree Model

Electronic trees (e-trees) usually use L-systems to simulate growth. L-systems are very important in the field of complexity science and A-life. A universally accepted system for describing changes in plant morphology at the cellular or modular level has yet to be devised. The most widely implemented tree generating algorithms are described in the papers "Creation and Rendering of Realistic Trees", and Real-Time Tree Rendering

Ecological Models

Ecosystem models are mathematical representations of ecosystems. Typically they simplify complex foodwebs down to their major components or trophic levels, and quantify these as either numbers of organisms, biomass or the inventory/concentration of some pertinent chemical element (for instance, carbon or a nutrient species such as nitrogen or phosphorus).

Models in Ecotoxicology

The purpose of models in ecotoxicology is the understanding, simulation and prediction of effects caused by toxicants in the environment. Most current models describe effects on one of many different levels of biological organization (e.g. organisms or populations). A challenge is the development of models that predict effects across biological scales. Ecotoxicology and models discusses some types of ecotoxicological models and provides links to many others.

Modelling of Infectious Disease

It is possible to model the progress of most infectious diseases mathematically to discover the likely outcome of an epidemic or to help manage them by vaccination. This field tries to find parameters for various infectious diseases and to use those parameters to make useful calculations about the effects of a mass vaccination programme.

Protein–protein Interaction Prediction

Protein–protein interaction prediction is a field combining bioinformatics and structural biology in an attempt to identify and catalog physical interactions between pairs or groups of proteins. Understanding protein–protein interactions is important for the investigation of intracellular signaling pathways, modelling of protein complex structures and for gaining insights into various biochemical processes. Experimentally, physical interactions between pairs of proteins can be inferred from a variety of experimental techniques, including yeast two-hybrid systems, protein-fragment complementation assays (PCA), affinity purification/mass spectrometry, protein microarrays, fluorescence resonance energy transfer (FRET), and Microscale Thermophoresis (MST). Efforts to experimentally determine the interactome of numerous species are ongoing, and a number of computational methods for interaction prediction have been developed in recent years.

Methods

Proteins that interact are more likely to co-evolve, therefore, it is possible to make inferences about interactions between pairs of proteins based on their phylogenetic distances. It has also been observed in some cases that pairs of interacting proteins have fused orthologues in other organisms. In addition, a number of bound protein complexes have been structurally solved and can be used to identify the residues that mediate the interaction so that similar motifs can be located in other organisms.

Phylogenetic Profiling

Phylogenetic profiling finds pairs of protein families with similar patterns of presence or absence across large numbers of species. This method is based on the hypothesis that potentially interacting proteins should co-evolve and should have orthologs in closely related species. That is, proteins that form complexes or are part of a pathway should be present simultaneously in order for them to function. A phylogenetic profile is constructed for each protein under investigation. The profile is basically a record of whether the protein is present in certain genomes. If two proteins are found to be present and absent in the same genomes, those proteins are deemed likely to be functionally related. A similar method can be applied to protein domains, where profiles are constructed for domains to determine if there are domain interactions. Some drawbacks with the phylogenetic profile methods are that they are computationally expensive to perform, they rely on homology detection between distant organisms, and they only identify if the proteins being investigated are functionally related (part of complex or in same pathway) and not if they have direct interactions.

Prediction of co-evolved Protein Pairs Based on Similar Phylogenetic Trees

It was observed that the phylogenetic trees of ligands and receptors were often more similar than due to random chance. This is likely because they faced similar selection pressures and co-evolved. This method uses the phylogenetic trees of protein pairs to determine if interactions exist. To do this, homologs of the proteins of interest are found (using a sequence search tool such as BLAST) and multiple-sequence alignments are done (with alignment tools such as Clustal) to build distance matrices for each of the proteins of interest. The distance matrices should then be used to build phylogenetic trees. However, comparisons between phylogenetic trees are difficult, and current methods circumvent this by simply comparing distance matrices. The distance matrices of the proteins are used to calculate a correlation coefficient, in which a larger value corresponds to co-evolution. The benefit of comparing distance matrices instead of phylogenetic trees is that the results do not depend on the method of tree building that was used. The downside is that difference matrices are not perfect representations of phylogenetic trees, and inaccuracies may result from using such a shortcut. Another factor worthy of note is that there are background similarities between the phylogenetic trees of any protein, even ones that do not interact. If left unaccounted for, this could lead to a high false-positive rate. For this reason, certain methods construct a background tree using 16S rRNA sequences which they use as the canonical tree of life. The distance matrix constructed from this tree of life is then subtracted from the distance matrices of the proteins of interest. However, because RNA distance matrices and DNA distance matrices have different scale, presumably because RNA and DNA have different mutation rates, the RNA matrix needs to be rescaled before it can be subtracted from the DNA matrices. By using molecular clock proteins, the scaling coefficient for protein distance/RNA distance can be calculated. This coefficient is used to rescale the RNA matrix.

Rosetta Stone (Gene Fusion) Method

A Rosetta stone protein is a protein chain composed of two fused proteins. It is observed that proteins or domains that interact with one another tend to have homologs in other genomes that are fused into a Rosetta stone protein , such as might arise by gene fusion when two previously separate genes form a new composite one. This evolutionary mechanism can be used to predict protein interactions. If two proteins are separate in one organism but fused in the other, then it is very likely that they will interact in the case where they are expressed as two separate products. The STRING database makes use of this to predict protein-protein interactions. Gene fusion has been extensively studied and large amounts of data are available. Nonetheless, like phylogenetic profile methods, the Rosetta stone method does not necessarily find interacting proteins, as there can be other reasons for the fusion of two proteins, such as optimizing co-expression of the proteins. The most obvious drawback of this method is that there are many protein interactions that cannot be discovered this way; it relies on the presence of Rosetta stone proteins.

Classification Methods

Classification methods use data to train a program (classifier) to distinguish positive examples of interacting protein/domain pairs with negative examples of non-interacting pairs. Popular classifiers used are Random Forest Decision (RFD) and Support Vector Machines. RFD produces results based on the domain composition of interacting and non-interacting protein pairs. When given a protein pair to classify, RFD first creates a representation of the protein pair in a vector. The vector contains all the domain types used to train RFD, and for each domain type the vector also contains a value of 0, 1, or 2. If the protein pair does not contain a certain domain, then the value for that domain is 0. If one of the proteins of the pair contains the domain, then the value is 1. If both proteins contain the domain, then the value is 2. Using training data, RFD constructs a decision forest, consisting of many decision trees. Each decision tree evaluates several domains, and based on the presence or absence of interactions in these domains, makes a decision as to if the protein pair interacts. The vector representation of the protein pair is evaluated by each tree to determine if they are an interacting pair or a non-interacting pair. The forest tallies up all the input from the trees to come up with a final decision. The strength of this method is that it does not assume that domains interact independent of each other. This makes it so that multiple domains in proteins can be used in the prediction. This is a big step up from previous methods which could only predict based on a single domain pair. The limitation of this method is that it relies on the training dataset to produce results. Thus, usage of different training datasets could influence the results.

Inference of Interactions from Homologous Structures

This group of methods makes use of known protein complex structures to predict and structurally model interactions between query protein sequences. The prediction process generally starts by employing a sequence based method (e.g. Interolog) to search for protein complex structures that are homologous to the query sequences. These known complex structures are then used as templates to structurally model the interaction between query sequences. This method has the advantage of not only inferring protein interactions but also suggests models of how proteins interact structurally, which can provide some insights into the atomic level mechanism of that interaction. On the other hand, the ability for these methods to make a prediction is constrained by a limited number of known protein complex structures.

Association Methods

Association methods look for characteristic sequences or motifs that can help distinguish between interacting and non-interacting pairs. A classifier is trained by looking for sequence-signature pairs where one protein contains one sequence-signature, and its interacting partner contains another sequence-signature. They look specifically for sequence-signatures that are found together more often than by chance. This uses a log-odds score which is computed as $log2(Pij/PiPj)$, where Pij is the observed frequency of domains i and j occurring in one protein pair; Pi and Pj are the background frequencies of domains i and j in the data. Predicted domain interactions are those with positive log-odds scores and also having several occurrences within the database. The downside with this method is that it looks at each pair of interacting domains separately, and it assumes that they interact independently of each other.

Identification of Structural Patterns

This method builds a library of known protein–protein interfaces from the PDB, where the interfaces are defined as pairs of polypeptide fragments that are below a threshold slightly larger than the Van der Waals radius of the atoms involved. The sequences in the library are then clustered based on structural alignment and redundant sequences are eliminated. The residues that have a high (generally >50%) level of frequency for a given position are considered hotspots. This library is then used to identify potential interactions between pairs of targets, providing that they have a known structure (i.e. present in the PDB).

Bayesian Network Modelling

Bayesian methods integrate data from a wide variety of sources, including both experimental results and prior computational predictions, and use these features to assess the likelihood that a particular potential protein interaction is a true positive result. These methods are useful because experimental procedures, particularly the yeast two-hybrid experiments, are extremely noisy and produce many false positives, while the previously mentioned computational methods can only provide circumstantial evidence that a particular pair of proteins might interact.

Domain-pair Exclusion Analysis

The domain-pair exclusion analysis detects specific domain interactions that are hard to detect using Bayesian methods. Bayesian methods are good at detecting nonspecific promiscuous interactions and not very good at detecting rare specific interactions. The domain-pair exclusion analysis method calculates an E-score which measures if two domains interact. It is calculated as log(probability that the two proteins interact given that the domains interact/probability that the two proteins interact given that the domains don't interact). The probabilities required in the formula are calculated using an Expectation Maximization procedure, which is a method for estimating parameters in statistical models. High E-scores indicate that the two domains are likely to interact, while low scores indicate that other domains form the protein pair are more likely to be responsible for the interaction. The drawback with this method is that it does not take into account false positives and false negatives in the experimental data.

Supervised Learning Problem

The problem of PPI prediction can be framed as a supervised learning problem. In this paradigm the known protein interactions supervise the estimation of a function that can predict whether an interaction exists or not between two proteins given data about the proteins (e.g., expression levels of each gene in different experimental conditions, location information, phylogenetic profile, etc.).

Relationship to Docking Methods

The field of protein–protein interaction prediction is closely related to the field of protein–protein docking, which attempts to use geometric and steric considerations to fit two proteins of known structure into a bound complex. This is a useful mode of inquiry in cases where both proteins in the pair have known structures and are known (or at least strongly suspected) to interact, but since so many proteins do not have experimentally determined structures, sequence-based interaction prediction methods are especially useful in conjunction with experimental studies of an organism's interactome.

Interactome

In molecular biology, an interactome is the whole set of molecular interactions in a particular cell. The term specifically refers to physical interactions among molecules (such as those among proteins, also known as protein–protein interactions, PPIs) but can also describe sets of indirect interactions among genes (genetic interactions). The interactomes based on PPIs should be associated to the proteome of the corresponding specie in order to provide a global view ("omic") of all the possible molecular interactions that a protein can present. A recent compendium of interactomes can be obtained in the resource: APID interactomes.

Part of the DISC1 interactome with genes represented by text in boxes and interactions noted by lines between the genes. From Hennah and Porteous, 2009.

The word "interactome" was originally coined in 1999 by a group of French scientists headed by Bernard Jacq. Mathematically, interactomes are generally displayed as graphs. Though interactomes may be described as biological networks, they should not be confused with other networks such as neural networks or food webs.

Molecular Interaction Networks

Molecular interactions can occur between molecules belonging to different biochemical families (proteins, nucleic acids, lipids, carbohydrates, etc.) and also within a given family. Whenever such molecules are connected by physical interactions, they form molecular interaction networks that are generally classified by the nature of the compounds involved. Most commonly, *interactome* refers to *protein–protein interaction* (PPI) network (PIN) or subsets thereof. For instance, the Sirt-1 protein interactome and Sirt family second order interactome is the network involving Sirt-1 and its directly interacting proteins where as second order interactome illustrates interactions up to second order of neighbors (Neighbors of neighbors). Another extensively studied type of interactome is the protein–DNA interactome, also called a *gene-regulatory network*, a network formed by transcription factors, chromatin regulatory proteins, and their target genes. Even *metabolic networks* can be considered as molecular interaction networks: metabolites, i.e. chemical compounds in a cell, are converted into each other by enzymes, which have to bind their substrates physically.

In fact, all interactome types are interconnected. For instance, protein interactomes contain many enzymes which in turn form biochemical networks. Similarly, gene regulatory networks overlap substantially with protein interaction networks and signaling networks.

Size of Interactomes

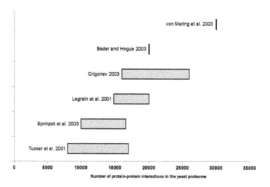

Estimates of the yeast protein interactome.

It has been suggested that the size of an organism's interactome correlates better than genome size with the biological complexity of the organism. Although protein–protein interaction maps containing several thousand binary interactions are now available for several species, none of them is presently complete and the size of interactomes is still a matter of debate.

Yeast

The yeast interactome, i.e. all protein–protein interactions among proteins of *Saccharomyces cerevisiae*, has been estimated to contain between 10,000 and 30,000 interactions. A reasonable estimate may be on the order of 20,000 interactions. Larger estimates often include indirect or predicted interactions, often from affinity purification/mass spectrometry (AP/MS) studies.

Genetic Interaction Networks

Genes interact in the sense that they affect each other's function. For instance, a mutation may be harmless, but when it is combined with another mutation, the combination may turn out to be lethal. Such genes are said to "interact genetically". Genes that are connected in such a way form *genetic interaction networks*. Some of the goals of these networks are: develop a functional map of a cell's processes, drug target identification, and to predict the function of uncharacterized genes.

In 2010, the most "complete" gene interactome produced to date was compiled from about 5.4 million two-gene comparisons to describe "the interaction profiles for ~75% of all genes in the budding yeast," with ~170,000 gene interactions. The genes were grouped based on similar function so as to build a functional map of the cell's processes. Using this method the study was able to predict known gene functions better than any other genome-scale data set as well as adding functional information for genes that hadn't been previously described. From this model genetic interactions can be observed at multiple scales which will assist in the study of concepts such as gene conservation. Some of the observations made from this study are that there were twice as many negative as positive interactions, negative interactions were more informative than positive interactions, and genes with more connections were more likely to result in lethality when disrupted.

Interactomics

Interactomics is a discipline at the intersection of bioinformatics and biology that deals with studying both the interactions and the consequences of those interactions between and among proteins, and other molecules within a cell. Interactomics thus aims to compare such networks of interactions (i.e., interactomes) between and within species in order to find how the traits of such networks are either preserved or varied.

Interactomics is an example of "top-down" systems biology, which takes an overhead, as well as overall, view of a biosystem or organism. Large sets of genome-wide and proteomic data are collected, and correlations between different molecules are inferred. From the data new hypotheses are formulated about feedbacks between these molecules. These hypotheses can then be tested by new experiments.

Experimental Methods to Map Interactomes

The study of interactomes is called interactomics. The basic unit of a protein network is the protein–protein interaction (PPI). While there are numerous methods to study PPIs, there are relatively few that have been used on a large scale to map whole interactomes.

The yeast two hybrid system (Y2H) is suited to explore the binary interactions among two proteins at a time. Affinity purification and subsequent mass spectrometry is suited to identify a protein complex. Both methods can be used in a high-throughput (HTP) fashion. Yeast two hybrid screens allow false positive interactions between proteins that are never expressed in the same time and place; affinity capture mass spectrometry does not have this drawback, and is the current gold standard. Yeast two-hybrid data better indicates non-specific tendencies towards sticky interactions rather while affinity capture mass spectrometry better indicates functional in vivo protein–protein interactions.

Computational Methods to Study Interactomes

Once an interactome has been created, there are numerous ways to analyze its properties. However, there are two important goals of such analyses. First, scientists try to elucidate the systems properties of interactomes, e.g. the topology of its interactions. Second, studies may focus on individual proteins and their role in the network. Such analyses are mainly carried out using bioinformatics methods and include the following, among many others:

Validation

First, the coverage and quality of an interactome has to be evaluated. Interactomes are never complete, given the limitations of experimental methods. For instance, it has been estimated that typical Y2H screens detect only 25% or so of all interactions in an interactome. The coverage of an interactome can be assessed by comparing it to benchmarks of well-known interactions that have been found and validated by independent assays. Other methods filter out false positives calculating the similarity of known annotations of the proteins involved or define a likelyhood of interaction using the subcellular localization of these proteins.

Predicting PPIs

Using experimental data as a starting point, *homology transfer* is one way to predict interactomes. Here, PPIs from one organism are used to predict interactions among homologous proteins in another organism ("*interologs*"). However, this approach has certain limitations, primarily because the source data may not be reliable (e.g. contain false positives and false negatives). In addition, proteins and their interactions change during evolution and thus may have been lost or gained. Nevertheless, numerous interactomes have been predicted, e.g. that of *Bacillus licheniformis*.

Schziophrenia PPI.

Some algorithms use experimental evidence on structural complexes, the atomic details of binding interfaces and produce detailed atomic models of protein–protein complexes as well as other protein–molecule interactions. Other algorithms use only sequence information, thereby creating unbiased complete networks of interaction with many mistakes.

Some methods use machine learning to distinguish how interacting protein pairs differ from non-interacting protein pairs in terms of pairwise features such as cellular colocalization, gene co-expression, how closely located on a DNA are the genes that encode the two proteins, and so on. Random Forest has been found to be most-effective machine learning method for protein interaction prediction. Such methods have been applied for discovering protein interactions on human interactome, specifically the interactome of Membrane proteins and the interactome of Schizophrenia-associated proteins.

Text Mining of PPIs

Some efforts have been made to extract systematically interaction networks directly from the scientific literature. Such approaches range in terms of complexity from simple co-occurrence statistics of entities that are mentioned together in the same context (e.g. sentence) to sophisticated natural language processing and machine learning methods for detecting interaction relationships.

Protein Function Prediction

Protein interaction networks have been used to predict the function of proteins of unknown functions. This is usually based on the assumption that uncharacterized proteins have similar functions as their interacting proteins (*guilt by association*). For example, YbeB, a protein of unknown function was found to interact with ribosomal proteins and later shown to be involved in translation. Although such predictions may be based on single interactions, usually several interactions are found. Thus, the whole network of interactions can be used to predict protein functions, given that certain functions are usually enriched among the interactors.

Perturbations and Disease

The *topology* of an interactome makes certain predictions how a network reacts to the perturbation (e.g. removal) of nodes (proteins) or edges (interactions). Such perturbations can be caused by mutations of genes, and thus their proteins, and a network reaction can manifest as a disease. A network analysis can identified drug targets and biomarkers of diseases.

Network Structure and Topology

Interaction networks can be analyzed using the tools of graph theory. Network properties include the degree distribution, clustering coefficients, betweenness centrality, and many others. The distribution of properties among the proteins of an interactome has revealed that the interactome networks often have scale-free topology where functional modules within a network indicate specialized subnetworks. Such modules can be functional, as in a signaling pathway, or structural, as in a protein complex. In fact, it is a formidable task to identify protein complexes in an interactome, given that a network on its own does not directly reveal the presence of a stable complex.

Studied Interactomes

Viral Interactomes

Viral protein interactomes consist of interactions among viral or phage proteins. They were among the first interactome projects as their genomes are small and all proteins can be analyzed with limited resources. Viral interactomes are connected to their host interactomes, forming virus-host interaction networks. Some published virus interactomes include

Bacteriophage

- *Escherichia coli* bacteriophage lambda
- *Escherichia coli* bacteriophage T7
- *Streptococcus pneumoniae* bacteriophage Dp-1
- *Streptococcus pneumoniae* bacteriophage Cp-1

The lambda and VZV interactomes are not only relevant for the biology of these viruses but also for technical reasons: they were the first interactomes that were mapped with multiple Y2H vectors, proving an improved strategy to investigate interactomes more completely than previous attempts have shown.

Human (Mammalian) Viruses

- Human varicella zoster virus (VZV)

- Chandipura virus

- Epstein-Barr virus (EBV)

- Hepatitis C virus (HPC), Human-HCV interactions

- Hepatitis E virus (HEV)

- Herpes simplex virus 1 (HSV-1)

- Kaposi's sarcoma-associated herpesvirus (KSHV)

- Murine cytomegalovirus (mCMV)

Bacterial Interactomes

Relatively few bacteria have been comprehensively studied for their protein–protein interactions. However, none of these interactomes are complete in the sense that they captured all interactions. In fact, it has been estimated that none of them covers more than 20% or 30% of all interactions, primarily because most of these studies have only employed a single method, all of which discover only a subset of interactions. Among the published bacterial interactomes (including partial ones) are

Species	proteins total	interactions	type
Helicobacter pylori	1,553	~3,004	Y2H
Campylobacter jejuni	1,623	11,687	Y2H
Treponema pallidum	1,040	3,649	Y2H
Escherichia coli	4,288	(5,993)	AP/MS
Escherichia coli	4,288	2,234	Y2H
Mesorhizobium loti	6,752	3,121	Y2H
Mycobacterium tuberculosis	3,959	>8000	B2H
Mycoplasma genitalium	482		AP/MS
Synechocystis sp. PCC6803	3,264	3,236	Y2H
Staphylococcus aureus (MRSA)	2,656	13,219	AP/MS

The *E. coli* and *Mycoplasma* interactomes have been analyzed using large-scale protein complex affinity purification and mass spectrometry (AP/MS), hence it is not easily possible to infer direct interactions. The others have used extensive yeast two-hybrid (Y2H) screens. The *Mycobacterium tuberculosis* interactome has been analyzed using a bacterial two-hybrid screen (B2H).

Note that numerous additional interactomes have been predicted using computational methods.

Eukaryotic Interactomes

There have been several efforts to map eukaryotic interactomes through HTP methods. While no biological interactomes have been fully characterized, over 90% of proteins in *Saccharomyces cerevisiae* have been screened and their interactions characterized, making it the best-characterized interactome. Species whose interactomes have been studied in some detail include

- *Schizosaccharomyces pombe*
- *Caenorhabditis elegans*
- *Drosophila melanogaster*
- *Homo sapiens*

Recently, the pathogen-host interactomes of Hepatitis C Virus/Human (2008), Epstein Barr virus/Human (2008), Influenza virus/Human (2009) were delineated through HTP to identify essential molecular components for pathogens and for their host's immune system.

Predicted Interactomes

As described above, PPIs and thus whole interactomes can be predicted. While the reliability of these predictions is debatable, they are providing hypotheses that can be tested experimentally. Interactomes have been predicted for a number of species, e.g.

- Human (*Homo sapiens*)
- Rice (*Oryza sativa*)
- *Xanthomonas oryzae*
- *Arabidopsis thaliana*
- Tomato
- *Brassica rapa*
- Maize, corn (*Zea mays*)
- *Populus trichocarpa*

Network Properties of Interactomes

Protein interaction networks can be analyzed with the same tool as other networks. In fact, they share many properties with biological or social networks. Some of the main characteristics are as follows.

Degree Distribution

The degree distribution describes the number of proteins that have a certain number of connections. Most protein interaction networks show a scale-free (power law) degree distribution where the connectivity distribution $P(k) \sim k^{-\gamma}$ with k being the degree. This relationship can also be seen as a straight line on a log-log plot since, the above equation is equal to $\log(P(k)) \sim -\gamma \cdot \log(k)$. One characteristic of such distributions is that there are many proteins with few interactions and few proteins that have many interactions, the latter being called "hubs".

Hubs

Highly connected nodes (proteins) are called hubs. Han et al. have coined the term "party hub" for hubs whose expression is correlated with its interaction partners. Party hubs also connect proteins within functional modules such as protein complexes. In contrast, "date hubs" do not exhibit such a correlation and appear to connect different functional modules. Party hubs are found predominantly in AP/MS data sets, whereas date hubs are found predominantly in binary interactome network maps. Note that the validity of the date hub/party hub distinction was disputed. Party hubs generally consist of multi-interface proteins whereas date hubs are more frequently single-interaction interface proteins. Consistent with a role for date-hubs in connecting different processes, in yeast the number of binary interactions of a given protein is correlated to the number of phenotypes observed for the corresponding mutant gene in different physiological conditions.

Modules

Nodes involved in the same biochemical process are highly interconnected.

Interactome Evolution

The evolution of interactome complexity is delineated in a study published in Nature. In this study it is first noted that the boundaries between prokaryotes, unicellular eukaryotes and multicellular eukaryotes are accompanied by orders-of-magnitude reductions in effective population size, with concurrent amplifications of the effects of random genetic drift. The resultant decline in the efficiency of selection seems to be sufficient to influence a wide range of attributes at the genomic level in a nonadaptive manner. The Nature study shows that the variation in the power of random genetic drift is also capable of influencing phylogenetic diversity at the subcellular and cellular levels. Thus, population size would have to be considered as a potential determinant of the mechanistic pathways underlying long-term phenotypic evolution. In the study it is further shown that a phylogenetically broad inverse relation exists between the power of drift and the structural integrity of protein subunits. Thus, the accumulation of mildly deleterious mutations in populations of small size induces secondary selection for protein–protein interactions that stabilize key gene functions, mitigating the structural degradation promoted by inefficient selection. By this means, the complex protein architectures and interactions essential to the genesis of phenotypic diversity may initially emerge by non-adaptive mechanisms.

Criticisms, Challenges, and Responses

Kiemer and Cesareni raise the following concerns with the state (circa 2007) of the field especially with the comparative interactomic: The experimental procedures associated with the field are error prone leading to "noisy results". This leads to 30% of all reported interactions being artifacts. In fact, two groups using the same techniques on the same organism found less than 30% interactions in common. However, some authors have argued that such non-reproducibility results from the extraordinary sensitivity of various methods to small experimental variation. For instance, identical conditions in Y2H assays result in very different interactions when different Y2H vectors are used.

Techniques may be biased, i.e. the technique determines which interactions are found. In fact, any method has built in biases, especially protein methods. Because every protein is different no method can capture the properties of each protein. For instance, most analytical methods that work fine with soluble proteins deal poorly with membrane proteins. This is also true for Y2H and AP/MS technologies.

Interactomes are not nearly complete with perhaps the exception of *S. cerevisiae*. This is not really a criticism as any scientific area is "incomplete" initially until the methodologies have been improved. Interactomics in 2015 is where genome sequencing was in the late 1990s, given that only a few interactome datasets are available.

While genomes are stable, interactomes may vary between tissues, cell types, and developmental stages. Again, this is not a criticism, but rather a description of the challenges in the field.

It is difficult to match evolutionarily related proteins in distantly related species. While homologous DNA sequences can be found relatively easily, it is much more difficult to predict homologous interactions ("interologs") because the homologs of two interacting proteins do not need to interact. For instance, even within a proteome two proteins may interact but their paralogs may not.

Each protein–protein interactome may represent only a partial sample of potential interactions, even when a supposedly definitive version is published in a scientific journal. Additional factors may have roles in protein interactions that have yet to be incorporated in interactomes. The binding strength of the various protein interactors, microenvironmental factors, sensitivity to various procedures, and the physiological state of the cell all impact protein–protein interactions, yet are usually not accounted for in interactome studies.

Flow Cytometry Bioinformatics

Flow cytometry bioinformatics is the application of bioinformatics to flow cytometry data, which involves storing, retrieving, organizing and analyzing flow cytometry data using extensive computational resources and tools. Flow cytometry bioinformatics requires extensive use of and contributes to the development of techniques from computational statistics and machine learning. Flow cytometry and related methods allow the quantification of multiple independent biomarkers on large numbers of single cells. The rapid growth in the multidimensionality and throughput of flow cytometry data, particularly in the 2000s, has led to the creation of a variety of computational analysis methods, data standards, and public databases for the sharing of results.

Computational methods exist to assist in the preprocessing of flow cytometry data, identifying cell populations within it, matching those cell populations across samples, and performing diagnosis and discovery using the results of previous steps. For preprocessing, this includes compensating for spectral overlap, transforming data onto scales conducive to visualization and analysis, assessing data for quality, and normalizing data across samples and experiments. For population identification, tools are available to aid traditional manual identification of populations in two-dimensional scatter plots (gating), to use dimensionality reduction to aid gating, and to find populations automatically in higher-dimensional space in a variety of ways. It is also possible to characterize data in more comprehensive ways, such as the density-guided binary space partitioning technique known as probability binning, or by combinatorial gating. Finally, diagnosis using flow cytometry data can be aided by supervised learning techniques, and discovery of new cell types of biological importance by high-throughput statistical methods, as part of pipelines incorporating all of the aforementioned methods.

Open standards, data and software are also key parts of flow cytometry bioinformatics. Data standards include the widely adopted Flow Cytometry Standard (FCS) defining how data from cytometers should be stored, but also several new standards under development by the International Society for Advancement of Cytometry (ISAC) to aid in storing more detailed information about experimental design and analytical steps. Open data is slowly growing with the opening of the CytoBank database in 2010, and FlowRepository in 2012, both of which allow users to freely distribute their data, and the latter of which has been recommended as the preferred repository for MIFlowCyt-compliant data by ISAC. Open software is most widely available in the form of a suite of Bioconductor packages, but is also available for web execution on the GenePattern platform.

Data Collection

Flow cytometers operate by hydrodynamically focusing suspended cells so that they separate from each other within a fluid stream. The stream is interrogated by one or more lasers, and the resulting fluorescent and scattered light is detected by photomultipliers. By using optical filters, particular fluorophores on or within the cells can be quantified by peaks in their emission spectra. These may be endogenous fluorophores such as chlorophyll or transgenic green fluorescent protein, or they may be artificial fluorophores covalently bonded to detection molecules such as antibodies for detecting proteins, or hybridization probes for detecting DNA or RNA.

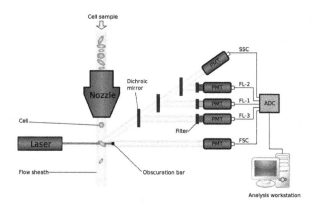

Schematic diagram of a flow cytometer, showing focusing of the fluid sheath, laser, optics (in simplified form, omitting focusing), photomultiplier tubes (PMTs), analogue-to-digital converter, and analysis workstation.

The ability to quantify these has led to flow cytometry being used in a wide range of applications, including but not limited to:

- Monitoring of CD4 count in HIV

- Diagnosis of various cancers

- Analysis of aquatic microbiomes

- Sperm sorting

- Measuring telomere length

Until the early 2000s, flow cytometry could only measure a few fluorescent markers at a time. Through the late 1990s into the mid-2000s, however, rapid development of new fluorophores resulted in modern instruments capable of quantifying up to 18 markers per cell. More recently, the new technology of mass cytometry replaces fluorophores with rare earth elements detected by time of flight mass spectrometry, achieving the ability to measure the expression of 34 or more markers. At the same time, microfluidic qPCR methods are providing a flow cytometry-like method of quantifying 48 or more RNA molecules per cell. The rapid increase in the dimensionality of flow cytometry data, coupled with the development of high-throughput robotic platforms capable of assaying hundreds to thousands of samples automatically have created a need for improved computational analysis methods.

Data

Markers

	FSC-A	FSC-H	SSC-A	B515-A	R780-A	R710-A	R660-A	V800-A	V655-A	V585-A	V450-A	G780-A	G710-A	G660-A	G610-A	G560-A
[1,]	27700.75	27291.75	177.52505	1964.485	625.6796	1232.1000	740.5101	1553.0295	1359.2565	3175.717	2330.1038	2206.1799	1758.4244	2550.914	1862.9043	1371.4854
[2,]	41264.25	39764.25	320.12296	3639.620	539.7032	1433.3112	2476.2059	2217.6750	2305.3516	5603.995	4767.4976	2617.9441	2063.0974	3401.507	2471.2236	2268.0318
[3,]	65054.75	57606.25	203.01697	2101.061	198.6541	726.9796	766.2196	802.2521	809.9579	1763.534	2870.2639	721.3501	750.2025	1156.690	879.6395	802.7821
[4,]	30504.60	31804.50	130.60890	1873.409	1304.0095	2520.7003	704.6980	1702.3671	1185.8608	2963.256	1839.7667	3945.7107	2489.2170	2585.430	3850.5399	2768.0043
[5,]	39505.75	39626.00	203.25166	2540.620	323.2025	857.1525	715.0004	1117.4775	1746.5790	3810.514	3442.1065	1766.7100	1595.8044	2746.546	2118.4902	1560.5364
[6,]	33171.50	34794.00	333.64246	2192.864	1408.8563	2573.5095	1604.2236	2128.1740	1727.5091	3734.910	2551.4509	5490.1421	2989.3867	3295.179	2938.3291	4603.7070
[7,]	62711.00	54475.50	1122.48340	3879.844	1730.0005	3573.5652	1691.8744	5106.0596	1570.0332	9183.305	7264.0634	7260.0550	4263.6313	4767.073	4025.7312	5758.2100
[8,]	46000.75	46213.50	236.54282	2545.050	1081.6753	2313.5952	1411.0963	2989.7524	1920.4047	4386.033	3081.6461	3615.0461	2552.7622	3304.552	2666.3181	3532.8064
[9,]	49206.00	49102.50	78.61045	1601.092	123.2634	493.6394	242.0285	633.3533	759.2227	1920.717	2082.5084	996.4405	805.6166	1197.744	957.8304	937.6376
[10,]	32209.75	33360.25	203.29097	2387.361	1056.0723	1769.4005	939.7758	1693.8635	1579.7000	3308.004	2106.1416	2835.7053	2057.3567	2653.473	1879.0623	2386.1431
[11,]	35937.25	36212.50	220.66590	2901.591	1218.1395	3202.3853	1059.7604	2443.6205	2253.0146	4684.219	2664.9727	5502.5425	3703.0475	4023.313	3111.4429	4476.1655
[12,]	32905.50	33097.50	233.90933	2726.246	1952.0721	3495.7139	2726.1091	2960.6882	2011.0159	4644.849	2661.8582	7000.1994	3540.6592	3915.086	3308.4014	6423.2324
[13,]	36028.50	35045.50	219.10874	3221.600	2542.3389	3895.0371	2203.0444	3331.6290	2479.6500	5253.362	2692.4919	9067.0859	4306.0105	4652.118	4095.7131	7948.1416
[14,]	38616.00	38775.00	218.46069	3218.305	502.6001	1022.7971	1255.5050	1516.4185	1993.2601	4657.159	1001.8761	2058.4124	1753.6392	2576.016	1914.5718	2386.2065
[15,]	45282.25	42223.25	1173.74407	6941.545	705.4651	1649.9570	1615.0811	4287.2036	3778.2302	11158.718	6247.2236	3130.5720	2382.1287	3487.720	2436.5006	3200.1677
[16,]	36246.25	36207.75	199.15569	3040.417	1726.7026	2823.7206	1031.6308	2624.6592	1053.8043	4669.628	2530.0605	6049.0901	3479.7073	3642.755	2085.2795	4767.1269
[17,]	29202.75	29004.00	289.64102	1836.197	612.2673	1149.7164	870.3303	1720.2170	1525.6914	2782.762	2335.3994	2180.0403	1855.0010	2702.035	1291.8840	1730.4067
[18,]	57757.25	54440.25	1098.17517	12972.077	4364.5900	11298.7070	6745.5039	20934.3457	17057.1934	30293.180	7082.0604	14765.4705	13275.3628	16369.047	14707.2540	9409.2637
[19,]	33301.00	33093.50	206.47181	2146.622	429.5022	855.5901	840.9418	1297.8069	1297.2603	2751.205	1001.5309	1716.1721	1479.2037	2510.357	1566.1290	1371.2155
[20,]	34470.25	35390.75	211.20921	3060.505	2016.3651	3442.5460	1340.4852	2673.9729	2259.0494	3781.046	1290.9741	7142.1543	3906.1693	4301.971	3506.8269	5097.7954
[21,]	29400.25	28219.50	231.55798	3060.300	997.8875	2319.5779	1514.2091	1757.2463	1875.9983	3019.569	1565.1250	4966.3364	2470.9639	2938.509	2288.2273	3631.0906
[22,]	49978.50	40517.75	537.64224	3122.343	901.1232	2252.1109	1861.3472	2518.4731	2306.9327	5010.112	3615.4170	4111.9141	2611.4641	3379.042	2634.6746	3722.1040
[23,]	39872.50	37020.75	198.75706	2719.222	1657.0030	2945.5713	1825.1293	3283.6527	1870.1367	3072.603	1079.3605	6735.8099	3531.4177	3501.812	2901.9954	4790.6758
[24,]	33395.00	35331.75	220.46056	2664.632	690.1926	1483.6096	1736.9537	1397.0316	1902.9124	3473.234	1987.4607	2142.7542	1793.1940	2844.251	2057.5003	2655.7776
[25,]	46976.60	47355.25	231.33037	2530.461	537.1376	1194.0661	1072.7603	1511.7494	1766.5041	3532.332	3593.0466	3967.0032	1918.4053	3249.490	2566.3657	3608.4010
[26,]	56663.75	51450.25	223.66416	3217.000	206.6222	1279.4000	1207.4561	1260.9965	1553.0804	3397.091	2623.9312	1606.0220	1583.9100	2461.450	1874.0762	2013.9438
[27,]	56818.75	48556.25	305.77102	3714.351	577.0732	1364.4095	1064.0903	1633.2513	2077.9406	3332.029	2654.2678	2074.0388	1966.0965	2876.737	1987.8170	2010.1973
[28,]	36225.25	36106.75	180.30524	2638.406	946.7570	2130.4143	1095.8002	1007.0429	2857.7292	3673.460	2611.5057	3530.6289	2630.3755	3600.507	2727.3037	2884.0163
[29,]	28509.25	30715.50	230.27397	1872.201	1067.2069	1843.1423	802.4011	1201.5806	668.1475	1810.260	618.8154	3604.4263	1530.6611	1353.209	1167.5325	2577.3455
[30,]	37198.75	36200.50	237.67776	3046.719	1376.3452	2580.9207	1326.2197	2509.6101	2196.7250	5525.000	3065.0623	4946.4224	3421.0040	3996.500	3045.4102	4413.9908

Cells (row label axis)

Representation of flow cytometry data from an instrument with three scatter channels and 13 fluorescent channels. Only the values for the first 30 (of hundreds of thousands) of cells are shown.

Flow cytometry data is in the form of a large matrix of intensities over M wavelengths by N events. Most events will be a particular cell, although some may be doublets (pairs of cells which pass the laser closely together). For each event, the measured fluorescence intensity over a particular wavelength range is recorded.

The measured fluorescence intensity indicates the amount of that fluorophore in the cell, which indicates the amount that has bound to detector molecules such as antibodies. Therefore, fluorescence intensity can be considered a proxy for the amount of detector molecules present on the cell. A simplified, if not strictly accurate, way of considering flow cytometry data is as a matrix of M measurements of amounts of molecules of interest by N cells.

Steps in Computational Flow Cytometry Data Analysis

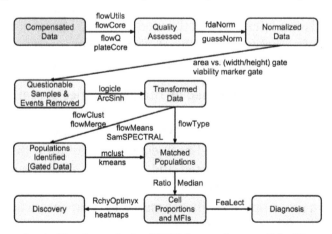

An example pipeline for analysis of FCM data and some of the Bioconductor packages relevant to each step.

The process of moving from primary FCM data to disease diagnosis and biomarker discovery involves four major steps:

1. Data pre-processing (including compensation, transformation and normalization)

2. Cell population identification (a.k.a. gating)

3. Cell population matching for cross sample comparison

4. Relating cell populations to external variables (diagnosis and discovery)

Saving of the steps taken in a particular flow cytometry workflow is supported by some flow cytometry software, and is important for the reproducibility of flow cytometry experiments. However, saved workspace files are rarely interchangeable between software. An attempt to solve this problem is the development of the Gating-ML XML-based data standard (discussed in more detail under the standards section), which is slowly being adopted in both commercial and open source flow cytometry software.

Data Pre-processing

Prior to analysis, flow cytometry data must typically undergo pre-processing to remove artifacts and poor quality data, and to be transformed onto an optimal scale for identifying cell populations of interest. Below are various steps in a typical flow cytometry preprocessing pipeline.

Compensation

When more than one fluorochrome is used with the same laser, their emission spectra frequently overlap. Each particular fluorochrome is typically measured using a bandpass optical filter set to a narrow band at or near the fluorochrome's emission intensity peak. The result is that the reading for any given fluorochrome is actually the sum of that fluorochrome's peak emission intensity, and the intensity of all other fluorochromes' spectra where they overlap with that frequency band. This overlap is termed spillover, and the process of removing spillover from flow cytometry data is called compensation.

Compensation is typically accomplished by running a series of representative samples each stained for only one fluorochrome, to give measurements of the contribution of each fluorochrome to each channel. The total signal to remove from each channel can be computed by solving a system of linear equations based on this data to produce a spillover matrix, which when inverted and multiplied with the raw data from the cytometer produces the compensated data. The processes of computing the spillover matrix, or applying a precomputed spillover matrix to compensate flow cytometry data, are standard features of flow cytometry software.

Transformation

Cell populations detected by flow cytometry are often described as having approximately log-normal expression. As such, they have traditionally been transformed to a logarithmic scale. In early cytometers, this was often accomplished even before data acquisition by use of a log amplifier. On modern instruments, data is usually stored in linear form, and transformed digitally prior to analysis.

However, compensated flow cytometry data frequently contains negative values due to compensation, and cell populations do occur which have low means and normal distributions. Logarithmic transformations cannot properly handle negative values, and poorly display normally distributed cell types. Alternative transformations which address this issue include the log-linear hybrid transformations Logicle and Hyperlog, as well as the hyperbolic arcsine and the Box-Cox.

A comparison of commonly used transformations concluded that the biexponential and Box-Cox transformations, when optimally parameterized, provided the clearest visualization and least variance of cell populations across samples. However, a later comparison of the flowTrans package used in that comparison indicated that it did not parameterize the Logicle transformation in a manner consistent with other implementations, potentially calling those results into question.

Quality Control

Particularly in newer, high-throughput experiments, there is a need for visualization methods to help detect technical errors in individual samples. One approach is to visualize summary statistics, such as the empirical distribution functions of single dimensions of technical or biological replicates to ensure they are the similar. For more rigor, the Kolmogorov–Smirnov test can be used to determine if individual samples deviate from the norm. The Grubbs' test for outliers may be used to detect samples deviating from the group.

A method for quality control in higher-dimensional space is to use probability binning with bins fit to the whole data set pooled together. Then the standard deviation of the number of cells falling in the bins within each sample can be taken as a measure of multidimensional similarity, with samples that are closer to the norm having a smaller standard deviation. With this method, higher standard deviation can indicate outliers, although this is a relative measure as the absolute value depends partly on the number of bins.

With all of these methods, the cross-sample variation is being measured. However, this is the combination of technical variations introduced by the instruments and handling, and actual biological information that is desired to be measured. Disambiguating the technical and the biological contributions to between-sample variation can be a difficult to impossible task.

Normalization

Particularly in multi-centre studies, technical variation can make biologically equivalent populations of cells difficult to match across samples. Normalization methods to remove technical variance, frequently derived from image registration techniques, are thus a critical step in many flow cytometry analyses. Single-marker normalization can be performed using landmark registration, in which peaks in a kernel density estimate of each sample are identified and aligned across samples.

Identifying Cell Populations

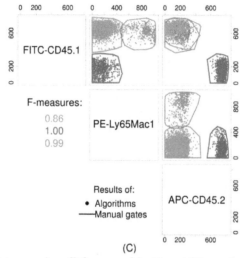

(C)

Two-dimensional scatter plots covering all three combinations of three chosen dimensions. The colours show the comparison of consensus of eight independent manual gates (polygons) and automated gates (colored dots). The consensus of the manual gates and the algorithms were produced using the CLUE package. Figure reproduced from.

The complexity of raw flow cytometry data (dozens of measurements for thousands to millions of cells) makes answering questions directly using statistical tests or supervised learning difficult. Thus, a critical step in the analysis of flow cytometric data is to reduce this complexity to something more tractable while establishing common features across samples. This usually involves identifying multidimensional regions that contain functionally and phenotypically homogeneous groups of cells. This is a form of cluster analysis. There are a range of methods by which this can be achieved, detailed below.

Gating

The data generated by flow-cytometers can be plotted in one or two dimensions to produce a histogram or scatter plot. The regions on these plots can be sequentially separated, based on fluorescence intensity, by creating a series of subset extractions, termed "gates". These gates can be produced using software, e.g. Flowjo, FCS Express, Win-MDI, CytoPaint (aka Paint-A-Gate), VenturiOne, CellQuest Pro, Cytospec, or Kaluza.

In datasets with a low number of dimensions and limited cross-sample technical and biological variability (e.g., clinical laboratories), manual analysis of specific cell populations can produce effective and reproducible results. However, exploratory analysis of a large number of cell populations in a high-dimensional dataset is not feasible. In addition, manual analysis in less controlled settings (e.g., cross-laboratory studies) can increase the overall error rate of the study. In one study, several computational gating algorithms performed better than manual analysis in the presence of some variation. However, despite the considerable advances in computational analysis, manual gating remains the main solution for the identification of specific rare cell populations that are not well-separated from other cell types.

Gating Guided by Dimension Reduction

The number of scatter plots that need to be investigated increases with the square of the number of markers measured (or faster since some markers need to be investigated several times for each group of cells to resolve high-dimensional differences between cell types that appear to be similar in most markers). To address this issue, principal component analysis has been used to summarize the high-dimensional datasets using a combination of markers that maximizes the variance of all data points. However, PCA is a linear method and is not able to preserve complex and non-linear relationships. More recently, two dimensional minimum spanning tree layouts have been used to guide the manual gating process. Density-based down-sampling and clustering was used to better represent rare populations and control the time and memory complexity of the minimum spanning tree construction process. More sophisticated dimension reduction algorithms are yet to be investigated.

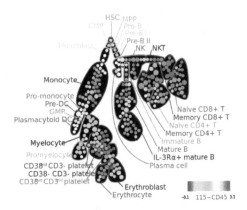

Cell populations in a high-dimensional mass-cytometry dataset manually gated after dimension reduction using 2D layout for a minimum spanning tree. Figure reproduced from the data provided in.

Automated Gating

Developing computational tools for identification of cell populations has been an area of active research only since 2008. Many individual clustering approaches have recently been developed, including model-based algorithms (e.g., flowClust and FLAME), density based algorithms (e.g. FLOCK and SWIFT, graph-based approaches (e.g. SamSPECTRAL) and most recently, hybrids of several approaches (flowMeans and flowPeaks). These algorithms are different in terms of memory and time complexity, their software requirements, their ability to automatically determine the required number of cell populations, and their sensitivity and specificity. The FlowCAP (Flow Cytometry: Critical Assessment of Population Identification Methods) project, with active participation from most academic groups with research efforts in the area, is providing a way to objectively cross-compare state-of-the-art automated analysis approaches. Other surveys have also compared automated gating tools on several datasets .

Probability Binning Methods

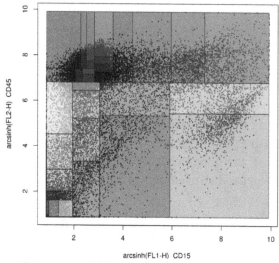

An example of frequency difference gating, created using the flowFP Bioconductor package. The dots represent individual events in an FCS file. The rectangles represent the bins.

Probability binning is a non-gating analysis method in which flow cytometry data is split into quantiles on a univariate basis. The locations of the quantiles can then be used to test for differences between samples (in the variables not being split) using the chi-squared test.

This was later extended into multiple dimensions in the form of frequency difference gating, a binary space partitioning technique where data is iteratively partitioned along the median. These partitions (or bins) are fit to a control sample. Then the proportion of cells falling within each bin in test samples can be compared to the control sample by the chi squared test.

Finally, cytometric fingerprinting uses a variant of frequency difference gating to set bins and measure for a series of samples how many cells fall within each bin. These bins can be used as gates and used for subsequent analysis similarly to automated gating methods.

Combinatorial Gating

High-dimensional clustering algorithms are often unable to identify rare cell types that are not well separated from other major populations. Matching these small cell populations across multiple samples is even more challenging. In manual analysis, prior biological knowledge (e.g., biological controls) provides guidance to reasonably identify these populations. However, integrating this information into the exploratory clustering process (e.g., as in semi-supervised learning) has not been successful.

An alternative to high-dimensional clustering is to identify cell populations using one marker at a time and then combine them to produce higher-dimensional clusters. This functionality was first implemented in FlowJo. The flowType algorithm builds on this framework by allowing the exclusion of the markers. This enables the development of statistical tools (e.g. RchyOptimyx) that can investigate the importance of each marker and exclude high-dimensional redundancies.

Diagnosis and Discovery

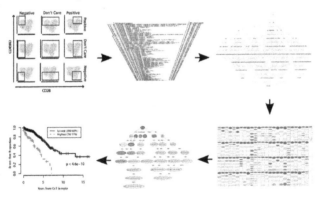

Overview of the flowType/RchyOptimyx pipeline for identification of correlates of protection against HIV: First, tens of thousands of cell populations are identified by combining one-dimensional partitions (panel one). The cell populations are then analyzed using a statistical test (and bonferroni's method for multiple testing correction) to identify those correlated with the survival information. The third panel shows a complete gating hierarchy describing all possible strategies for gating that cell population. This graph can be mined to identify the "best" gating strategy (i.e., the one in which the most important markers appear earlier). These hierarchies for all selected phenotypes are demonstrated in panel 4. In panel 5, these hierarchies are merged into a single graph that summarized the entire dataset and demonstrates the trade-off between the number of markers involved in each phenotype and the significance of the correlation with the clinical outcome (e.g., as measured by the Kaplan–Meier estimator in panel 6). Figure reproduced in part from and.

After identification of the cell population of interest, a cross sample analysis can be performed to identify phenotypical or functional variations that are correlated with an external variable (e.g., a clinical outcome). These studies can be partitioned into two main groups:

Diagnosis

In these studies, the goal usually is to diagnose a disease (or a sub-class of a disease) using variations in one or more cell populations. For example, one can use multidimensional clustering to identify a set of clusters, match them across all samples, and then use supervised learning to construct a classifier for prediction of the classes of interest (e.g., this approach can be used to improve the accuracy of the classification of specific lymphoma subtypes). Alternatively, all the cells from the entire cohort can be pooled into a single multidimensional space for clustering before classification. This approach is particularly suitable for datasets with a high amount of biological variation (in which cross-sample matching is challenging) but requires technical variations to be carefully controlled.

Discovery

In a discovery setting, the goal is to identify and describe cell populations correlated with an external variable (as opposed to the diagnosis setting in which the goal is to combine the predictive power of multiple cell types to maximize the accuracy of the results). Similar to the diagnosis use-case, cluster matching in high-dimensional space can be used for exploratory analysis but the descriptive power of this approach is very limited, as it is hard to characterize and visualize a cell population in a high-dimensional space without first reducing the dimensionality. Finally, combinatorial gating approaches have been particularly successful in exploratory analysis of FCM data. Simplified Presentation of Incredibly Complex Evaluations (SPICE) is a software package that can use the gating functionality of FlowJo to statistically evaluate a wide range of different cell populations and visualize those that are correlated with the external outcome. flowType and Rchy-Optimyx (as discussed above) expand this technique by adding the ability of exploring the impact of independent markers on the overall correlation with the external outcome. This enables the removal of unnecessary markers and provides a simple visualization of all identified cell types. In a recent analysis of a large (n=466) cohort of HIV+ patients, this pipeline identified three correlates of protection against HIV, only one of which had been previously identified through extensive manual analysis of the same dataset.

Data Formats and Interchange

Flow Cytometry Standard

Flow Cytometry Standard (FCS) was developed in 1984 to allow recording and sharing of flow cytometry data. Since then, FCS became the standard file format supported by all flow cytometry software and hardware vendors. The FCS specification has traditionally been developed and maintained by the International Society for Advancement of Cytometry (ISAC). Over the years, updates were incorporated to adapt to technological advancements in both flow cytometry and computing technologies with FCS 2.0 introduced in 1990, FCS 3.0 in 1997, and the most current specification FCS 3.1 in 2010. FCS used to be the only widely adopted file format in flow cytometry. Recently, additional standard file formats have been developed by ISAC.

netCDF

ISAC is considering replacing FCS with a flow cytometry specific version of the Network Common Data Form (netCDF) file format. netCDF is a set of freely available software libraries and machine independent data formats that support the creation, access, and sharing of array-oriented scientific data. In 2008, ISAC drafted the first version of netCDF conventions for storage of raw flow cytometry data.

Archival Cytometry Standard (ACS)

The Archival Cytometry Standard (ACS) is being developed to bundle data with different components describing cytometry experiments. It captures relations among data, metadata, analysis files and other components, and includes support for audit trails, versioning and digital signatures. The ACS container is based on the ZIP file format with an XML-based table of contents specifying relations among files in the container. The XML Signature W3C Recommendation has been adopted to allow for digital signatures of components within the ACS container. An initial draft of ACS has been designed in 2007 and finalized in 2010. Since then, ACS support has been introduced in several software tools including FlowJo and Cytobank.

Gating-ML

The lack of gating interoperability has traditionally been a bottleneck preventing reproducibility of flow cytometry data analysis and the usage of multiple analytical tools. To address this shortcoming, ISAC developed Gating-ML, an XML-based mechanism to formally describe gates and related data (scale) transformations. The draft recommendation version of Gating-ML was approved by ISAC in 2008 and it is partially supported by tools like FlowJo, the flowUtils library in R/BioConductor, and FlowRepository. It supports rectangular gates, polygon gates, convex polytopes, ellipsoids, decision trees and Boolean collections of any of the other types of gates. In addition, it includes dozens of built in public transformations that have been shown to potentially useful for display or analysis of cytometry data. In 2013, Gating-ML version 2.0 was approved by ISAC's Data Standards Task Force as a Recommendation. This new version offers slightly less flexibility in terms of the power of gating description; however, it is also significantly easier to implement in software tools.

Classification Results (CLR)

The Classification Results (CLR) File Format has been developed to exchange the results of manual gating and algorithmic classification approaches in a standard way in order to be able to report and process the classification. CLR is based in the commonly supported CSV file format with columns corresponding to different classes and cell values containing the probability of an event being a member of a particular class. These are captured as values between 0 and 1. Simplicity of the format and its compatibility with common spreadsheet tools have been the major requirements driving the design of the specification. Although it was originally designed for the field of flow cytometry, it is applicable in any domain that needs to capture either fuzzy or unambiguous classifications of virtually any kinds of objects.

Public Data and Software

As in other bioinformatics fields, development of new methods has primarily taken the form of free open source software, and several databases have been created for depositing open data.

Bioconductor

The Bioconductor project is a repository of free open source software, mostly written in the R programming language. As of July 2013, Bioconductor contained 21 software packages for processing flow cytometry data. These packages cover most of the range of functionality described earlier in this article.

GenePattern

GenePattern is a predominantly genomic analysis platform with over 200 tools for analysis of gene expression, proteomics, and other data. A web-based interface provides easy access to these tools and allows the creation of automated analysis pipelines enabling reproducible research. Recently, a GenePattern Flow Cytometry Suite has been developed in order to bring advanced flow cytometry data analysis tools to experimentalists without programmatic skills. It contains close to 40 open source GenePattern flow cytometry modules covering methods from basic processing of flow cytometry standard (i.e., FCS) files to advanced algorithms for automated identification of cell populations, normalization and quality assessment. Internally, most of these modules leverage functionality developed in BioConductor.

Much of the functionality of the Bioconductor packages for flow cytometry analysis has been packaged up for use with the GenePattern workflow system, in the form of the GenePattern Flow Cytometry Suite.

FACSanadu

FACSanadu is an open source portable application for visualization and analysis of FCS data. Unlike Bioconductor, it is an interactive program aimed at non-programmers for routine analysis. It supports standard FCS files as well as COPAS profile data.

Public Databases

The Minimum Information about a Flow Cytometry Experiment (MIFlowCyt), requires that any flow cytometry data used in a publication be available, although this does not include a requirement that it be deposited in a public database. Thus, although the journals Cytometry Part A and B, as well as all journals from the Nature Publishing Group require MIFlowCyt compliance, there is still relatively little publicly available flow cytometry data. Some efforts have been made towards creating public databases, however.

Firstly, CytoBank, which is a complete web-based flow cytometry data storage and analysis platform, has been made available to the public in a limited form. Using the CytoBank code base, FlowRepository was developed in 2012 with the support of ISAC to be a public repository of flow cytometry data. FlowRepository facilitates MIFlowCyt compliance, and as of July 2013 contained 65 public data sets.

Datasets

In 2012, the flow cytometry community has started to release a set of publicly available datasets. A subset of these datasets representing the existing data analysis challenges is described below. For comparison against manual gating, the FlowCAP-I project has released five datasets, manually gated by human analysts, and two of them gated by eight independent analysts. The FlowCAP-II project included three datasets for binary classification and also reported several algorithms that were able to classify these samples perfectly. FlowCAP-III included two larger datasets for comparison against manual gates as well as one more challenging sample classification dataset. As of March 2013, public release of FlowCAP-III was still in progress. The datasets used in FlowCAP-I, II, and III either have a low number of subjects or parameters. However, recently several more complex clinical datasets have been released including a dataset of 466 HIV-infected subjects, which provides both 14 parameter assays and sufficient clinical information for survival analysis.

Another class of datasets are higher-dimensional mass cytometry assays. A representative of this class of datasets is a study which includes analysis of two bone marrow samples using more than 30 surface or intracellular markers under a wide range of different stimulations. The raw data for this dataset is publicly available as described in the manuscript, and manual analyses of the surface markers are available upon request from the authors.

Open Problems

Despite rapid development in the field of flow cytometry bioinformatics, several problems remain to be addressed.

Variability across flow cytometry experiments arises from biological variation among samples, technical variations across instruments used, as well as methods of analysis. In 2010, a group of researchers from Stanford University and the National Institutes of Health pointed out that while technical variation can be ameliorated by standardizing sample handling, instrument setup and choice of reagents, solving variation in analysis methods will require similar standardization and computational automation of gating methods. They further opined that centralization of both data and analysis could aid in decreasing variability between experiments and in comparing results.

This was echoed by another group of Pacific Biosciences and Stanford University researchers, who suggested that cloud computing could enable centralized, standardized, high-throughput analysis of flow cytometry experiments. They also emphasised that ongoing development and adoption of standard data formats could continue to aid in reducing variability across experiments. They also proposed that new methods will be needed to model and summarize results of high-throughput analysis in ways that can be interpreted by biologists, as well as ways of integrating large-scale flow cytometry data with other high-throughput biological information, such as gene expression, genetic variation, metabolite levels and disease states.

Biodiversity Informatics

Biodiversity Informatics is the application of informatics techniques to biodiversity information for improved management, presentation, discovery, exploration and analysis. It typically builds on a foundation of taxonomic, biogeographic, or ecological information stored in digital form, which, with the application of modern computer techniques, can yield new ways to view and analyse existing information, as well as predictive models for information that does not yet exist. Biodiversity informatics is a relatively young discipline (the term was coined in or around 1992) but has hundreds of practitioners worldwide, including the numerous individuals involved with the design and construction of taxonomic databases. The term "Biodiversity Informatics" is generally used in the broad sense to apply to computerized handling of any biodiversity information; the somewhat broader term "bioinformatics" is often used synonymously with the computerized handling of data in the specialized area of molecular biology.

Overview

Biodiversity informatics (different but linked to bioinformatics) is the application of information technology methods to the problems of organizing, accessing, visualizing and analyzing primary biodiversity data. Primary biodiversity data is composed of names, observations and records of specimens, and genetic and morphological data associated to a specimen. Biodiversity informatics may also have to cope with managing information from unnamed taxa such as that produced by environmental sampling and sequencing of mixed-field samples. The term biodiversity informatics is also used to cover the computational problems specific to the names of biological entities, such as the development of algorithms to cope with variant representations of identifiers such as species names and authorities, and the multiple classification schemes within which these entities may reside according to the preferences of different workers in the field, as well as the syntax and semantics by which the content in taxonomic databases can be made machine queryable and interoperable for biodiversity informatics purposes...

History of the Discipline of Biodiversity Informatics

Biodiversity Informatics can be considered to have commenced with the construction of the first computerized taxonomic databases in the early 1970s, and progressed through subsequent developing of distributed search tools towards the late 1990s including the Species Analyst from Kansas University, the North American Biodiversity Information Network NABIN, CONABIO in Mexico, and others, the establishment of the Global Biodiversity Information Facility in 2001, and the parallel development of a variety of niche modelling and other tools to operate on digitized biodiversity data from the mid-1980s onwards. In September 2000, the U.S. journal Science devoted a special issue to "Bioinformatics for Biodiversity", the journal "Biodiversity Informatics" commenced publication in 2004, and several international conferences through the 2000s have brought together Biodiversity Informatics practitioners, including the London e-Biosphere conference in June 2009. A supplement to the journal BMC Bioinformatics (Volume 10 Suppl 14) published in November 2009 also deals with Biodiversity Informatics.

History of the Term "Biodiversity Informatics"

According to correspondence reproduced by Walter Berendsohn, the term "Biodiversity Informatics" was coined by John Whiting in 1992 to cover the activities of an entity known as the Canadian Biodiversity Informatics Consortium, a group involved with fusing basic biodiversity information with environmental economics and geospatial information in the form of GPS and GIS. Subsequently it appears to have lost any obligate connection with the GPS/GIS world and be associated with the computerized management of any aspects of biodiversity information.

Current Biodiversity Informatics Issues

Global List of all Species

One major issue for biodiversity informatics at a global scale is the current absence of a complete master list of currently recognised species of the world, although this is an aim of the Catalogue of Life project which has ca. 1.65 million species of an estimated 1.9 million described species in its 2016 Annual Checklist. A similar effort for fossil taxa, the Paleobiology Database documents some 100,000+ names for fossil species, out of an unknown total number.

Problems with Genus and Species Scientific Names as Unique and Persistent Identifiers

Application of the Linnaean system of binomial nomenclature for species, and uninomials for genera and higher ranks, has led to many advantages but also problems with homonyms (the same name being used for multiple taxa, either inadvertently or legitimately across multiple kingdoms), synonyms (multiple names for the same taxon), as well as variant representations of the same name due to orthographic differences, minor spelling errors, variation in the manner of citation of author names and dates, and more. In addition, names can change through time on account of changing taxonomic opinions (for example, the correct generic placement of a species, or the elevation of a subspecies to species rank or vice versa), and also the circumscription of a taxon can change according to different authors' taxonomic concepts. One proposed solution to this problem is the usage of Life Science Identifiers (LSIDs) for machine-machine communication purposes, although there are both proponents and opponents of this approach.

Achieving a Consensus Classification of Organisms

Organisms can be classified in a multitude of ways, which can create design problems for Biodiversity Informatics systems aimed at incorporating either a single or multiple classification to suit the needs of users, or to guide them towards a single "preferred" system. Whether a single consensus classification system can ever be achieved is probably an open question, however the Catalogue of Life has commissioned activity in this area which has been succeeded by a published system proposed in 2015 by M. Ruggiero and co-workers.

Mobilizing Primary Biodiversity Information

"Primary" biodiversity information can be considered the basic data on the occurrence and diversity of species (or indeed, any recognizable taxa), commonly in association with information regarding their distribution in either space, time, or both. Such information may be in the form of retained specimens and associated information, for example as assembled in the natural history collections of museums and herbaria, or as observational records, for example either from formal faunal or floristic surveys undertaken by professional biologists and students, or as amateur and other planned or unplanned observations including those increasingly coming under the scope of citizen science. Providing online, coherent digital access to this vast collection of disparate primary data is a core Biodiversity Informatics function that is at the heart of regional and global biodiversity data networks, examples of the latter including OBIS and GBIF.

As a secondary source of biodiversity data, relevant scientific literature can be parsed either by humans or (potentially) by specialized information retrieval algorithms to extract the relevant primary biodiversity information that is reported therein, sometimes in aggregated / summary form but frequently as primary observations in narrative or tabular form. Elements of such activity (such as extracting key taxonomic identifiers, keywording / index terms, etc.) have been practiced for many years at a higher level by selected academic databases and search engines. However, for the maximum Biodiversity Informatics value, the actual primary occurrence data should ideally be retrieved and then made available in a standardized form or forms; for example both the Plazi and INOTAXA projects are transforming taxonomic literature into XML formats that can then be read by client applications, the former using TaxonX-XML and the latter using the taXMLit format. The Biodiversity Heritage Library is also making significant progress in its aim to digitize substantial portions of the out-of-copyright taxonomic literature, which is then subjected to OCR (optical character recognition) so as to be amenable to further processing using Biodiversity Informatics tools.

Biodiversity Informatics Standards and Protocols

In common with other data-related disciplines, Biodiversity Informatics benefits from the adoption of appropriate standards and protocols in order to support machine-machine transmission and interoperability of information within its particular domain. Examples of relevant standards include the Darwin Core XML schema for specimen- and observation-based biodiversity data developed from 1998 onwards, plus extensions of the same, Taxonomic Concept Transfer Schema, plus standards for Structured Descriptive Data and Access to Biological Collection Data (ABCD); while data retrieval and transfer protocols include DiGIR (now mostly superseded) and TAPIR (TDWG Access Protocol for Information Retrieval). Many of these standards and protocols are currently maintained, and their development overseen, by the Taxonomic Databases Working Group (TDWG).

Current Biodiversity Informatics Activities

At the 2009 e-Biosphere conference in the U.K., the following themes were adopted, which is indicative of a broad range of current Biodiversity Informatics activities and how they might be categorized:

- Application: Conservation / Agriculture / Fisheries / Industry / Forestry

- Application: Invasive Alien Species

- Application: Systematic and Evolutionary Biology

- Application: Taxonomy and Identification Systems

- New Tools, Services and Standards for Data Management and Access

    o New Modeling Tools

    o New Tools for Data Integration

- o   New Approaches to Biodiversity Infrastructure

- o   New Approaches to Species Identification

- o   New Approaches to Mapping Biodiversity

- National and Regional Biodiversity Databases and Networks

A post-conference workshop of key persons with current significant Biodiversity Informatics roles also resulted in a Workshop Resolution that stressed, among other aspects, the need to create durable, global registries for the resources that are basic to biodiversity informatics (e.g., repositories, collections); complete the construction of a solid taxonomic infrastructure; and create ontologies for biodiversity data.

Biodiversity Informatics Projects of the World

Global projects:

- The Global Biodiversity Information Facility (GBIF), and the Ocean Biogeographic Information System (OBIS) (for marine species)

- The Species 2000, ITIS (Integrated Taxonomic Information System), and Catalogue of Life projects

- Global Names

- EOL, The Encyclopedia of Life project

- The Consortium for the Barcode of Life project

- The Map of Life project

- The uBio Universal Biological Indexer and Organizer, from the Woods Hole Marine Biological Laboratory

- The Index to Organism Names (ION) from Thomson Reuters, providing access to scientific names of taxa from numerous journals as indexed in the Zoological Record

- ZooBank, the registry for nomenclatural acts and relevant systematic literature in zoology

- The Index Nominum Genericorum, compilation of generic names published for organisms covered by the International Code of Botanical Nomenclature, maintained at the Smithsonian Institution in the U.S.A.

- The International Plant Names Index

- MycoBank, documenting new names and combinations for fungi

- The List of Prokaryotic names with Standing in Nomenclature (LPSN) - Official register of valid names for bacteria and archaea, as governed by the International Code of Nomenclature of Bacteria

- The Biodiversity Heritage Library project - digitising biodiversity literature

- Wikispecies, open source (community-editable) compilation of taxonomic information, companion project to Wikipedia

- TaxonConcept.org, a Linked Data project that connects disparate species databases

- Instituto de Ciencias Naturales. Universidad Nacional de Colombia. Virtual Collections and Biodiversity Informatics Unit

- ANTABIF. The Antarctic Biodiversity Information Facility gives free and open access to Antarctic Biodiversity data, in the spirit of the Antarctic Treaty.

- Genesys (website), database of plant genetic resources maintained in national, regional and international gene banks

Regional and national projects:

- Fauna Europaea

- Atlas of Living Australia

- A Pan-European Species-directories Infrastructure (PESI)

- Symbiota

- i4Life project

- Sistema de Información sobre Biodiversidad de Colombia

- LifeWatch is proposed by ESFRI as a pan-European research (e-)infrastructure to support Biodiversity research and policy-making.

A listing of over 600 current biodiversity informatics related activities can be found at the TDWG "Biodiversity Information Projects of the World" database.

References

- Bourne, P.E., and Gu, J. (2009) Structural Bioinformatics (2nd edition), John Wiley & Sons, New York, ISBN 978-0-470-18105-8.

- Leach, Andrew (2001) Molecular Modelling: Principles and Applications (2nd edition), Prentice Hall, ISBN 978-0-582-38210-7.

- Peitsch, M.C., and Schwede, T. (2008) Computational Structural Biology: Methods and Applications World Scientific, ISBN 978-9812778772.

Permissions

Index

A

Automated Gating, 233-234

B

Bacterial Interactomes, 223
Bayesian Network Modelling, 216
Bioclipse, 14, 192, 202-203
Bioconductor, 14, 165, 170-173, 176, 208, 227, 229, 234, 237-238
Biodiversity Informatics, 13, 240-245
Bioengineering, 3, 99, 131
Bioinformatics Workflow Management Systems, 14
Biojava, 14, 165, 176-180, 182, 185-186, 188-192, 203
Biojs, 14, 176, 192-193, 208
Bioperl, 14, 22, 165-166, 174-177, 189-190, 194
Biopython, 14, 22, 165-170, 176-177, 189, 194, 208
Bioruby, 14, 22, 165, 176-177, 189, 194-198, 201-202
Bridge Amplification, 75, 77-78
Bridge Pcr, 56

C

Chain-termination Methods, 54, 70, 93
Chromosome Topology, 9
Clonal Amplification, 56, 59, 77
Combinatorial Gating, 227, 235-236
Comparative Genomics, 6, 88, 114-119, 130, 140, 147
Computational Evolutionary Biology, 5-6, 132, 134
Computational Phylogenetics, 134, 151
Conservation Genomics, 99

D

Data Analysis, 12, 15, 53, 78, 82, 229, 237-239
Dna Nanoball Sequencing, 61
Dna Sequencing, 4, 16, 18, 41, 43, 48-50, 52-53, 56, 58, 62-70, 72-73, 75, 79, 83, 87-90, 93, 95, 101, 108, 115, 119-122
Domain-pair Exclusion Analysis, 216-217
Dot-matrix Methods, 23

D

Dye-terminator Sequencing, 71, 73
Dynamic Programming, 20-27, 29, 33-34, 36-37, 84, 86, 146, 156-157, 177

E

Ecological Models, 145, 212
Emboss, 14, 22, 25, 165, 170, 177, 203-204
Epigenomics, 97, 106, 133
Eukaryotic Interactomes, 224

F

Fine-mapping, 129
Fitch-margoliash Method, 154
Flow Cytometry Bioinformatics, 209, 227, 239
Functional Genomics, 96, 106, 130, 137

G

Gating, 227, 230, 232-237, 239-240
Gene Expression, 3, 8, 11, 13, 58, 67, 96-97, 111, 117, 119, 126, 128, 138, 147, 238, 240
Gene Prediction, 19, 95, 121, 136-142, 181-182
Genetics of Disease, 7
Genocad, 13-14, 205-208
Genome Annotation, 5, 95-96, 121, 136, 164, 171-172
Genome Assemblers, 41
Genome Project, 4-5, 17, 44, 88, 91-92, 102, 105-106, 111, 115, 119-123, 130, 132, 173-174
Genome-wide Association Studies, 3, 7, 100, 149
Genomic Medicine, 99
Genomics, 1-2, 5-7, 45, 54-55, 59, 67, 86, 88, 91, 96-103, 105-108, 114-119, 123, 130-133, 137, 140, 146-148, 150
Greedy Algorithm, 44

H

Heliscope Single Molecule Sequencing, 62
High-throughput Image Analysis, 12
High-throughput Sequencing, 53, 56-59, 62, 65, 67, 75, 82, 93, 129
High-throughput Single Cell Data Analysis, 12
Horizontal Gene Transfer, 6, 99, 138, 152, 155, 162

I

Illumina Dye Sequencing, 75, 79

Illumina Sequencing, 61, 75, 77, 79

Interactome, 209, 213, 217-226

Ion Semiconductor

Sequencing, 16, 79-82

Ion Torrent

Semiconductor

Sequencing, 61, 83

Iterative Methods, 27, 35, 38

M

Mapping Assembly, 42

Massively Parallel Signature Sequencing (mpss), 8, 53, 58

Maxam-gilbert Sequencing, 53-54

Metagenomic Gene Prediction, 141

Metagenomics, 18, 50, 63, 75, 98, 130, 141

Microfluidic Sanger Sequencing, 65, 72

Mitochondrial Dna, 64-65, 112-113

Modelling Biological Systems, 142, 209

Molecular Interaction Networks, 11, 192, 218

Motif Finding, 13, 27, 38-39

Multi-cellular Organism Simulation, 144, 211

Multiple Sequence Alignment, 14, 17-18, 23, 26-28, 30, 32-33, 35-37, 39, 151, 153, 159, 182-183, 192, 201, 204

N

Nanopore Dna Sequencing, 62

Non-coding Multiple Sequence Alignment, 39

O

Oncogenomics, 88, 105, 107, 109, 111

Open-source Bioinformatics Software, 13

Operomics, 108

P

Pan Genomics, 6

Phylogenetic Analysis, 29, 33, 40, 153, 161-162

Phylogenetic Signal, 163

Phylogeny-aware Methods, 37

Polony Sequencing, 55, 58

Probability Binning Methods, 234

P (continued)

Protein Expression, 2, 8, 205

Protein Folding, 144, 211

Protein Localization, 9

Protein Structure Prediction, 3, 9, 19, 27-28, 34, 37, 144, 211

Protein-protein Interaction Prediction, 209, 213, 217

Pseudogene Prediction, 141

R

Reduced Cycle Amplification, 76-77

S

Sanger Sequencing, 16-17, 43-44, 53-54, 59, 65-66, 68, 72-74, 79, 82, 92-93, 98, 101

Sankoff-morel-cedergren Algorithm, 156

Sequence Alignment, 2-4, 14, 16-18, 20-23, 26-33, 35-37, 39, 41, 85, 151, 153, 159, 165, 182-183, 192, 194, 201, 203-204

Sequence Analysis, 2, 4, 14, 16-17, 19-21, 23, 25, 27, 29, 31, 33, 35, 37, 39, 41, 43, 45, 47, 49, 51, 53, 55, 57, 59, 61, 63, 65, 67, 69, 71, 73, 75-77, 79, 81, 83, 85, 87, 118, 154, 192, 194, 203

Sequence Assembly, 4, 16, 18, 41-43, 67, 75, 79, 95, 98, 136, 138, 159

Sequencing Chemistry, 59, 61, 73, 78, 81

Shotgun Sequencing, 5, 8, 41, 43, 53, 56, 92-93, 95, 98, 101, 120

Signal Detection, 81, 138

Simulated Annealing, 28, 37, 86

Solid Sequencing, 55, 60

Structural Bioinformatics, 9, 11, 97, 177, 209, 245

Synthetic Biology, 99, 130, 205, 208

T

Tagmentation, 76

Transcriptomes, 79, 108-109, 111

Tree Model, 145, 212

V

Viral Interactomes, 222

W

Web Services In

Bioinformatics, 14

www.ingramcontent.com/pod-product-compliance
Lightning Source LLC
Jackson TN
JSHW052157130125
77033JS00004B/186

* 9 7 8 1 6 3 5 4 9 0 4 5 9 *